MINÉ OKUBO FOLLOWING HER OWN ROAD

EDITED BY

GREG ROBINSON &
ELENA TAJIMA CREEF

UNIVERSITY OF WASHINGTON PRESS

SEATTLE AND LONDON

MINÉ

FOLLOWING HER OWN ROAD

OKUBO

Miné Okubo: Following Her Own Road is published with the assistance of a grant from the Naomi B. Pascal Editor's Endowment, supported through the generosity of Janet and John Creighton, Patti Knowles, Mary McLellan Williams, and other donors.

University of Washington Press
P.O. Box 50096, Seattle, WA 98145 U.S.A.
www.washington.edu/uwpress

Library of Congress Cataloging-in-Publication Data
Miné Okubo : following her own road / edited by Greg Robinson and Elena Tajima Creef.
p.   cm.
Includes bibliographical references and index.
ISBN 978-0-295-98774-3 (pbk. : alk. paper)
1. Okubo, Miné—Criticism and interpretation.   2. Okubo, Miné.
3. Japanese American artists—Biography.   I. Robinson, Greg, 1966–
II. Creef, Elena Tajima.
N6537.O395M56 2008
759.13—dc22   2007053065

TO MINÉ AND HER FRIENDS AND COMRADES

WHO HELPED US ON OUR JOURNEYS—

MITSUYE YAMADA, SHIRLEY GEOK-LIN LIM,

AIKO HERZIG-YOSHINAGA, AND THE LATE JACK HERZIG—

THIS WORK IS LOVINGLY DEDICATED.

CONTENTS

PART II. SCHOLARLY ESSAYS

PREFACE

GREG ROBINSON AND ELENA TAJIMA CREEF

The artist who lived a few stalls down tried to solve her need for privacy by tacking a large "Quarantined—Do Not Enter" sign on her door. But rather than keeping people away, it only drew further attention to her reluctant presence. "What's wrong with you?" her friends would call. And she would shout back, "Hoof and mouth disease. Go away!"

—YOSHIKO UCHIDA, *DESERT EXILE: THE UPROOTING OF A JAPANESE-AMERICAN FAMILY*

I visited most of the relocation centers, where WRA officials made it possible for me to move about freely, interviewing anyone I wished. On these visits I met evacuees who became and have remained close friends, including Miné Okubo, the distinguished artist. . . . When I first met Miné, she was sloshing about in the mud and snow at the Topaz Center.

—CAREY MCWILLIAMS, *THE EDUCATION OF CAREY MCWILLIAMS*

Miné Okubo was first and foremost an artist, and an artist lives through the creation of images. Such images enlighten—in the sense both of inform-ing and of brightening up—but they can also contain mysteries, secret and unknowable messages. Miné's special gift was the creation of images of herself.

Her signature work, *Citizen 13660*, is composed of a series of self-portraits, which together constitute a narrative of her experience as a Japanese American taken from her home and confined by official order during World War II. She continued fashioning herself throughout her later life. She gave the world enduring images of her talent and personality but deftly controlled her self-creation, never letting anyone see more of herself than she wanted them to see.

We came upon these two epigraphs recently, and together they rather neatly sum up our feelings about Miné Okubo. Yoshiko Uchida's unnamed artist is Miné in her cranky glory. Although one side of Miné was always trying to withdraw into herself and give herself space for her art, and she raged loudly against the idle curiosity of the ignorant, she simultaneously craved attention and recognition. As Carey McWilliams's comment testifies, Miné made friends with whole numbers of people, famous and unknown, who were drawn to her extraordinary wit and vitality as much as by her artistic talent. We were astounded at first to discover that McWilliams, the minority rights advocate and editor of *The Nation*, had considered Miné a close friend. She certainly never mentioned him in any of her recorded writings or interviews. Yet, as countless friends would later testify, Miné was secretive about her extensive acquaintance, and spoke only cryptically of her other acquaintances, referring to "the dancer," "the tall guy," or one of the other nicknames she took mischievous delight in inventing for her friends. We feel a certain justice in the fact that, although both of us counted ourselves as friends of Miné's, we never actually met until we both attended her memorial service at the Japanese American Church in New York.

Miné Okubo: Following Her Own Road pays tribute to this legendary artist. It is divided into three sections. The first section introduces readers to the artist's oeuvre by reproducing a selection of her art and writing from different periods of her life. These selections represent a variety of artistic formats—paintings, drawings, illustrations, photographs, and prints—and encompass such diverse literary genres as letters, memoir, and testimony before a public commission. The section begins with a transcription of the artist's childhood recollections based on the last conversations she had with her close friend, the poet Fay Chiang. This is followed by a series of Miné's published and unpublished writings that include her "Artist's Credo"—a personal statement of her philosophy, which she would send out together with her annual Christmas cards (mailed to some five hundred friends each year). We also include an essay she wrote from Topaz Relocation Center for the *San Francisco Chronicle* in 1943, "An Evacuee's Hopes—and Memories," along with the personal testimony she gave in 1981 before the Commission on Wartime Relocation and Internment of Civilians. The section concludes with some of Miné's personal letters, written from camp, to fellow artist Isamu Noguchi as well as a selection from her forty-year correspondence with her patrons and friends Dr. Roy Leeper and Dr. Gaylord Hall of San Francisco.

The second section of this volume is composed of scholarly essays on the artist's career and work, primarily on *Citizen 13660* and also on her wartime contributions to the literary arts magazine *Trek*. Written by specialists from across a wide range of fields, including American Studies, ethnic studies, literature, architecture, and American political history, these essays examine the importance and multiple meanings of Miné Okubo's contributions. Although *Citizen 13660* occupies a central place in both historical and literary studies of the wartime Japanese American experience, this illustrated memoir has, ironically, received very little critical attention from scholars. This section builds off the work we began with *Amerasia Journal*'s special tribute to Okubo in the summer 2004 issue. However, with the exception of the essay by Vivian Fumiko Chin (chapter 7 of this volume)—which appeared in *Amerasia Journal* 30, no. 2 (2004)—all of the scholarly essays were commissioned as original explorations of Okubo's work from across a variety of disciplinary perspectives.

It is our hope that the essays in this volume will offer readers a wide array of critical tools and background materials that enrich the scant scholarship on *Citizen 13660* and place it more concretely in its various historical and literary contexts.

Vivian Fumiko Chin chronicles Okubo's subtle—and not so subtle—visual language of resistance in *Citizen 13660*, which, she argues, both challenges and undoes the language of racism permeating wartime depictions of Japanese and Japanese Americans. Heather Fryer examines Okubo's memoir as a form of protest against Executive Order 9066. She contends that *Citizen 13660* is a much more confrontational work than early reviewers realized. Her discussion brings to light the multilayered and multifaceted nature of what Okubo leaves unsaid and hidden in the text while exposing the camps as a great hypocrisy of "barbed-wire democracies." Kimberley L. Phillips looks at Okubo's work in the context of a longer tradition of Japanese immigrant print culture and the radical political dissent of 1930s public art. Her insightful commentary places Okubo's autographic work within a comic-book tradition that combines social criticism of a horrific personal and group experience and which was not seen again in American print until Art Spiegelman's *Maus*. Lynne Horiuchi and Laura Card each expand the critical discussion of Okubo's wartime work as they examine her contributions as art editor of the literary magazine, *Trek*, produced at Topaz Relocation Center. Horiuchi offers a unique comparative reading of Okubo's stylistic representation of space, location, and movement in *Trek* and *Citizen 13660*. Card adds to the critical discussion by offering an analysis of Okubo's use of symbolism and form as the artist wavers between resisting and complying with official camp administration rules regarding censorship and representation. Stella Oh examines the complexities of Okubo's representation of surveillance in *Citizen 13660*. She foregrounds the myriad ways in which the spectacle of the gaze is embedded in relationship to power and the production of knowledge. Oh also demonstrates how the inconsistencies and contradictions between text and image in

Okubo's memoir perform nothing less than a theory of citizenship. Finally, Greg Robinson concludes this section with a contrary reading of how Okubo's memoir functions as a "masterpiece of ambiguity." After raising questions about why there has been a tendency among scholars (including those in this collection) to read beneath the textual surface of *Citizen 13660* in search of subversive meanings and gestures of resistance, Robinson traces the historical evolution of Okubo's wartime artwork and writing that led to the 1946 publication of *Citizen 13660*. In particular, he examines the complicity between Okubo's own agenda as an artist and writer and that of the War Relocation Authority administrators who, he argues, kept her well within their sights.

The third section of this volume is composed of reminiscences and tributes that describe Miné's unusual and irrepressible character and illuminate the breadth of influence she exerted on so many people as an artist, friend, teacher, militant, collaborator, witness, and role model. We are honored to include poems by James Masao Mitsui and Sohei Hohri as well as essays by Shirley Geok-lin Lim and Greg Robinson. These writers each bear witness to Miné's rightful place in American history and to her gift of genius.

Like any other small business, even one run for love, this enterprise could not have survived without contracting some sizable debts, which we are glad to acknowledge: Russell Leong, editor of *Amerasia Journal*, agreed to publish a special issue on Miné Okubo—the *Journal*'s first-ever issue devoted to a visual artist—and then enthusiastically supported the creation of a book-length anthology. Mary Uyematsu Kao did a super job of laying out the *Amerasia* issue and took a day off to photograph the artwork on the cover.

Aiko Yoshinaga-Herzig, a Nisei hero and the godmother of the Japanese American redress movement, generously shared her files of Okubo material, including correspondence with Okubo, clippings and ephemera, and her personal collection of Miné's artwork.

The late Roy Leeper and Gaylord Hall, who were Miné's greatest patrons and who supported her emotionally and financially over decades, gave indispensable support to this tribute. After leading us on an unforgettable tour through their home, they offered us full permission to photograph their unequaled collection of Okubo works, and they generously contributed funds to permit the making of a color insert for the volume. They also graciously allowed us to use excerpts from the large archive of Okubo letters they donated to the Archives of American Art.

Seiko Buckingham, Miné's niece and the executor of the estate, gave us the green light to put together our compilation of Okubo materials and pledged her cooperation, without which this project would have never been able to proceed.

Mary H. Curtin, co-author with Theresa Larkin of the play *Miné: A Name for Her-*

self, took time from her work on Miné's biography to exchange documents and information with us, and her enthusiasm for Okubo was infectious. Marian Yoshiki-Kovinick, archivist at the now-defunct southern California branch of the Smithsonian Institution's Archives of American Art, searched for Okubo material and shared her wide knowledge of Asian American artists. Vicki Onufriu, an intelligent graduate student at the Université du Québec À Montréal, pored over the Okubo collections at the main branch of the Archives of American Art in Washington, D.C., and copied the Leeper letters. Fay Chiang, Roger Daniels, Arthur Hansen, Karin Higa, Setsuko Matsunaga Nishi, and Ann Yonemura provided recollections of Okubo or insights into her work. Heng Gun Ngo, a favorite of Miné's in her lifetime, shared art and memories of "Okubos."

The late Masumi Hayashi, Clemens Kalischer, and Irene Poon also agreed to share their photographic portraits of Miné. Taken at different stages of Miné's life, the images capture the beauty and mischief of the artist. Heng Wee Tan produced the vibrant color photos of Miné's work featured in the insert. Dean Keesey gave us permission to honor his mother, Masumi Hayashi, by using her photograph of Miné on the cover.

And finally, we are deeply indebted to Naomi Pascal, at the University of Washington Press, who embraced this project with great enthusiasm from the very beginning. Her generous feedback and unfailing support were instrumental in ushering this collection into print.

On a personal note, Greg Robinson wishes to thank his parents, Ed Robinson and the late Toni Robinson; his conjoint and his far-flung family, which includes Judy and the late Russell Baker, Ann Dwornik and Bob Sandler, Ellen Fine, Ken Feinour, Ronald Seely, Deborah Malamud and Neal Plotkin, Adron Nguyen, Sydelle Postman, Julio Perez, Frieda and Dan Post, Katherine Quittner, Alex and Jennifer Robinson-Gilden, Ariella and Jocelyn Robinson, Ian Robinson, the late Lillian Robinson, Tracy Robinson, and Robert Rosen—all of whom offered long and loving support.

Elena Tajima Creef wishes to thank her mother, Chiyohi Creef, and other family members Art, Val, Ed, Cheryl, Karen, and Dottie for their support; her friends Leslie Bow, Nora Okja Keller, Jeni Yamada, Meret Keller, Yvonne Keller, and Carp Ferrari, who have always stood behind this project with great enthusiasm; her students and colleagues at Wellesley College, who have studied Okubo with delight; and finally, Mark and Skylar Schmidt, for their years of encouragement, cheerleading, and infinite patience.

NOTE

The epigraphs are from Yoshiko Uchida, *Desert Exile: The Uprooting of a Japanese-American Family* (Seattle: University of Washington Press, 1982), 96, and Carey McWilliams, *The Education of Carey McWilliams* (New York: Simon & Schuster, 1979), 104–5.

COLOR PLATES

1 Hippo and cat with umbrellas and man (no date)

2 Blue green vases (no date)

3 Red man, boy, and cat (no date)

4 Blue woman with contented cat (1975)

5 Blue nude with cat (no date)

6 Two small pink nudes (1972)

7 Pink woman (no date)

8 Orange and blue vase (no date)

9 Pink woman with three children (no date)

10 Lilac nude, green background (no date)

11 Hippo, cat, and man on black (no date)

12 Red nude with blue (1973)

13 Geometric rectangle in yellow, blue, and teal (1981)

14   Geometric in grey and yellow (1980)

15 Pink woman in blue hat (1973)

16 Large vase with peeking girl (no date)

17 Pink girl with hat and vase (1975)

18 Girl with sailboats (1978)

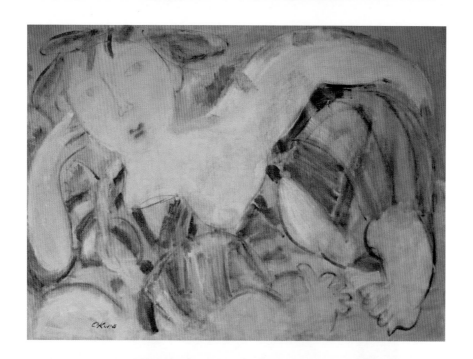

19 Blue-eyed woman (no date)

20 Green nude in pink hat (1975)

21 Blue figure with red border (1974)

22 Male portrait in blue (no date)

23 Purple woman with flowers (1980)

24   Photograph of Miné Okubo by Cecil J. Thompson

25   Photograph of Miné Okubo by Cecil J. Thompson

MINÉ OKUBO FOLLOWING HER OWN ROAD

FOLLOWING HER OWN ROAD

THE ACHIEVEMENT OF MINÉ OKUBO

ELENA TAJIMA CREEF

The world is all shot to hell, but you still have to go on hope.

—MINÉ OKUBO

I'm an individual . . . who wants to contribute to the betterment of this world. To me, life and art are one and the same. It took me fifty years to find this out, but now I have arrived.

—MINÉ OKUBO

In the fall of 1993, I had just finished writing a dissertation chapter on Miné Okubo's famous illustrated memoir of the internment camps, *Citizen 13660*, and had also just moved from California to begin my first job teaching women's studies on the East Coast. During my first trip to New York, I resolved to look up this artist who also hailed from my hometown of Riverside, California. I was thrilled when my friend and colleague Shirley Geok-lin Lim offered to make the introduction. Besieged with requests for visits and information by a battery of graduate students, researchers, educators, art collectors, filmmakers, and journalists, Miné was wary of using up her time to entertain the endless stream of visitors who called her at home and showed up on her doorstep at all hours of the day and night. "People are always calling me and stopping by, interrupting me from doing my work. It's so bad I have to stay up all night just to get anything done. I don't even sleep."

Still, I persisted, and I will always consider it an honor that she welcomed me up to her one-room third-floor apartment. This was the same tiny Greenwich Village apartment that *Fortune* magazine originally helped Miné find in 1944 when she made her way from a concentration camp in Topaz, Utah, to the magazine's office, armed with nothing but two packed suitcases and determination to begin work as an illustrator for their special issue on Japan. Rumor had it that Miné was the oldest surviving rent-control tenant in her building, outliving and outlasting several generations of landlords who tried their best to push her out. Many winters, she went without heat. Friends would bring her hand warmers, down-filled parkas, and coverlets. Her "pocket sized studio" looked as if all maintenance and upkeep had abruptly ceased sometime in the 1960s.[1] Yet, in spite of the faded, chipped green walls and plumbing that didn't always work, the back wall of her apartment had a lovely set of old French windows that let in sunlight from floor to ceiling.[2] Miné said that when she first moved in, there was a beautiful wooden terrace outside these windows where she entertained friends and visitors who would enjoy the view of surrounding courtyards and buildings. Decades earlier, one of her landlords had ripped out the entire structure in an attempt to dispirit and dislodge her. His efforts were in vain.

Miné lived simply and humbly in this cramped space for more than fifty years. To visit her living quarters was to grasp that, for her, "life and art" were indeed one and the same. Her furniture consisted of old folding lawn chairs and a small folding card table covered (for guests) with a fresh white tablecloth. First-time visitors were most struck by the remarkable lack of modern conveniences: no television, stereo, computer, or extra lighting. In other words, there was nothing to distract her from the daily task of dedicating herself to her work. The only modern object in her tiny apartment was a simple radio given to her by friends.

Visitors to Miné's apartment were always treated like VIP guests, whom she would entertain with tea and a table spread with Pepperidge Farm cookies, bowls of sliced fruit, and Ben & Jerry's ice cream—Cherry Garcia, her favorite flavor. This ritual of tea and treats was always followed by the highlight of the visit: a private showing of Miné's lifetime body of work. These private showings were always dependent on the amount of daylight streaming into the back of her apartment through the French windows. As she revealed and displayed dozens of canvases, the sheer range of her paintings would take your breath away. Some stretched more than six feet tall; others were miniatures no larger than two by three inches. Hundreds filled her apartment and were stacked together against the walls, piled one on top of another. Other than her folded futon bed, there was not a single empty surface in her apartment, and the only decorations that adorned her walls were her own paintings—abstract expressionist compositions of color and lines. Miné showed the work she was most proud of, and the canvases included her most recent pieces as well as others stretching back over the decades. There were female nudes sunbathing on the beach; geometric portraits in which the body was reduced to abstract shapes, lines, and colors; and gorgeous oversize canvases of the joyful figures of children, cats, birds, and flowers in a range of surreal pastel colors. Each painting gave evidence of her dazzling command of color, technique, and composition.

While most people familiar with Miné's work know only of her published internment camp sketches, the breadth and immensity of the paintings she produced in the last fifty years of her life will certainly anchor her place as one of the great twentieth-century American artists. In addition to her art, Miné also had several unpublished manuscripts she had written years ago. These witty, creative, and original graphic works, written in the same visual narrative style of *Citizen 13660*, capture what Deborah Gesensway and Mindy Roseman call her "creative, playful, even mischievous" sense of humor in observing the daily world.[3] One manuscript recorded the absurdity of the human world from a chicken's point of view, and another captured the circuslike pleasures and oddities of a crowded and colorful Manhattan, observed from the perspective of Santa Claus during a Christmas Eve visit to the Big Apple.

From our first meeting in 1993 until our last in 2000, it was always clear that Miné would belong to a future in which she would be remembered and honored as one of the pioneers of Asian American art and literature. To those who were lucky enough to know her—and to those who will know her only through her lasting work—her legacy is a dazzling combination of talent, genius, and the tenacious gift of what art educator Betty LaDuke has called "persistent vision."[4] Miné's friend, the poet Fay Chiang, has observed that in another culture, Miné would have been cherished as a "living treasure" and her work "would have been viewed in its entirety. Not fragmented for what was most marketable, recognizable . . . her body of evacuation work. She moved on as an artist, a persona growing in her life and work. In some other place, there would be interest in this artistic growth. Art making would be viewed through the lens of process."[5]

Many do not know that Miné enjoyed several retrospective exhibitions of her work on both coasts during her lifetime. She also received numerous honors for her painting and writing, including the American Book Award in 1984. In 1987, Miné was selected by the California State Department of Education as one of twelve women pioneers for the historical poster "California since 1800." In 1991, she was honored by the National Museum for Women in the Arts for her lifetime contributions. In addition, her work currently hangs in such prestigious locations as the Japanese American National Museum, the Oakland Museum of California, and the Smithsonian Institution. She was the contemporary and colleague of such great twentieth-century artists and writers as Willem de Kooning, Franz Kline, Toshio Mori, Isamu Noguchi, Jackson Pollock, and Diego Rivera.

Born in Riverside, California, on June 27, 1912, to Issei parents, Miné was a middle child—a self-proclaimed "misfit"—in a family of seven.[6] Her mother, a calligrapher and painter, was an honors graduate from the Tokyo Art Institute and arrived in the United States in 1904 to participate in the Saint Louis Exposition of Arts and Crafts.[7] Like her mother, Miné's father also participated in the Saint Louis fair. Miné remembered him as a learned scholar who made his living working as a gardener and landscaper. Her older brother, Benji Okubo, was a notable painter who offered a model of artistic creation.

During her childhood in prewar southern California, Riverside was still a rural farming town on the famous De Anza Trail, renowned for its magnificent orange groves and spectacular ring of surrounding mountains. Miné's memories of childhood were filled with nostalgic colorful stories of the crowds that gathered around campfires in her family's backyard at night to tell tales and entertain one another. In many interviews, Miné recalled how she watched the burden of motherhood and marriage thwart her mother's artistic ambitions, as she sacrificed her creative work in order to take care of the family. As a result, Miné resolved from an early age to devote herself to painting rather than to the traditional roles expected of a Nisei daughter: "Oh, I knew I was never going to get married. Look at my poor mother. Her life was ruined working so hard for the children. She never had time to do anything. She stopped painting. I wasn't going to wash anybody's socks, cook their dinner. Forget it!"[8]

Miné attended Riverside Community College and later transferred to the University of California, Berkeley, to study art. She completed a bachelor's degree in 1935 and a master's of fine arts in 1936. In 1938, she won the prestigious Bertha Taussig Traveling Scholarship, and for eighteen months she traveled alone across Europe, studying art and visiting the great museums. When war was declared in 1939, Miné found herself stranded, like many other international travelers, and struggled to get back to the safety of home.

Upon her return, Miné moved back to the Bay Area, where she worked on mosaics and frescoes for the Federal Art Project at Fort Ord; the Golden Gate International Exposition on Treasure Island, where Diego Rivera was at work on his famous 1,800-square-foot movable mural on Pan-American unity; and the Oakland Hospitality House for Service Men. Over the years, Miné would mischievously recall that when people saw her back then, a lone Japanese American woman artist literally working beneath the legendary Mexican painter, they would say that she must be "Diego's sixth child by a third marriage."[9]

As a Japanese American, Miné found that her life was forever changed by the events of December 7, 1941, and their aftermath. Executive Order 9066 sent her packing along with more than one hundred thousand others—for "their own protection"—for what would turn out to be the duration of the war. Miné's family was splintered by evacuation and relocation. Her father was sent to a prison camp in Missoula, Montana, and later to Louisiana. Miné and her youngest brother went to Tanforan Assembly Center and later to Central Utah Relocation Camp in Topaz. Her older sister was sent to Heart Mountain in Wyoming, and another brother was drafted early in the war.[10]

At Topaz, Miné taught art classes for children and worked on the camp newspaper, the *Topaz Times*. She also served as the arts editor for *Trek*—the now legendary literary arts magazine produced in camp—and designed the striking covers for the three issues that were produced. (During her years at Tanforan and Topaz, she also produced the hundreds of pen-and-ink sketches that would serve as the basis for her camp memoir, *Citizen 13660*.) *Fortune* magazine saw her illustrations for *Trek* and recruited her in 1944 to work on a special issue on Japan. Over the next ten years, Miné worked as an illustrator who drew, as she put it, "everything from soup to nuts" for mainstream magazines, newspapers, novels, children's literature, and even psychology and anatomy books.[11] The latter, she argued, "taught [her] to investigate into all the facts like a scientist," and she "simplified and simplified [her] drawing until all interpretations and mannerisms [were] out and only the clear facts remained."[12] Throughout these decades, her painting, always idiosyncratic, underwent continual shifts, passing through a range of styles and formats.

In 1951, Miné gave up freelance and commercial work and devoted the next half decade to painting as an independent artist. In countless interviews, she recalled her decision to turn away from the commercial and politicized world of art galleries and critics in order to follow her own path:

> If you're not following the current art trends, they think you're really cracked. . . . You either pursue the art business–show business system as a promotion game, or you're on your own, which often means that your works don't sell. I didn't follow any trend or anyone. My work was not accepted because you are judged by those who play the game—the critics and the dealers. Because my paintings are different and don't fit the ongoing trend, the museums and galleries don't know where to place me. . . . Luckily the people saved me—the little people from whom I borrowed money and [a] few collectors who helped me with the rent.[13]

Although trained in the Western tradition of great European artists, Miné's mission was always simple: to take art "back to zero." Toward the end of her career, she felt she had finally arrived:

> My beginning training in art has been completely Western. I followed the French Impressionists because they went the furthest in oils. I don't use

watercolor because I like solid things. If you use watercolor, you might end up being pretty. I think in big, simple, monumental terms. . . . In the end, I returned to "the Primitives"; to the flat usage of color and form used by Egyptians, Mayans, and Orientals. By going the full route and by proving it myself, I went back again.[14]

Miné's work received significant exposure in numerous gallery and museum shows on the East and West coasts, although she remained aloof from and somewhat disdainful of the mainstream art world. Her art was featured in books, Asian American journals, and exhibition catalogs. She continued to paint until a few months before her death.

Miné Okubo: Following Her Own Road is much more than simply a Festschrift or memorial volume. Rather, it recovers and illuminates a pioneering Nisei artist, writer, and activist who spent her almost seventy-year-long career challenging conventional role expectations for women, Japanese Americans, and modern artists. Miné's legacy is centered primarily on her landmark book *Citizen 13660* (1946), the first and arguably one of the best autobiographical narratives of the Japanese American relocation and internment experience. Yet, despite the visibility of this book and her historic importance, Miné Okubo herself remains little understood. This volume attempts to shed light on her work by placing it within critical discussions of wartime and postwar history and Asian American literature. As the first critical anthology on Miné Okubo, this volume does not pretend to be comprehensive in its treatment of her life and work. It would be impossible to fully capture in any one text the career of an individual who so defied categorization. Indeed, the disciplinary and demographic range of the contributors to this collection testifies to the remarkable multiplicity of the artist's interests and to the breadth of fields covered by her work. Nevertheless, a few essential themes do recur with frequency in the selections that compose the volume. These include Miné's simultaneous position as insider and outsider in the various worlds she inhabited and her self-proclaimed status as a "misfit"; her fierce independence and her idiosyncratic but powerful feminism; and her remarkable ability to reach out and connect with diverse groups of people. Miné requested that her work be divided after her death into collections that would go to the Japanese American National Museum, the Oakland Museum of California, her alma mater, Riverside Community College, and her family. In the years to come, as this lifetime body of work finally becomes available for study by historians and critics, we hope to see other scholarly treatments of her postwar art as well as a full biographical chronicling of her rightful place in American history.

Miné's friend Nobuo Kitagaki once observed that while "Georgia O'Keeffe went to the desert to seek her inner vision, . . . Miné went to New York and found a desert in which she created her own garden."[15] Although she was a native daughter of the

Golden West, there is no doubt that the only true place Miné ever considered home was New York City. During my last visit with her, we went out for Japanese food in Greenwich Village. I enjoyed lingering with her afterward as we hunted for snacks and trinkets in a Japanese grocery store. Later, as it was getting dark, I asked her if I could walk her back to her apartment. "Nah. I know my way home." We hugged good-bye, and I watched as she disappeared into the teeming crowds of young, black-clad Village people, all hurrying to get somewhere. If you didn't know who she was, you might have mistaken her for somebody's tiny, eccentric Japanese grandmother, not the genius who devoted her life to following her own road. In a personal credo she had once written, Miné made this final observation: "beauty and truth are the only two things which live timeless and ageless."[16] If one looks at the substantial body of artwork and writing that she left behind, it is abundantly clear that she devoted herself to pursuing both with passion, commitment, and not an ounce of compromise.

NOTES

1   Shirley Sun, *Miné Okubo: An American Experience*, exh. cat. (San Francisco: East Wind Printers, 1972), 11.

2   Photographer Masumi Hayashi took her collage portrait of Miné outside the artist's Greenwich Village studio in 1997. Hayashi remembers that Miné stubbornly would not let her take the photographs inside; as a result, one can see multiple collaged incarnations of the artist against these black French windows. According to Hayashi, the photo-collage was taken in the rain under cover of Miné's purple umbrella.

3   Deborah Gesensway and Mindy Roseman, *Beyond Words: Images from America's Concentration Camps* (Ithaca, N.Y.: Cornell University Press, 1987), 66. Gesensway and Roseman interviewed Miné in 1982.

4   See the video *Persistent Women Artists: Pablita Velarde, Mine Okubo, Lois Mailou Jones*, presented by Betty LaDuke, directed by Brian Varaday (Botsford, Conn: Reading & O'Reilly, 1996).

5   Fay Chiang, "Miné Okubo," *Dialogue: New York Asian American Arts Alliance* (Fall 1998): 33.

6   Sun, *Miné Okubo*, 12.

7   Ibid.

8   Chiang, "Miné Okubo," 31.

9   Miné repeatedly told this story. I cite it here from her interview in Sun, *Miné Okubo*, 18. She also relates a version in her interview with Betty LaDuke in *Persistent Women Artists*.

10 Miné's widowed father was relocated several times, eventually remarried, and was repatriated to Japan after the war.

11 Sun, *Miné Okubo*, 41.

12 Ibid.

13 Barbara J. Marvis, *Contemporary American Success Stories: Famous People of Asian Ancestry* (Childs, Md.: Mitchell Lane Publishers, 1994), 4, 43.

14 Sun, *Miné Okubo*, 41.

15 Ibid., 42.

16 Miné Okubo, "An Artist's Credo: A Personal Statement," unpublished. For the entire statement, see chapter 2 of this volume.

I

AN ARTISTIC
AND LITERARY
PORTFOLIO

Miné Okubo, *Drawing of Redress Cases before U.S. Supreme Court*, 1987, pen and ink

Miné Okubo, *Drawing of Redress Cases before U.S. Supreme Court*, 1987, pen and ink

Miné Okubo, *Girl and Cat*, 1977, brush and ink

Miné Okubo, cover of *Trek* 1, no. 1 (December 1942)

Miné Okubo, cover of *Trek* 1, no. 2 (February 1943)

Miné Okubo, cover of *Trek* 1, no. 3 (June 1943)

Miné Okubo, illustration for *Where the Carp Banners Fly* by Grace W. McGavran

Miné Okubo, illustration for *Where the Carp Banners Fly* by Grace W. McGavran

Miné Okubo, illustration for *Where the Carp Banners Fly* by Grace W. McGavran

Miné Okubo, illustration for *Ten Against the Storm* by Marianna Nugent Prichard

Miné Okubo, illustration for *The Waiting People* by Peggy Billings

Miné Okubo, illustration for *The Seven Stars* by Toru Matsumoto

Miné Okubo, *Fish*, 1942, oil on canvas

Miné Okubo, *Men's Hall Line-up*, 1942, oil on canvas

Miné Okubo, *Dust Storm*, 1942

Miné Okubo at a tea in her honor sponsored by the Common Council for American Unity, New York, March 6, 1945

Clemens Kalischer, *Miné Okubo*, 1948

Clemens Kalischer, *Miné Okubo*, 1948

Clemens Kalischer, *Miné Okubo*, 1955

Masumi Hayashi, photo-collage of Miné Okubo, 1997

Irene Poon, photograph of *Portrait of Miné Okubo*, 1996

Miné Okubo, *Untitled Abstract*, oil on canvas

Miné Okubo, *Girl*, oil on canvas
Miné Okubo, *Untitled Abstract*, oil on canvas

1

RIVERSIDE

MINÉ OKUBO AND FAY CHIANG

In the last months of her life, from a hospital bed at New York University Medical Center and then Cabrini Nursing Home, Miné vividly recounted stories about her hometown Riverside: her childhood, her mother and father, her older brothers and sister, and how she was so very shy she hardly spoke, but watched with great curiosity the people and events around her.—FAY CHIANG

Oh, Papa and Mama worked so hard for us kids. Papa made candies in a store. At night he'd come home late from work and wake us up, the ice cream dripping. And Mama was always cleaning and cooking and sewing. I said to myself, I'm never going to get married and wash someone else's socks. Forget it.

What a bunch we were. One autumn the leaves were falling to the ground and Papa and Mama told us, "Rake up those leaves." Well, we kids shook those trees so the leaves would fall off, and the ones that didn't, we climbed up the branches and pulled them off. That way we only had to rake the leaves once. When our parents saw what we had done, they said, "Ah! Bakatari! Bakatari!"

Another time we left our clothes hanging from the bedposts. Mama told us to put them away instead of leaving them all over the place. Well, we kids took care of that: we sawed off the bedposts!

We were a handful, but lively and imaginative.

When my brothers were older, every night when the weather was warm, we built a bonfire. Oh, my brothers were good looking! Girls falling all over them, even fighting one another for one of them! They were colorful, hair slicked back like Valentino and beautiful wide sashes tied around their waists.

Me? I was just a kid watching everything. It was very interesting. Riverside was filled with orchards then. Oh, that smell at night and the sky full of stars.

We had all kinds of people coming around: tramps, hobos, friends, and even criminals! Neighbors? Oh, we had everybody: a Mexican family, two other Japanese families, Irish, Italian, a school nearby for American Indians, and yes! Gypsies.

There was music and singing and dancing all through the night! And when we got hungry, the boys would go off and steal a couple of chickens, pick some ears of corn or whatever was growing at the time and cook it in the fire.

Papa and Mama? They were with all their kids.

Next door there was a house that was empty for the longest time. Whoever lived there before had planted a lot of fruit trees—apples, peach, lemons, pears. Since there was no one to pick the ripe fruit, we just ate it off the trees. Nah, we were never hungry. We loved to eat!

Did you ever eat a green apple with salt? My brother and I would climb into an apple tree with a salt shaker and just sit taking bites out of apples like squirrels.

Oh, it was the best childhood. I would lie in the grass staring at the sky and clouds, the blades of grass, and watch the ants on the ground. It's all in nature. We can only simplify the Creator's work.

I walked everywhere for miles by myself as a little kid, and sometimes, all the way to town where I would climb the highest building to look-see all around.

At school they didn't know what to do with me, but they knew I had it in art from when I was little, from the very beginning, so the teachers left me pretty much alone.

When I went to Riverside Community College, I could hardly read or write. I kept asking questions, "How do you write that?" "What does that mean?" I had teachers, people who believed in me, helped me.

My mother was a renowned calligrapher. She came to America to represent Japan in the St. Louis Exposition, but look at what happened to her taking care of all those kids.

When I was traveling through Europe after graduating from Berkeley, I sent her a postcard every day telling her about my adventures. I came back when she was sick and she died shortly after. I found those postcards after she died. She had saved every one.

I want to be cremated. Scatter my ashes over Mama's grave in Riverside. I planted an olive tree there for her a long time ago. Me? A lemon tree.

Like your mother.[1] Oh, they put her in a nice spot on a hill. Next to a tall, tall tree and a flowering bush. Surrounded by her family. Your mother looked so young. But what you going to do?

No, I wasn't going to get married to anyone. Cook his dinner, do laundry all the time. Look at you! I don't know how you have so much laundry! (Miné often sat in the laundromat waiting for me to finish my family's wash, so we could go to the movies together. She loved the movies.)

I only know how to do one thing: Art.

My sister—a tiny thing—is so capable. She could drive a car, even a tractor. She had a gallery in the Mission for about a year before she got married. She painted, worked on the chicken farm, had kids. I don't know how she did it.

What are you waiting for? Do it while you're young, while you can. Look at me. At the end. But I had a good life. I've done everything I wanted to do.

I like it here [the Cabrini Nursing Home]. It's clean and people are so nice. Nah, I can't eat all this stuff. All these visitors bring me so many cookies and fruit. How is one person supposed to eat all that food? You eat it!

I'm right next to the window. It's quiet around here. At night I watch the airplanes and the bridge lights look so pretty, all lit up.

Who brought those flowers? I have so many visitors. You know they're going to do a big show of my work at Riverside. The president of the college came to see me.[2] Look it. They're building a new gallery and they want me to open it. I guess they think I'm a big shot! Can you imagine, all my paintings.

Well, I got it now. I'm finishing up you see. My art is the mastery of drawing, color and craft staying with subject and reality, but simplifying like the primitives. It took all those years, but I got it.

What you think? I'd have to get on an airplane. You would come? We could bring the whole gang—Xian, your sister, Kathy, and the art store kids.[3] I'll see people I haven't seen in a long time. Show them my paintings. It will be one big party with lots of food, people.

NOTES

This essay was read at Miné Okubo's memorial services at Riverside Community College in Riverside, California, on March 18, 2001, and at the Japanese American United Church in New York City on April 7, 2001.

1 Miné attended the wake and funeral of my mother, who passed away two years ago. Miné and my mother knew each other from encounters at art openings at the Basement Workshop where I worked, or from joining our family for Lunar New Year dinner, or from meeting up at the South Street Seaport or near Miné's apartment in Washington Square Park. Whenever they met, they would run toward one another and say, "Oh! How young you look!" "How do you do it!" Watching my mother and Miné holding each other warmly by the elbows, I would just shake my head.

2 President Salvatore G. Rotella and consultant Mary Curtin from Riverside Community

College visited Miné in December 2000 at the nursing home and took her to lunch at a wonderful midtown Italian restaurant. It was Miné's last trip outside.

3 In 1990, when Xian was five and a half months, I brought her to meet Miné for the first time at her apartment. As Miné took out her latest paintings to show me, Xian sat Buddha-like, unblinking on Miné's bed, staring at the paintings with their beautiful colors and shapes. Miné said, looking at Xian, "Now that one has a business head, no poor artist for her!" Miné was prophetic! We sat in the Washington Square Park children's playground in the afternoons through the passing seasons, sipping coffee while Xian played in the sandbox with other children. Often we were joined by Teru Kanazawa and her two young sons, Mikio and Terence Sheehan. Teru's father is the writer Tooru Kanazawa and a friend and contemporary of Miné's during the war and in the years after the war in New York City.

2

AN ARTIST'S CREDO

A PERSONAL STATEMENT

MINÉ OKUBO

My interest from the beginning has been a concern for the humanities. Having traveled and studied people and art in Europe, experienced the commercial world of New York, and lived [through] the Japanese Evacuation, I decided to follow the individual road of dedication in art instead of the popular arts of the times. By using all my technical ability and knowledge of art, I followed the difficult road of research and study.

I took everything back to the basics—workable and universal truth again. In the process I found my own identity, my handwriting, the content of reality. I mastered drawing, color, and craft—each to its simplest possible usage. Beauty and statements of truth revealed themselves in the simple and the sensitive and all the concocted and false fell aside. I found myself working with definite "what's" and "how's." The seemingly unimportant, minute undefined areas even became form and color and every act a direct statement which related and interrelated.

To me life and art are one and the same, for the key lies in one's knowledge of people and life. In art one is trying to express it in the simplest imaginative way, as in the art of past civilizations, for beauty and truth are the only two things which live timeless and ageless.

3

AN EVACUEE'S HOPES—AND MEMORIES

MINÉ OKUBO

A third-generation Japanese American, Miss Miné Okubo is an art graduate of the University of California and a young woman with a healthy sense of humor. As an artist she needs no introduction to the Bay Area. Her debut as a writer was accidental—her explanatory notes with her sketches were so much more [that] "This World" simply incorporated them into an article.—EDITORS OF "THIS WORLD," *SAN FRANCISCO CHRONICLE*, AUGUST 29, 1943

Following the attack on Pearl Harbor, evacuation of citizens and aliens of Japanese descent from the West Coast area was authorized by the Government. One hundred and ten thousand people were evacuated. Twelve assembly centers and ten relocation centers were established.

In all of them the situation has been more or less the same, so I feel that in picturing Tanforan Assembly Center and the Central Utah Relocation Center (Topaz), I am expressing the whole.

"Relocation centers were never intended as concentration camps or prisons. They were established primarily as an expedient . . ."

Approximately 7,500 people, former residents of the San Francisco Bay area, were interned at Tanforan Center for a period of six months. All were later transferred to Topaz Center. Former residents of the Bay region who were at the Santa Anita Assembly Center joined this group along with some Hawaiian evacuees. The maximum population was 8,779, making Topaz the fifth largest community in Utah.

40

Fig. 3.1 Miné Okubo, illustration from "An Evacuee's Hopes—and Memories"

Bewilderment was expressed by most of the evacuees with loss of home and security. There are many who were embittered but I think as a whole, despite evacuation, most of us look forward to a better tomorrow. To date, 1,050 indefinite leaves have been granted from this center alone so that the evacuee may go out of camp

Fig. 3.2 Miné Okubo, illustration from "An Evacuee's Hopes—and Memories"

and renew life as a normal American citizen. They are leaving at the rate of eight a day.

"*The evacuees read the same newspapers as the rest of us and listen to the same radio programs. Many are reluctant to leave the centers to face a public that seems predominantly hostile.*"

Here are some of the memories they will take with them: First, buses were chartered for our transportation from our homes to the different assembly centers. Race tracks and fair grounds were transformed overnight with barbed wire and military police. Family numbers and identification cards were given to everybody. On moving day each person and every single piece of baggage had to have tags bearing these numbers. After induction and from then on he or she was identified by these numbers.

"*The names of nearly 90 percent of the adult evacuees have now been checked through FBI.*"

We were all vaccinated for typhoid and for small pox. Young and old were lined up and given shots at a mass production rate.

At Tanforan, most of the cotton mattresses were late in arriving. We were given canvas bags for mattresses.

The lower section of the grandstand served as the mess hall. Young and old, 7,500 people stood out in line waiting to be served. There were often four or five lines, each about a block long, and they had begun forming two hours before mess time. It was a blessing when the 17 mess halls opened.

Fig. 3.3   Miné Okubo, illustration from "An Evacuee's Hopes—and Memories"

Fig. 3.4 Miné Okubo, illustration from "An Evacuee's Hopes—and Memories"

"Costs of feeding over the past several months has ranged from 34 to 42 cents per person per day. All rationing restrictions applicable to the civilian population are strictly followed."

Pre-schools were very important in the center. Busy parents' children were not only assured of good care but good training in these schools. The kiddies of this age are darlings and these schools were a good counter-influence to the bad camp atmosphere.

Then there was the typical Tanforan scene with the old bachelors lying around on the grass and the neighbors visiting and passing on the rumors of the day.

Just when we were settled it was moving day again. We received our orders to prepare for the Utah trip. Improvised box furniture and shelves came down and packing started. Tags with family numbers were brought out. There was inspection for contraband.

The train trip from Tanforan to Topaz was a nightmare. It was the first train trip for most of us and we were excited, but many were sad to leave California and the Bay region. To most of the people, to this day, the world is only as large as from San Francisco to Tanforan to Topaz.

"We have assumed that the great majority of the people of Japanese ancestry now in this country will remain here after the war and continue to be good citizens or law-abiding aliens."

Buses were waiting for us in Delta to take us to Topaz. Seventeen miles of alfalfa farms and greasewood were what we saw. Some people cried on seeing the utter desolation of the camp. Fine alkaline dust hovered over it like San Francisco fog.

Then home life centered around the pot-bellied coal stove which was provided in each of the rooms. Mother hung up clothes, daughter cooked, papa read the newspapers and the kiddies played in the sand pit which was often placed underneath the stove for fire prevention.

"In the barracks there is no running water, no cooking facilities, no bath or toilets. However, each block of 12 or 14 barracks—accommodating between 250 and 300 people—is provided with a mess hall and a bath and laundry building."

During the winter trees and shrubs were transported from the distant mountains and transplanted in camp. Many people were skeptical about them living, but to the surprise of all in the spring green started to appear. Right now Topaz looks a little green in spots and it is a treat. The typical Topaz scene is the watch tower, barbed wire, low tar-covered barracks and the distant mountains.

"The W.R.A. . . . carried out a vast registration program of all evacuees at centers over 17 years of age . . . Aliens were asked to swear they would abide by the laws of the U.S. and not interfere with the war effort. Citizen evacuees were asked to make a definite declaration of loyalty. Eighty-eight percent answered 'yes.'"

Schools were late in opening and difficult to organize because of the lack of school buildings and necessary supplies. Teachers were not available, so they used inexperienced teachers to take over. Sometimes the students knew more than the teachers and there was lack of discipline in the classrooms However, this was not true of all of the classes.

"We believe it is possible to distinguish between the loyal and disloyal people of Japanese ancestry to a degree that will safeguard the national security. We believe that loyalty grows and sustains itself only when it is given a chance."

NOTE

This essay was originally published in the *San Francisco Chronicle* in 1943. The newspaper added the italicized sections, which were taken from a speech by War Relocation Authority director Dillon S. Myer on Executive Order 9066. We reprint the interpolated text to show the constraints under which Okubo was operating and how her work was viewed by a wartime audience.

4

STATEMENT BEFORE THE COMMISSION ON WARTIME RELOCATION AND INTERNMENT OF CIVILIANS

MINÉ OKUBO

M S. OKUBO: This is a new experience for me. My name is Miné Okubo. I am an artist. I was traveling and studying in Europe for almost two years on a fellowship from the University of California. I made the last American ship leaving Bordeaux, France.

When I returned to California, I worked on the Federal Arts Project. At the time of Pearl Harbor and the declaration of World War II, I had been commissioned to do several mosaic murals for the new Oakland Serviceman's Center and for Fort Ord by the Federal Arts Project for the Army.

Shortly after Pearl Harbor all American citizens and aliens of Japanese ancestry were restricted to an 8:00 P.M. to 6:00 A.M. curfew and were not allowed to travel outside a five-mile radius of their home. However, I received a special permit from the Government and those in authority to go to work every day from Berkeley to Oakland to complete these murals.

I finished the murals work but I only had three days to prepare for evacuation. My brother was attending the University of California and lived with me, so it was a big help. We had to clean the house of everything quick and fast. We gave away almost everything and left our important things with our Caucasian friends and left a couple of bulky crates at some of our friends to store with the Government.

We were exhausted and weary from lack of sleep, no eating, and packing, but with friends picking us up in their station wagon, we managed to make the control station on time.

It was a pathetic sight to see mountains and mountains of number-tagged [bags] and hundreds and hundreds of people number-tagged of different ages. The buses were lined up for blocks on this quiet residential street. The First Congregational Church was our control station. Church people served us sandwiches and fruit. We marched to the bus with soldiers on guard. Our friends waved goodbye and people gawked. Our destination was Tanforan Assembly Center.

Cameras were confiscated. Photography was not allowed in any of the camps. Being an artist, I decided to record my whole camp experience. I had many, many friends on the outside and I thought this would be a good way to repay them for their kindness in sending letters and food packages and telling us that we were not forgotten.

I was interested in people and life, so the camp gave me an opportunity to study the human race from cradle to grave and to see what happens to people when they are reduced to one status and one condition.

I was all over the camp sketching everything from the very first day. There were untold hardships and sadness everywhere and humor because everything was so insane.

There were no plans or preparations for this forced evacuation. Everybody of Japanese ancestry was evacuated: the young, the old, the children, babies, pregnant mothers, sick—110,000 were evacuated in three months. One cannot know what it was like unless you lived it.

Since evacuees were not allowed to return to California and the West, and I knew nobody in the East, I decided to remain in camp until the gates closed, but in March 1944 *Fortune* magazine asked me to come to New York to help illustrate their special April 1944 Japan issue and I decided to stay in New York.

When the *Fortune* magazine people saw the vast collection of drawings that I had on the evacuation, they were surprised and excited and when they learned that American citizens were evacuated, they were ashamed, and they decided to look into the matter more, and they wrote an article called "Issei, Nisei, Kibei." It's one of the first illustrated articles that came out in one of the largest periodicals of the time, because anything Japanese was not quite known in the East yet.

These drawings were originally made for my friends on the outside, and the *Fortune* magazine people told me that I should continue and make it into a book. So the factual account of the Japanese evacuation and internment is in *Citizen 13660*, which was published in 1946 by the Columbia University Press. It was the first inside-the-camp documentary story of the Japanese evacuation and internment coming out when the subject was not too well known in the East, and when everything Japanese was still unpopular. It was too soon after the war's ending.

I kept the drawings objective, and the brief text was not only to interest the reader but to record this tragic incident of the war.

I believe an apology and some form of reparation are due in order to prevent this from happening to others. Textbooks and history studies on this subject should be taught to children when young in grade and high schools. Many generations do not know that this ever happened in the United States.

Whenever I speak about evacuation, they think it happened in Japan.

I wish to present a copy of *Citizen 13660* to the Commission for the record.

I also have a copy of the *Fortune* article, "Issei, Nisei, Kibei," and for the public I have put together an exhibition of my sketches, drawings, and paintings for you in the back of the room.

CHAIRMAN FLEMMING: Thank you. First of all, may I say that we appreciate your presenting a copy of the book for the record, and certainly do accept it for the record along with the article from *Fortune* magazine, which made quite an impression on me. You said that you explained to them or that they learned for the first time, I gather, as a result of their conversation with you that U.S. citizens were involved.

MS. OKUBO: Yes, and that they were ashamed and very angry—many were—so they decided that they would write this article and put it into the same issue of *Fortune* in Japan.

They wanted to tell the world what is happening to the Japanese in the United States.

CHAIRMAN FLEMMING: That tells a story by itself in terms of the complete lack of understanding of what was happening.

COMMISSIONER MITCHELL: The reason the people at *Fortune* didn't understand this, it's rather hard to comprehend.

MS. OKUBO: Well, in the East the Japanese weren't well known before this.

COMMISSIONER MITCHELL: They just hadn't thought about it at all?

MS. OKUBO: No. It was political—and then they had this problem of LaGuardia and other mayors who didn't want the Japanese here, you see, and so there was something going on in higher political places.

So *Fortune*, I guess, just avoided it until this Japanese issue came up, and then they didn't look into it that much until they saw the pictures and they saw that everybody was involved, everybody with Japanese ancestry was evacuated, and the people that I worked for, many were ashamed.

CHAIRMAN FLEMMING: As an artist you brought up another point that hasn't been brought up before today—it was brought up at a number of our other hearings— namely, the failure to make an adequate presentation of this part of our history in the history books that are used in our elementary and secondary schools.

I was just wondering whether any publisher of textbooks for use in elementary and secondary schools had ever asked you for help in illustrating it or asked for these pictures.

MS. OKUBO: Well, I think in about 1975 the different publishers have been asking for the history books and so these same drawings are reproduced for many of the textbooks in history and then in social studies.

CHAIRMAN FLEMMING: That started about 1975?

MS. OKUBO: Yes. Then I think—I really should think that it should be started earlier, you know. In the grade schools.

CHAIRMAN FLEMMING: There's no question about it.

MS. OKUBO: And that's one way to get it across, and I think that this redress is very important. Hearings are important because many generations don't know this happened. It's bringing it all to them and they are all asking questions now.

COMMISSIONER MITCHELL: I had just one brief question: Do you have a list of the textbooks in which these articles are published?

MS. OKUBO: I have quite a few.

COMMISSIONER MITCHELL: Could you supply that to the Commission?

MS. OKUBO: Yes, I could later.

CHAIRMAN FLEMMING: That would be very helpful. We would like to have that for the record.

MS. OKUBO: Yes.

CHAIRMAN FLEMMING: Anything else? We are grateful to you for coming and giving us this testimony.

NOTE

This statement is taken from transcripts in the Records of the Commission on Wartime Relocation and Internment of Civilians, Record Group 220: Records of Temporary Committees, Commissions, and Boards, 1893–1999, National Archives, Unsolicited Testimony files, 1981–1982.

5

LETTERS FROM MINÉ OKUBO
TO ISAMU NOGUCHI

[TANFORAN]

July 1, 1942

Dear Mr. Noguchi:

Your letter arrived today. I am sorry I didn't get around to writing you a letter as I have promised in the card. I just had too much to do so I let my letter writing slide.

It is good policy to not believe all that you hear. Don't let that gal in the nurse's uniform fool you. Beauty, talent and wit—the last trait explains me—I'm a nit-wit.

I personally would rather leave the pioneering to others who are more steady and rugged. I prefer to introduce culture later. Har! Har! The picture you paint of Poston is too marvelous to be true! Post Toasties to you and Boy! I can smell the heat and see the dust rising. Tanforan is good enough for me.

All my good friends are located in this area and as I am a person whose first and last thought is food, I would be a nut to move away from the extra delicacies which are brought in now and then.

Teaching is alright but it is a headache. My students are doing really fair work but I would much rather get something done for myself—I keep puttering on with my painting but I feel that I must get out somewhere miles away from civilization (if you can call this setup thus). I can do my best work in quiet. There is no privacy in these camps and therefore I feel that if possible I must get out.

I have no desire to go south for many reasons. Heat for one and the idea of the camp life forever is too much (I prefer a padded cell).

50

My brother states the place is H—— spelled in capital letters with a few exclamation points around it. Since I am the one to follow facts I am at loss to dream of (paradise) as the Caucasians around here speak of so often. They say relocation camps are paradise compared to Assembly Centers. You can't kid a horse fly. No I'm remaining here until they move me or if I should have good fortune to fly east.

It isn't such a big world so I will perhaps run into you someday. I should like to go east but may be sent to Poston. Who knows what may happen. At present I just grin and bear it.

Give my best regards to that lopsided family (Kobayashi). Poor (Y) must be a human skeleton by now. Tell Fumi another reason I won't come is because I might end up having her as a nurse.

As ever.

Miné

[TANFORAN, UNDATED, SEPTEMBER 1942]

Dear Mr. Noguchi:

I left your letter unanswered because I was busy and lazy. For the past three weeks I have been more or less on the sick side. I had a terrible cold. I thought I was a goner but the Good Lord wanted me to continue my existence in this earth so here I am well again.

Anne & Mitch Kunitani of Tanforan left for Poston not long ago. You have probably come across them by now. They wanted me to come down there but I think the question of my coming there is out for I definitely plan to hit the eastward trail. On September 15th I plan to go to Abraham, Utah, to join up with the Mormons. (Relocation camp). From there God only knows where.

More I think of it I want to get out of here so I can get some work done. In this camp it is like living in the Monkey Block or on Telegraph Hill. I have a quarantine sign on the door but even that doesn't faze the time-wasters. I could ambulate a few of them.

Fumi wrote me a long letter and even mentioned your rat hole apartment. What a description! I'm glad to know you are getting work done.

This is my 21st letter and I'm not half through so please excuse writing, etc.

May it get cooler in Poston.

Very sincerely yours,

Miné Okubo

p.s. when rest of the radicals arrive there, you will have friends.

6

LETTERS FROM MINÉ OKUBO
TO DR. ROY W. LEEPER

Miné corresponded with Dr. Roy W. Leeper for nearly fifty years, beginning in 1957. Dr. Leeper was both a longtime friend and a collector of her artwork. His collection of letters from Okubo has been donated to the Smithsonian Institution's Archives of American Art. (Note: Some of the letters are addressed to Dr. Leeper and Dr. Gaylord Hall and their cats, Ringo and Ling.) —GR

May 23, 1957

Dear Roy. You must have a big place in S.F. I can't recall the Filbert area. It's wonderful your mother can be with you. I had a laugh when you mentioned your relations ganging upon you for making a stupid purchase. My mind's eye made a hilarious cartoon of this. Also I pictured your best friend's jaw drop when you unwrapped the "flower painting": Yak! Nothing like being "mad" in your own right.

San Francisco is a charming place but for me N.Y. offers a place where one can disappear and at the same time one must keep the blood flowing in the veins. It's a place where one has got to be alive in order to stay alive. Everybody is fighting and bickering and kept constantly hopping. It's very rich and healthy for a creative brain.

To be classified as a legend is a new one. I've been called everything from a nut to a crackpot simply because I have a mind of my own and I am following my own convictions. It is not the easiest of roads to travel but it has had my share of hilarity because one is completely at odds with everything. Sincerely. Miné.

July 26, 1957

Dear Roy. I have a habit of answering letters right away but forgetting to mail them if I don't happen to have stamp and envelope on hand. In the meantime letters get jammed between piles of sketches and I find these letters decades later. I remember writing a letter to you before my last note but I don't know if I mailed it. . . . It is hot as hell here. Pools of sweat at end of pencil just from holding the pencil. Have been getting pretty weary of meeting all these deadlines, now I've got most of them controlled for the first rechecking but I'm jammed up with nut problems among them the landlord. (Trying to raise rent double because I work at home). We are both determined so it all amounts to head pain. To the mirth of my friends they say at last maybe then you will have an exhibition on the sidewalk. That is when I am kicked out. Sincerely. Miné.

August 3, 1957

Dear Roy. Other day on 14th St., on one of the hottest of days, I saw my first Santa Claus. He was complete with flowing whiskers and knee-high boots and sweating like a plow horse. This is no joke. Santa is symbol of July here in NY and your gift of candy (apple cotlets) arriving now had me amused. I said, "It must be Christmas!" It was a surprise and they are delicious. I am eating them as I slave on this Christianity book. Many thanks to you Roy, but you shouldn't be sending me gifts.

I'm completely tied up with this awful job which is very technical and time taking with no grand result and in the end the whole thing will amount to Siberian labor camp pay plus experience. It will take about a week more.

I'm having a rough time now as the rent thing has started to take action. It's going to be one of those sickeningly long drawn-out affairs of battle of wits. Sincerely. Miné.

August 26, 1957

Dear Roy. I [have a] vision terrific stuff coming in my work but I do not kid myself ever as to the uncompromising challenges yet to be faced in order to fulfill the perfection that I seek. I had a pretty good undisturbed week to work despite the eviction threats. I can picture myself being hauled out with brush in hand. Yuk!

September 5, 1957

Dear Roy. Labor Day Holiday I had some good painting sessions except for some dinner engagements and nonsense. Work getting more solid, richer in color and spontaneous: lots of (naïve) humans, also serious ones: limited few who have seen work [are] delighted. Still work [is] small. I can hardly wait to get into big stuff and major productions.

The landlord business is still in suspension but coming to some conclusion where I still maintain and fight principle but may give him a slight raise provided he paints place and gives me a lease. This will mean a major task because of the accumulated junk. I have a feeling I will throw out everything but for the very necessities. We are all a bunch of pack rats in analysis.

September 19, 1957
Dear Roy. Yes, I know Islam area art is loaded with motifs and color for when I came to N.Y., I lived at the Metropolitan Museum. I have had a great fascination for [oriental] stuff and one of the things I studied lots were rugs. Persian stuff also intrigued me as I am a great one for color. In painting, French impressionists took painting farthest in oil.

October 17, 1957
Dear Roy. What a nightmare task! Every muscle and bone aches. I have been at this since I last wrote you and I will be at it for sometime so I can forget it when I get into production. A tornado or an earthquake would relieve me of all these decisions as to [what I should discard].

October 23, 1957
Dear Roy. The Queen of England was in town. Everybody stark raving. I went to see the procession too. Had a good spot on the street but by the time the cars came I was pushed against the wall of the building. A man behind me looked at his wrist watch and said, "2 minutes!" What a show. Yuk! The cars were traveling so fast all was like a swift wind.

November 28, 1957
Dear Roy. Chicago for me is a dreadful city. I remember one winter when I saw frozen words come out of people's mouths. Yes—it can get windy, cold and pretty nasty in that ville . . . Had a good laugh about [your] wish to hear me talk—most people think I should have my mouth washed with soap as 2, 3, and 4 letter words flow out with greatest of ease—far from quaint!

March 31, 1958
Dear Roy. Your nice neat letters reflect on my chicken-scratch scribble. Some friends have written that they don't know about my paintings but that my letters have completely left the representational field. . . . After all these weeks of silence I finally went to Yale for conferences this week and I failed completely because I was killing myself not to fulfill their supposed conservative minds—now they think they want something completely new—it is the usual procedure as they all don't know what they

want in the first place and [are] always wrapped up in terms of getting off the normal and accepted. All of it will mean a complete new start.

January 3, 1959

Dear Roy. This is to say I'm bringing down the gates on everybody. My whole life I went out to understand and listen to people and as the result my life is deluged and pestered by people (the weak, sick, empty, lonely, lost, dead) to whom I am the last Indian. No more of this nonsense. They can all take their ills elsewhere. Starting [in] 1959 I think of myself. No letters and no nothing, no more. I must free my mind from [the every day] to follow the creative [years before they fly away]. I have had 4 beautiful fights over the holidays and I feel good. No more the silent smiling idiot for others to latch on to but a sharp-tongued TNT. I blast out what I see in each of them and good riddance. It is awareness of the frailties in people and life that make me an artist dedicated.

February 1, 1960

Dear Roy. The Guggenheim museum to me is a monstrosity of unbeauty and wasted space. To top matters fluorescent lights destroy paintings. The circular idea start is okay but the building didn't come off as a thing of simple beauty—as a Coney Island attraction it draws people in droves and at 50 cents entrance fee the building should already be paid for. To each is one's own judge.

July 28, 1960

Dear Roy. If you are serious about collecting Okubo and hope to leave collection to a museum later, the idea is to make an interesting group as well as the individual good paintings. Be critical and selective, you don't have to buy everything I send to you. Later I will have some good abstracts. Would you be interested in drawings and [watercolors]? If so I will keep some good ones in mind. . . . Build your own world and don't envy others[,] for if one studied closely one will find Peyton Place or vast emptiness in the most heavenly—Frailty of people and life is a lulu—a set of paradox, a free circus. However, as an artist in this mess-pot I see wonders. [So I have dedicated myself to the pursuit of perfect] beauty and truth in hopes that others may see too.

Serious decisions came about in the forties. I myself was on top of the ladder with a lucrative career as a commercial artist and I knew everybody important. I could have had the moon but I decided all was one Big Dung Heap and blew all to the winds to follow the humanitarian journey of a dedicated artist. Everybody thought I was nuts. If any regrets, it's because I did not decide earlier for now I realize the waste of time and the value of time.

Fig. 6.1 "Season's Greetings," 1963–64

July 11, 1961

I am beating my brains out. Whatever I have to say to the world is in paints.

October 26, 1969

Dear Roy. So Gaylord has got to California again and army boy Innes showed up and others too. Sounds like you should have gone into the hotel business. Too bad the cats can't take charge instead of fighting each other. Sorry to hear but normal that Ringo resents Ling. He has lost his place and on top of that has to take the insults from the growing brat cat which uses him for living plaything target, unless they are related or brought up together . . . sometime they don't get along like a dog and cat playmates. . . . Roy, I finally got something unique in painting. I stayed with the funny and the small all these years, and it has jelled 100% into something so simple and powerful everybody will have no doubts looking at work now. It's been coming for a long time but I had to play along until this total integration of loose shapes like calligraphy writing. . . . Things haven't been rose petals and I have lots of crack-up cases around here in every form and shape like everybody else has. When things get too goofy I go to the movies and am cured. Wow! The case studies there are lulus!

The world has gone to pot! Values at lowest! There was one great week here when the Mets won the World's Series and baseball pennant—people were really happy in spirit. Everything else to them is apathy.

June 1969
Dear Roy and Ringo. Weather hot now and I finally got the porch fixed and painted. Plan to put new bulbs in . . . and work on big paintings now. I lined up 3 hours to see Judy [Garland]—what an experience! What humanity! Squirrelville Okubo.

March 3, 1970
Dear Leeper. Hoist the American flag! Finally all the bells rang and I have [done] what I set out to do 23 years ago in painting. . . . The simplest art ever. Happy Spring! My best. Squirrelville Okubo.

September 5, 1970
This is Labor Day weekend and I have work piled up. I have been in paper work for over three weeks and I have had stupid interruptions of every kind. On top of all, the death of a dear friend this week. All these long time friends with mind, heart, and understanding are going and it is very sad. Now more than ever I realize the passing of time and that I am not getting younger and that my own years are numbered. . . . It is fall here. Can't say smell of fall as the city is so polluted one tries not to breathe much of it. Seems a gloomy labor day start but I hope the sun wins out before the 3 days are up. The Washington Square Art is in now; opened yesterday, but few artists came out because it was a stormy day with strong wind. They never had much luck weather-wise. It rained a lot on them in the Spring show.

September 22, 1970
It is a beautiful fall day now. The Washington Square Art folded on Sunday. More quality in realism but same old thing. Lots of young and new. The hippies and peddlers of all kinds join in to make the whole thing look like a flea market. The regular artists have to pay $15 so squawk but they can't do a thing for fear of causing a riot. Seems law can't do anything anymore. So many artists get work stolen in the show and the audacity of the stealers. If caught in the act they act as if nothing happened and it wasn't them and want to be friends and say let's shake hands. Weird ain't the world. Boy! . . . If you people think I've been killing myself for 24 years to become a professional artist you are out of your tortilla flats! . . . Sincerely. Squirrelville Okubo.

April 18, 1971
Dear Roy and Hall. Thank you for the vacation break from routine work. I enjoyed the plays, the dinners, the walking and the talking very much. I liked both plays but

I preferred "Follies" because it deals with reality of people and life as it is and it had so many fine qualities, and perfections here and there to admire and respect. . . . You fellows are blessed by the Gods to have fine weather all week and I must say you are living it up a la Ritz and why not if you can do so because you will pass through this way (planet) only once. With everybody I know retired and puttering in garden or sunning on foreign shores and I having to stay with the rock pile I can sometimes yell but I'm stuck with my pile. . . . I am aware of life and see each nut is loaded with nightmares. Life is harsh. It is a living circus. . . . Squirrelville Okubo.

May 5, 1971
Dear Roy [and cats]. . . . This Sunday to the stomach laughs of a few close friends who know of my Perils of Pauline life, I was hit by a baseball. Not in the head but on the leg and so I am with a painful black and blue spot. Luckily it missed the shin bone. With friends, covered Chinatown area and the East Village over where boys were using street and sidewalk for a ball park. You have no idea how hard those balls are.

October 8, 1972
Dear Roy and Weaselhead Hall. Thanks for plays, dinners, drinks, flowers, liquor and candy. I enjoyed the break and had a good time. "Superstar" was too much of the put-on and corn but I liked "Grease." Players were people and personalities so it radiated life. There was lots there to read too if one can see. . . . Best to everyone. Keep well and crazy. Despite the drinking, seem to be holding up fine. It was nice seeing both of you. Adios and hello to Ringo & Ling & Ting. Squirrelville Okubo.

April 6, 1973
Dear California Joe Hall. . . . The thing I can't make people see is that I am not a person trying to be an artist . . . but am a person born with insight and understanding so keen. I'm using art as my means to prove the truths of life and painting is the result.

August 7, 1973
Dear Roy and animals. . . . I am touched by Gaylord and your kindness to give me the first chance to rent a studio where I could have paintings out for work is a wonderful dream but all depends on my course of work and events. For the present New York is the best base for me in every possible way. Here I am totally independent and free and I have a feeling of being able to come and go as I please with every convenience possible at arm's reach and not much effort or time needed for maintenance. Also I am able to step out the door at will and enter the pulsating whirl of people and life activities which is a delight and also a necessity to me. . . . I wake up and this room

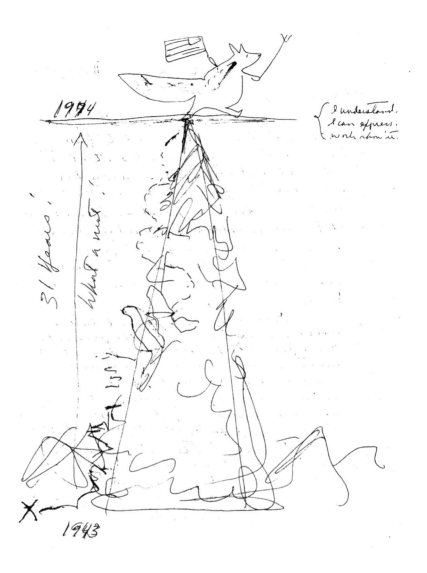

1974

31 years.

What a nut.

1943

{ I understand.
{ I can express.
{ work when it.

Fig. 6.2   "Squirrelville Okubo"

tower in the middle of people and life madness is perfect as I function on instincts and not plans. There is also the advantage of being where everybody comes and where I can be reached easily. . . .

   At the moment I don't feel so hot because this time the nervous wreck exhaustion aftermath from this apartment painting nightmare is shingles on face and neck.

Fortunately not in too conspicuous a spot. I am applying medication twice a day. No pains but bothersome. The way I drive myself it's a wonder I didn't end up with more damage. . . . Nothing much to report but to say summer is about shot and I'm one year older and this year will be shot soon. . . . My best. Squirrelhead Okubo.

August 13, 1973
Dear Roy and cats. My work has finally become one and I am now organizing place for production in the large sizes. My shingles is healing up so I feel like a human again. . . . For a person not driving a car remoteness is too inconvenient. New York to me as I am set up now is ideal for it is an ivory tower in midst of everything with not much time or effort wasted in the maintenance end of things and the minute I'm out the door is an adventure which is perfectly suitable for concentrated work. I am fine and independent to go and come at will anytime and when I please everywhere and this is important. Also I am in easy reach of anything important that comes like the Japanese TV thing last week. A possible interview for an evacuation documentary. These things always come and are done in a rush with not much preparation. . . . We are having a beautiful stretch of good weather. Two weeks now and a joy to see sun every day. Some days very hot and humid, but we survive. The light is very good now.

Save the tree climbing to Ringo. I can see tormented Ling now that he has had taste of freedom and the outer world. . . . Hello to all. Must run for appointment so will put this in mail.

August 31, 1973
Dear Roy. Your note and snaps of me and painting and Ling and Tai-Tai arrived. The snaps of me came out clear but I sure look like a sumo champion. Thank you! You should see what the final painting is! It's like everything opened up like a flower. The French Impressionists saw in the Japanese art the simplicity and understanding of Nature. I've found my own identity & writing . . . with the content of reality intact. . . . So ends summer 1973. I did it. Wow!

January 3, 1974
Dear Roy. I noticed one black squirrel in Washington Square Park. Other day saw a tree full of them. Really funny creatures. Should be a laugh to see them in the snow. . . . The Manzanar book came and I never read much, but I got the book read in a couple hours. After my book where I put all the facts down (to my surprise as not too bright then) everything reads about same but the father description was typical of the knuckleheaded Issei fathers so that I did get a laugh. Book was simple and well-written. I passed it on to others as a loan to read. . . .

I sent Xmas card to everybody (even the Oakland list) to remind them I'm still here on this planet. The Japanese paper in S.F. printed it, saying Miné Okubo sends greetings. I had several clippings coming in the mail. From different people. The Los Angeles paper (Japanese paper) as usual printed my full-page Christmas drawing. . . .

One night I went to the Mexican Folklore dance program at the City Center. Reminded me of Riverside Days—very colorful and happy with enough changes to breach the monotony of sameness. Well, it was one hell of a year and a mad ending. Hope to make 1974 sing forward despite the gloomy outlook everywhere and in everybody. . . . Well have a good 1974. It is the Tiger Year. Hi to everybody. Squirrelhead Okubo.

February 18 1974

Dear Roy and Hall. Happy Washington Day! . . . Something came out of the air which I think is an honor and is also beneficial for my going out to the public this year. I was selected by the Riverside City College (Junior College) as the alumnus of the year to be honoured with a plaque, a show, and a reception and the news media. So I will have to get a small show ready and be there June 18th. I'm accepting provided details can be worked out. I am weary and all feet and hands because I don't know where to begin. It will be repeat madness of 1972. . . .

Things seem to be opening up in my book thing too so I'm trying to push these at the same time so I can have books in print so I can sell at all these public places. All frightening and I'm not keen on all these things but I want to make headway and make it so I can pay back loans to everybody. I didn't think it would take all this time to throw out all the crap and get back to me and universal. . . . The Princeton speech thing which I received now verifies all. I will have to go there last part of March. Got to prepare that too. I plan to talk about my art with slides and give them another slant on art. It will be good to try to reach the young heads. So I accepted it. I am a shy person and don't give me that hot-shit talk. I am not only shy but very simple-witted as to words and such so a total failure at lectures and such but I do have a strong will and I have too many obligations to fulfill so got to s—— in pants to do all. I'll end up with shingles and eczema.

My best. Squirrelhead Okubo.

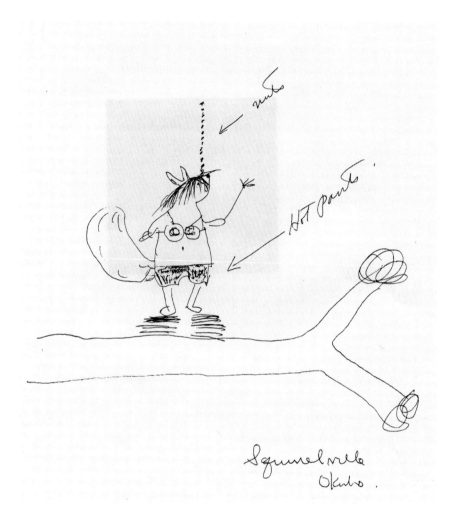

Fig. 6.3 "1943–1974: 31 Years! What a Nut! I understand. I can express. Work shows it."

May 9, 1979

After chaos, confusion, delay finally gave speech. (Lincoln Center mall and steps) Had it in a building nobody could even get to or find—a monster of a place. One can't go up steps but had to go way around back to the other side. Nobody showed so they had to announce over the loudspeaker at mall stage after delay of 30 minutes. By that time I was so mad I had forgotten what I was to say. Finally a full house and all went okay but I forgot all the amusing things I was to say. How can they plan such a confusion. Golly! My best. Squirrelhead Okubo.

October 24, 1983

Dear Roy [and cat]. . . . Opening of show I understand drew 250 plus people but not many after as timing is odd and way in Chinatown. Also non-profit so no selling place. . . . I learned lots by showing and seeing things hung. Show goes on to 29th so still one may come and see. Usually things pick up at end of show. I'm not worried about my work. I did something no artist did so will eventually find way out. It's a matter of fame today or fame after. Main thing is to fulfil one's goals in work. . . . It's a dark gloomy day. . . . Well that's it for now. My best. Miné.

October 1987

Dear Roy. . . . Finally had to be cruel to be kind to myself. I found that few understand art or life and what I was doing so I had to take control. Everything written about me has [said] that I was an individual following the universal values so automatically out in this political and economic oriented society where $ is value. I tried to build followers and believers en route but failed. So I must find my own imaginative way out against the tide of everything. It will be like jumping into the Atlantic as there are no values or integrity out there anymore. But I will challenge on. My generation gone and 30–40 people all disbanded to go individual roads so it will mean starting out new in every way. I'll keep you informed. A horrible road, but I chose it and knew what I would face. So I'm with it. Sincerely, Miné. p.s. I hope your pumpkin party will be successful and fun.

December 1992

Dear Leeper and Hall. Have finally put together 48 years of research in painting into one and I am finally with understanding, knowledge, and mastery. Actually it is to find one's own identity [and] handwriting, and to become a whole person again. The key here is understanding of people and life. As the highest top inner vision . . . the challenge is in the realm of God and science as everything attunes to truth and [the] universal. So it is a different alone road. I will be having a five decade sponsored retrospective exhibition in Boston on March 3, 1993. I will know more when things take shape. Hope things have been well your way. Merry Merry! And Happy Happy! My best, Miné Okubo. Ahooey! Haven't given up!

[Undated] 1994

Those who thought I was just one more nut old lady painting pretty pictures will get a surprise. To educate and to build a following was a laugh. My mistake was to leave the top minds of *Fortune* [magazine]. . . . The best years with idealism were 1940–1950—everything died with [the] flower children and [the] Vietnam War in 1960.

February 15, 1997

Dear Leeper. Hope what ails you will be successful in the operation. Getting old is the pits. All around in [New York] everybody in our generation is ending up with something. December and January were very sad months for me as I lost all the ones rooting for me since 1944 when I came here to New York. Suddenly, I'm beginning to feel old. With [my] black hair, people don't think I'm 84. But I've shrunk three inches and my cursing is . . . loud and to the point. . . . Anyway, I'll make it. I've proven everything so will move outwards soon. Be around. My best. Miné.

December 1998

Dear Roy. With my "it is and it isn't" clarity of mind and vision, and with my knowledge and keen insight into people and life, I decided to dedicate my life to this highest inner vision [of] beauty [and] art. It is one's own challenge and a hell road all the way for one is going towards universal truth. In the society and people world, [one is supposed] to follow and to play along. This research took 50 years and now, with the final integrity answers to life and art, I have arrived. . . . [It's been] a long, lonely journey but a joyous challenge towards wonders and betterment. My Christmas cards each year were to tell everybody that I was taking this difficult total odds road towards universal truth. A Merry Xmas and a Happy New Year. Wishing you good health and joy. Sincerely, Miné Okubo.

[Undated] 1998

Dear Roy and Hall. You weren't around when I was glorified like a movie star and a princess by the [big wigs] of the Bay Area in 1935 and 1936. . . . All the people of that time were all dead when you two appeared in 1958. I am working harder than I ever did . . . to finish up my life's work and I've started to clear away 50 years of accumulation. What a job! I'm packed solid like a sardine can. We have been having beautiful weather here. . . . My generation and organizations [are] all gone, but I will fight on and finish up. Stay around for the fireworks. My best. Miné.

II

SCHOLARLY

ESSAYS

7

GESTURES OF NONCOMPLIANCE

RESISTING, INVENTING, AND ENDURING
IN *CITIZEN 13660*

VIVIAN FUMIKO CHIN

Miné Okubo's *Citizen 13660* documents the ways in which Japanese American internees used gesture and invention to resist edicts based upon essentialist notions of race that demonized the "Japanese" body. In the book's preface, Okubo states, "I am not bitter"; however, this stated lack of bitterness contrasts with illustrations showing Okubo sticking her tongue out at figures of authority and with images of internees shielding themselves from their surroundings with their hands.[1] These physical gestures demonstrate acts of resistance toward environmental elements and serve as symbolic gestures of resistance against forced incarceration. Moreover, hands busy with knitting, making paper flowers, building, and gardening show how handiwork and productivity allowed for ways to fight boredom and inhumane treatment. *Citizen 13660* illustrates a spirit of endurance that helped internees withstand the experience of internment camp.

The conviction that the Japanese "race" was a product of biology that determined the making of national affiliations governed the decision to remove people of Japanese ancestry from the West Coast of the United States.[2] On February 19, 1942, two months after the bombing of Pearl Harbor, President Franklin D. Roosevelt signed Executive Order 9066, which authorized the secretary of war and military commanders "to prescribe military areas . . . from which any or all persons may be excluded."[3] This order was made more specific with civilian exclusion orders, which ruled that "all persons of Japanese ancestry, both alien and non-alien, be excluded" from "military areas," then designated as the West Coast.[4] This call for the exclusion of Japanese Americans was predicated upon a belief in a biological essentialist concept of race, in which Japanese ancestry meant a "natural" loyalty to Japan. In other words, people of Japanese ancestry would inherently hold an allegiance to Japan, despite their citizenship or residency.

Such a belief in a natural disloyalty to the United States stemmed from ideologies of "absolute difference."[5] As noted by David Palumbo-Liu in *Asian/America: Historical Crossings of a Racial Frontier*, this notion was put forth, for example, in 1914, by sociologist Robert E. Park. According to Park, "The Japanese, like the Negro, is condemned to remain among us as an abstraction, a symbol—and a symbol not merely of his own race but of the Orient and of that vague, ill-defined menace we sometimes refer to as the 'yellow peril.'"[6]

Thus classified, the Japanese "race" was a significant, if "vague and ill-defined" threat. Later arguments in favor of the exclusion of Japanese Americans echoed this contention. One month prior to the signing of Executive Order 9066, in a memo written by Major Carter Garver, acting assistant adjutant general of the army, to Lieutenant General John L. DeWitt, Garver warned: "From what is known of the Japanese character and mentality it is also considered dangerous to rely on the loyalty of native born persons of Japanese blood unless such loyalty can be affirmatively demonstrated."[7] According to Garver, American birth was no guarantee of American affiliation, and disloyalty based on blood should be assumed. Again naming "Japanese" as a race, DeWitt, who was responsible for West Coast security, wrote in the final recommendation he submitted to Secretary of War Henry Stimson:

> The Japanese race is an enemy race and while many second and third generation Japanese born on United States soil, possessed of United States citizenship, have become "Americanized," the racial strains are undiluted. To conclude otherwise is to expect that children born of white parents on Japanese soil sever all racial affinity and become loyal subjects, ready to fight, and, if necessary, to die for Japan in a war against the nation of their parents.[8]

Here, DeWitt conflates "racial affinity" and national loyalty, charging that race would overcome place of birth and citizenship. The racial characteristics that render the "Japanese race" an "enemy race" are inherited. Thus, no person of Japanese ancestry, even if born in the United States and an American citizen, could be expected to be loyal to the United States.

The military position regarding Japanese American loyalty remained informed by a reading of the "Japanese" body. Reiterating the significance of inherited "Japanese" physical characteristics, a document prepared by the War Relocation Authority maintained, "All Japanese look very much alike to a white person—it is hard for us to distinguish between them. It would be hard to tell a Japanese soldier from a resident Japanese."[9] Being of Japanese ancestry and looking "Japanese" were enough to cast suspicion regarding matters of national loyalty. A white person would not be able to distinguish between a Japanese person who was an enemy and a Japanese American person who was loyal to the United States.

Citizen 13660 depicts the language of racism in use in December 1941 and Okubo's response to it. "On the West Coast there was talk of possible sabotage and invasion by the enemy. It was 'Jap' this and 'Jap' that," the text reads, while the accompanying illustration shows Okubo meeting the reader's gaze, standing at a table. Her hands are braced against a newspaper opened flat on the table, while headline-style phrases in uppercase letters such as "A JAP IS A JAP" and "DON'T TRUST A JAP" fill the space around her, bombarding her body.[10] A small, derogatory cartoon face appears next to the caption "A JAP LOOKS LIKE THIS."[11] Okubo's elbows are locked straight, and her hands and arms support her as she stands stiffly. She is not actively fending off the racist language, but she is not cowering in shame and fear. Her posture is one of strength and resilience while she is being pelted with hate speech.

A reoccurring design on clothing worn by people in *Citizen 13660* counters the idea that all "Japs" looked the same. In the illustration, Okubo stands surrounded by the hateful slogans, wearing a shirt covered with crosses, a pattern that reappears throughout the book. Because it is so distinctive, a reader might expect this pattern to be used as an easy way to identify Okubo. But although it usually does appear on her clothing, this pattern at times appears on clothing worn by others—a headscarf, a woman's blouse, or a man's shirt—while Okubo is dressed in unpatterned fabric. In one illustration, a woman in a cross-patterned blouse who faintly resembles Okubo might be mistaken for Okubo.[12] One expects the pattern to signify Okubo. This expectation or visual trick mimics the misapprehension discussed in the War Relocation Authority document, which states, "All Japanese look very much alike."[13] To discern Okubo, one is forced to look more carefully at the drawing, to notice distinguishing features such as the shape of her hair; then one can see that these two women do not really look alike. An apparent sign—the crosses—does not serve to signify what is expected and thus disrupts the making of meaning based on appearances. Another illustration that plays with notions of indistinguishable people depicts three women wearing identical blouses, all marked with the same cross pattern. "Everyone was dressed alike, because of the catalog orders and the G.I. clothes," the text explains.[14] However, the three women look nothing alike. One is visibly pregnant; another is elderly, wears glasses, and has her hair in a bun; and the other is Okubo, arms akimbo, with a look of irritation on her face. Despite their matching clothing, each person is distinctive, and the women are easy to tell apart.

In her book *Masking Selves, Making Subjects*, Traise Yamamoto observes that "Nisei women's autobiographies are frustratingly *un*autobiographical, not given to personal disclosure or passages of intimate self-reflection."[15] In its written text, *Citizen 13660* complies with this observation by maintaining an emotional distance from its subject. Okubo declines to state how she feels and upholds an even, unemotional tone in the writing throughout the book. Even when describing a short leave from Tanforan, she does not bracket her language with phrases like "I felt...," instead stating, "That one day of liberty was wonderful. I was like a child." In contrast, the illustrations show the emotions the text elides. For example, when Okubo and her brother must leave their house for incarceration at Tanforan, the caption reads, "Our friends came to take us to the Civil Control Station. We took one last look at our happy home."[16] These two factual statements do not reveal Okubo's inner sentiments. The illustration, however, shows two tears on Okubo's cheek, supplementing the written text and disclosing her emotional state. By not explicitly discussing negative emotions, the written text does not risk publicly confessing personal feelings. Instead, Okubo's facial expressions in the drawings reveal her noncompliance through emotions of sadness, anger, and displeasure.

Yamamoto goes on to ask, "... is the very act of articulation, taking on the assumption of the right to speak the self, a gesture of resistance sufficient to refuse the pressures of hegemonic autobiographical representation?"[17] To apply this point to *Citizen 13660*, one might venture to state that Okubo's illustrated memoir is counterhegemonic simply because it was produced under conditions that would erase and silence her. If we acknowledge that the political context in which Okubo wrote her autobiographical work constructed her as an enemy who needed to be removed from mainstream American society, then we can read *Citizen 13660* as a gesture of resistance that sufficiently refuses to represent a compliant, invisible, and silenced Japanese American internee. Regarding autobiographies of Nisei women, Yamamoto asserts: "At issue are crucial acts of discursive agency and the (re)appropriation of representational power, both of which are directly related to whether one reads these autobiographies as simply benign remembrances of things past or as self-conscious narratives that construct and assert subjecthood and agency."[18]

Although Okubo avoids language that openly expresses bitterness or anger, *Citizen 13660* is not a "benign remembrance" but a text that consistently provides its narrator with a self-determined and critical perspective. This perspective is made clearly evident by Okubo's inclusion of herself in the illustrations. Throughout *Citizen 13660*, Okubo places herself in almost every illustration, in profile or facing the reader. Her profile reminds us that we are seeing through her eyes, while the gaze she returns to the reader prevents her from becoming merely an object of spectacle, something to be looked at and pitied. The reader is thus drawn into the text. In this way, Okubo grants herself agency and resists the notion of herself as an "Other." When she appears in profile, the reader shares Okubo's vision; when she faces the reader, Okubo asserts her subjectivity. She is present as an individual who cannot be made into a faceless member of the "yellow peril," and she is an individual who cannot be erased.

In contrast to, say, Ansel Adams's collection of photographs taken at Manzanar, Okubo's drawings in *Citizen 13660* do not accentuate the aesthetic beauty of her surroundings or subjects. These drawings are made up of harsh, strong lines, unlike the softer contours of her other artwork. While interned in Topaz, Okubo produced the covers for three issues of *Trek*, "a literary magazine spiced with wry humor in recording the day-to-day life experiences of the camp."[19] This magazine was published by and for internees. The cover for the February 1943 issue is similar to illustrations of people eating at Tanforan and Topaz in *Citizen 13660*.[20] However, the hands of the people on the cover of *Trek* are not marked with the lines that make the hands in *Citizen 13660* look clawlike and unappealing. Perhaps, through the more pleasing look of the hands on the *Trek* covers, Okubo wanted to provide a softer tone for readers who were already familiar with the harshness of camp life.

Okubo does not gloss over the challenging conditions of internment camp in *Citizen 13660*. One illustration depicts her trying to paint while swarms of insects fly in through the window and buzz around her. One hand is at rest, and the other awkwardly grasps a paintbrush.[21] The hands are crudely drawn in unattractive shapes, the fingers heavily lined with creases. This style of drawing refuses to make its subject palatable and easy to witness. These hands are "ugly," as if they have taken on the undesirable characteristics attributed to Japanese Americans by the U.S. government. Yet despite their "ugliness," these hands perform the everyday tasks necessary to maintain a certain standard of living—eating, washing, and building and also creating and protecting.

The stark rendering of hands augments the terse and careful language used to narrate the memoir. Okubo was first sent to live at the Tanforan Assembly Center, a racetrack near San Francisco where the War Relocation Authority saw fit to house people in stables. Okubo portrays the constraints imposed upon the Tanforan evacuees. In a grammatically passive construction that leaves the organizers unnamed, Okubo recalls, "Churches were early established to bolster the morale of the bewildered and humiliated people."[22] The passive form of expression used here echoes the restricted agency available to the internees. At the same time, in the very direct language of an empowered narrative voice, Okubo describes the evacuees as "bewildered and humiliated." Although such an unrestrained description of negative emotional states occurs infrequently, Okubo's voice is one of authority and certainty. Even in her reserved observations, she claims the right to name her experiences.

Unspoken language also appears throughout the book. Much of the body language shown in *Citizen 13660* involves people using their hands in practical and symbolic protective gestures. Okubo's somewhat grotesque hands shield people from windblown dust, intruding eyes and sounds, and bad smells. In an illustration of Tanforan, Okubo sweeps the floor with a small whisk broom after arriving at the horse stall in which she must live. She holds a handkerchief over her nose and mouth in an attempt to block out the dirt. Okubo and another woman repeat this gesture in a scene that concerns the weather at Tanforan, where it was "always windy and dusty." When Okubo and other internees were moved to an internment camp in Utah, they were greeted by a sign reading "Welcome to Topaz," and she recounts, ". . . we could hear band music and people cheering, but it was impossible to see anything through the dust." The expressions of welcome become ironic as the environment refuses to provide a welcome. In this picture, and in a picture showing Okubo and her brother being guided to their new living quarters, the internees struggle to use their bodies to shield themselves against the inhospitable surroundings. This struggle continues as time passes. When Easter comes to Topaz and a ceremony begins, "an unusually violent wind and dust storm struck the center. People ran in all directions for shelter." A crowd fills the image, with those in front covering their faces while the wind gusts and blows dust at them. The following page depicts a similar set of contrasts. The text begins "In spring the climate in Topaz was mild" and then elaborates, "But the wind blew from all points of the compass most of the time." Three figures in heavy coats make a great effort to walk while using their hands to fend off the wind. The next page further explains, "They tried everything to control the wind and the dust. . . . But nothing was successful; the elements won out."[23] Who constitutes this "they" is unclear, but in the illustration, Okubo covers her face with her hands while a fellow internee wearing a face mask wields a pick in an attempt to construct a defense against the wind and dust. Ultimately, resistance against these elements is futile. They can only wait for the weather to improve. If we compare this situation to the general political climate of the times, and to the experience of being interned, Okubo seems to suggest that some unfavorable conditions have no remedy. One must simply withstand the weather until it improves, and one must simply withstand living in internment camp until the situation improves.

Wind and dust were not the only aggravating environmental elements. Conditions caused not by nature but by crowding created problems for evacuees. In Tanforan, "The stench from the stagnant sewage was terrible," Okubo writes. She and two others use their hands to clamp their noses shut as they walk past workers who are "always digging up the camp" in an attempt to repair the pipes. In Topaz, "The sewage swamp was located half a mile directly west of the center . . . the stench came sailing into camp whenever the wind was in the right direction." Okubo and her brother pinch their noses, while another man covers his nose with his sleeve.[24] Despite their knowledge of the exact location of the sewage swamp at Topaz, and despite efforts at Tanforan to maintain the sewage system, nothing can alleviate the invasive and offensive odor, and they cannot simply move away from the stink. The noxious traces, the physical reality, the actual presence of the living bodies of those interned cannot be eradicated. Although completely unpleasant, this sign of their existence endures.

In other drawings, people shield themselves against intrusions upon their private space and against a general lack of power over the affairs of daily life. At suppertime on her first day at Tanforan, after waiting for an hour in a line that led nowhere, Okubo finds a friend in another line, and she and her brother crowd in. Her hands appear very large as she stands with her arms crossed firmly across her chest, protecting herself against the punishing glares of two men standing nearby in the line. Similarly, in an image that shows a cutaway view of two adjoining horse-stall living spaces, Okubo sits with her arms crossed. She watches a pot on a hot plate, while one neighbor replaces a lightbulb and another cradles a nursing infant in her arms. The text explains, "Although cooking was not permitted in the barracks and stalls, blown fuses often left us in the darkness, guiltily pondering whether it was our hot plate or our neighbor's that did the trick."[25] Defying a rule that restricts her power to control what she eats, Okubo shields herself from blame for breaking a rule or blowing a fuse. In a matching posture, her neighbor breastfeeds her baby. Despite the authorities' attempts to dictate the details of everyday life, internees manage to keep some semblance of control, and, as the nursing infant demonstrates, life goes on.

While life continues, Okubo shows people being subjected to physical discomfort while being transported by train from Tanforan to Topaz. "The trip was a nightmare that lasted two nights and a day," and passengers hold their heads in their hands while their faces show fatigue. Okubo curls up on top of a suitcase on her seat, her arms tightly crossed, containing her body, while, next to her, her brother assumes a reverse pose with arms folded behind his head, his body open and stretched out. The people around them are sitting in different positions, all uncomfortable-looking.[26] These illustrations show the effects of the exclusion orders on people's bodies, recording their physical realities. The passengers on the train are not merely numbers but people suffering from physical discomforts that bespeak their humanity.

One dehumanizing factor of camp life was the lack of privacy caused by overcrowding. "The flush toilets were always out of commission," and in the women's bathroom, "a half-partition separated the toilets conversationally in pairs." Okubo injects humor into this scene by describing the toilet placement as conversational, as if the private act of relieving oneself could easily become shared and public. Exposed by this design arrangement and by Okubo's pen, a woman seated on a toilet holds her head in her hands, shutting her eyes. Her posture rejects the idea of a relaxed conversation under those circumstances. Okubo continues on another page, "Many of the women could not get used to the community toilets. They sought privacy by pinning up curtains and setting up boards." In this picture, a woman without the benefit of a curtain or board covers her face with her hand and shuts her eyes.[27] In these pictures, the women's shielding hands seek to prevent the humiliating exposure of a private act. The gesture works on two levels: first, within the context of the image itself, it wards off the eyes of the other figures, and, second, from outside the image, it thwarts the reader's gaze, refusing to make the women a spectacle. The women's closed eyes serve to further close off their bodies and also function as a barrier, shutting out their surroundings.

In addition to portraying gestures and postures that attempt to assert boundaries between a subject and the exterior world, Okubo shows people engaged in physical acts of misbehavior. Describing the mess hall at Tanforan, Okubo observes, "Table manners were forgotten. . . . Mothers had lost all control over their children." Demonstrating this breakdown of normal habits, a child pours the contents of a spoon over his head, the man sitting next to him rests both elbows on the table, covering his face with an upturned bowl, while Okubo and the woman next to her seem to be engaged in a stare-down. Later on, closely packed together at a table in Topaz, a man clumsily clutches his fork and stretches his other arm in front of a person with clasped hands who is apparently saying grace. The bad manners extend beyond the mess hall. In Topaz, "Schools were late in opening and difficult to organize because of the lack of buildings and necessary supplies. . . . Classroom discipline was poor." Two children paint on each other's faces while one frowns and the other sticks out his tongue. In the background, a girl sticks out her tongue and pushes another girl. Okubo holds a paintbrush and looks at the girls. She appears to have no control over the students. These students and the diners are unruly and unmanageable. They are not docile, mild, or well-mannered.[28]

Okubo also depicts herself sticking out her tongue in a completely unrestrained expression of disapproval. Life in Tanforan involved being under surveillance. "Curfew was imposed, and roll call was held every day at 6:45 a.m. and 6:45 p.m. Each barrack had a house captain who made the rounds to check on us twice a day," Okubo relates. This house captain was a collaborator, an evacuee who was working with the authorities who ran the camp. Okubo shows her disdain by pointing her tongue at him. This gesture shows disrespect by enacting the "bad" manners involved in displaying one's body. Exposing an internal body part, the tongue, shows indifference toward maintaining "polite" boundaries between the inside and the outside. It is an undisciplined gesture because it rejects using the tongue for a more dignified or more controlled form of communication—speech.[29]

Building and constructing, creating objects, and gardening are among the more productive physical acts Okubo shows. Bricolage, making do with what is at hand, was a form of invention available to people at Tanforan and Topaz. Okubo writes of the internees' determination to transform uninhabitable spaces into livable homes. In a characteristically understated tone, she explains that at Tanforan, "The first month was the hardest because adjustments had to be made to the new mode of life." People scavenged for lumber, and "Everyone was building furniture and fixing up barracks and stalls. Many of the discomforts of the camp were forgotten in this activity." By actively engaging in reconstructing their environment, people at Tanforan resisted the undesirable living situation that had been forced upon them. Their productivity improved their living conditions. At Tanforan, "a group of landscape architects decided to build a lake to beautify the camp." The project was remarkable since "everyone knew the camp was not a permanent one." Okubo stands in profile, watching while two people, both with heavily lined hands, work amid a jumble of materials. Remarking on their perseverance and inventiveness, Okubo states, "The workmen struggled day after day with limited equipment." When their project was finished, Okubo notes, "The lake was a great joy to the residents and presented new material for the artists." Okubo shows herself standing at the lake's edge, working on a sketch. What might seem to be an extravagance serves the necessary function of fending off despair. In another area of the camp were a fountain and pond where "A former fisherman invented a sailboat out of a telephone pole and took children on as passengers."[30] Since Japanese American fishermen were considered particularly suspect by the U.S. government because they worked on the Pacific, this man's use of his manual skills to create an enjoyable activity seems particularly significant.

At Topaz, building materials were "scarce and well guarded." As a means of acquiring wood, "stealing no longer became a crime but an act of necessity." Shown in the middle of a search for lumber, Okubo removes a piece of wood while her brother struggles to right himself after having fallen between boards covering a trench. *Citizen 13660* remarks upon this reversal of morality as well as the irony and difficulty of maintaining a sense of ethics and decorum within the confines of internment camp. Beneath an illustration showing three men near a pile of lumber, each holding pieces of lumber as ready weapons—one leaning against a stick of wood, another brandishing a two-by-four like a club, and another seated cross-legged, facing a fire, with a piece of wood resting across his legs—the text reads, "The precious scrap-lumber piles were guarded night and day, but in the zero weather the guard burned up most of it in order to keep themselves warm."[31] The wood is successfully guarded, but because it is burned, no one can build with it. In this case, actions become self-defeating.

Another example of productive yet unproductive behavior appears in a view of a classroom in Topaz. "School organization was an improvement over Tanforan," the caption reads, but, in the picture, as the teacher looks away from the students, one girl knits, two boys play cards, a child naps with his head resting on his arms, and only one girl looks somewhat engaged, listlessly raising her hand. Although one student holds a sheet of paper close to his eyes, reading, none of the students is writing.[32] Not all busy hands participate in constructive or obedient behavior. This inappropriate classroom activity is similar to the impolite eating habits on display in mess halls and is related to the transformation of theft from a crime to a necessity. In these instances, people succumb to the socially distorted climate of the internment camp. For example, where food is served out of large containers with bare hands rather than utensils, upholding "normal" modes of behavior and etiquette is not always possible.

Yet other activities were creative and productive. While at Topaz, Okubo harks back to the creative landscaping at Tanforan, writing, "Art and hobby shows were of great interest." She portrays herself at one of these shows, viewing odd-looking ornamental objects. "Ingenious use was made of everything that could be found in the center," including "finger rings of cellophane or fashioned from toothbrush handles, peach seeds or beads, tools made of scrap iron, and beautiful hats made of citrus-fruit wrappings woven with potato-sack strings." With such examples of bricolage, hobbyists proved their ingenuity, resourcefulness, and ability to adapt. Producing handicrafts also provided an outlet for expressing emotions. When an elderly resident was killed by a guard, "The women of each block made enormous floral wreaths with paper flowers." A group of women sits around a table, busily making flowers, while Okubo offers one flower to the collection. Her portrayal of these rounded, bespectacled, gentle-looking women contrasts with her description of other responses to the killing. Okubo explains that "The anti-administration leaders again started to howl and the rest of the residents shouted for protection against soldiers with guns."[33] By calling the leaders' voices a "howl," Okubo dehumanizes them and reveals her more conservative, controlled stance. Although she shows herself surrounded by people weeping at the memorial service, she herself sheds no tears. In holding a flower, she suggests that making flowers is more appropriate than speaking out against the guard's abuse of power. In other words, constructive acts may be preferable to outspoken criticism.

In another illustration, Okubo sticks out her tongue at one of the "Strongly pro-Japanese leaders," further revealing her political position. In the previous drawing, surrounded by men with tears falling from their eyes, Okubo pinches her nose shut. She glances off to the side while listening to a weeping speaker discuss the "28 questions to determine loyalty and willingness to fight" as volunteers in the U.S. military. Her gesture is somewhat ambiguous. Is she squeezing her nose to protect herself from the words of the impassioned speaker as if they are a bad smell, or is she holding back tears? The text provides more details about the questionnaire: "The registration form was long and complicated. The questions were difficult to understand and answer. Center-wide meetings were held, and the anti-administration rabble rousers skillfully fanned the misunderstandings."[34] By naming this body of people "rabble rousers," Okubo diminishes their credibility and implies that they are not organized to promote an important perspective but are merely disruptive and disobedient. Okubo does not condone their style of noncompliance.[35]

Citizen 13660 consciously uses language in the service of Okubo's narrative positioning. Detailing life in Tanforan, Okubo carefully chooses noninflammatory language. "Day and night Caucasian camp police walked their beats within the center. ('Caucasian' was the camp term for non-evacuee workers)." Simply noting terminology, and in a very matter-of-fact tone, the text succinctly presents the racial divide that was responsible for Japanese American internment. Okubo also displays her awareness of semiotics and the power of language in an illustration of signs posted by evacuees: "On the barracks in the center field and on the stalls, ingenious family name plates and interesting signs were displayed with great pride. All signs in Japanese were ordered removed. . . . To discourage visitors, I nailed a quarantine sign on my door." This commentary appears next to a page describing a "huge sign, 'Enjoy Acme Beer,'" that "stood out like a beacon on a near-by hill," beyond the boundaries of Tanforan. "The sign was clearly visible from every section of the camp and was quite a joke to the thirsty evacuees, especially on warm days."[36] The evacuees are excluded from the advertisement's intended audience. The sign underscores their confinement, as they cannot follow its demands. The name plates claim living spaces but are controlled by the authorities. With the quarantine sign, Okubo is able to exert a certain degree of control over her living space by excluding unwanted visitors. It matters not that the sign's message is untrue. Okubo exposes language as utilitarian, not necessarily as a medium for conveying truth. In this way, the text suggests that language naming Japanese Americans as "the enemy" was not necessarily accurate but was intended only to serve certain ends.

In other sequences, Okubo uses page spreads to impose continuity on her experiences. One pairing shows her perched on a fence looking into a pigpen and, on the opposite page, evacuees packed into the back of a truck with wooden sides that resemble the fence.[37] The two images are connected by the visual parallel, while no written text points out the similarities. In this nonverbal fashion, Okubo compares the experiences of internees to those of caged livestock. A similar graphic match occurs in a page spread that shows, on one side, an older man flying a kite and, on the other, a woman in the same posture, doing what appears to be a hula dance. The two figures are similar and at the same time very different. Again, Okubo allows the images to speak for themselves and does not provide text to expose the pun. The images tell a story that may differ from the accompanying text. With such sequencing, Okubo shapes her story, connecting and disjoining language and images to reconstruct her experiences.

Regarding the production of a memoir, writer Vivian Gornick reflects:

A memoir is a work of sustained narrative prose controlled by an idea of the self under obligation to lift from the raw material of life a tale that will shape experience, transform event, deliver wisdom. Truth in a memoir is achieved not through a recital of actual events; it is achieved when the reader comes to believe that the writer is working hard to engage with the experience at hand. What happened to the writer is not what matters, what matters is the large sense that the writer is able to *make* of what happened.[38]

Although it does matter that Okubo was forcibly incarcerated in Tanforan and Topaz, Okubo remakes this experience into *Citizen 13660*, asserting her own subjectivity, voice, and vision. Her memoir conforms to the characteristics of Nisei women's autobiography, as stated by Yamamoto, by which "However strongly they might feel about their experiences, there is also a reluctance to speak about these experiences and feelings, a guardedness about the act of revelation."[39] Despite this verbal reticence, what Okubo does not speak about in the captions is often revealed in the drawings.

Okubo presents her experiences at Tanforan and Topaz as intertwined with the production of visual records of her life in each place. At Tanforan, "The humor and pathos of the scenes made me decide to keep a record of camp life in sketches and drawings." What she saw encouraged her to memorialize these images in her artwork. Much later, "In January of 1944, having finished my documentary sketches of camp life, I finally decided to leave."[40] The way Okubo puts it, the completion of her sketches allowed her to leave. In this telling, her sense that she has accomplished her task, rather than permission from the War Relocation Authority, enables her to get out. She becomes responsible for her departure from Topaz.

Ostensibly to protect national security, the government evacuated more than 110,000 American citizens and resident aliens of Japanese ancestry.[41] The civilian exclusion orders warned that "Any person subject to this order who fails to comply with any of its provisions . . . will be liable to . . . criminal penalties."[42] Given the threat of criminal prosecution for failing to comply with evacuation, the oft-quoted Japanese sayings *shikata ganai*, commonly translated as "it can't be helped," and *gaman suru*, "just endure it," do not necessarily voice complicit resignation.[43] Instead, these phrases show a will to persevere despite governmental policies that sought to disperse Japanese American communities.

The self-protecting gestures Okubo depicts block out various external and environmental factors. In *Oneself as Another*, Paul Ricouer explains that "shifting the position of a pawn on the chessboard is in itself simply a gesture, but taken in the context of the practice of the game of chess, this gesture has the meaning of a move in a chess game."[44] While the physical gestures shown in *Citizen 13660* serve practical functions, the context in which they take place, within the confines of the internment camp, imparts more significance to these gestures. One can read them as gestures of resistance against the notions that caused the internment of Japanese Americans. Moreover, the internees' creativity and invention are comparable to Okubo's own determination to create and record through her art in spite of her incarceration.

Although *Citizen 13660* depicts explicit forms of rebellion or disobedience, this behavior is displayed by students in classrooms, and by children and adults in mess halls, and thus is equated with immaturity or bad manners. In contrast, the internees' bricolage, shown in the making of gardens and crafts, enacts a more productive and therefore apparently more acceptable rebellion against the repressive conditions of incarceration. In the preface to *Citizen 13660*, Okubo explains: "I am often asked, why am I not bitter and could this happen again? I am a realist with a creative mind, interested in people, so my thoughts are constructive. I am not bitter. I hope that things can be learned from this tragic episode, for I believe it could happen again."[45]

Outright criticism of internment may not be found in the written text of *Citizen 13660*, yet the illustrations show a more critical eye. Regarding *Trek* magazine, the publication Okubo took part in producing while at Topaz, scholar Stan Yogi comments, "Although only three issues were produced, each one reflects tensions between 'optimistic' and 'critical' perspectives. 'Optimistic' writing is characterized by admonitions not to be bitter and to believe in America."[46] Similarly, *Citizen 13660* offers a perspective that is both optimistic and critical, at times on the same page.

Classifying resistance in internment camps, historian Gary Okihiro charts "internee resistance potential" as well as different types of resistance that took place in a number of internment camps. Rather than attempt to fit the gestures of resistance seen in *Citizen 13660* into Okihiro's classifications, we can view Okubo's memoir as evidence of a continuum of resistance that extends beyond an "optimistic" versus "critical" paradigm. Incorporating the negative and the positive, *Citizen 13660* reveals Okubo's realistic yet optimistic positioning. "Most people live in the positive—but it's the negative things that make you strong. Things against you make you strong. It's an endless struggle."[47]

NOTES

1 Miné Okubo, *Citizen 13660* (Seattle: University of Washington Press, 1983), xii. In the recorded testimonies of people who experienced internment, many comment on their feelings of bitterness or their lack of bitterness toward these experiences. See, for example, John Tateishi, *And Justice for All: An Oral History of the Japanese American Detention Camps* (New York: Random House, 1984). Bitterness is an emotional and sensorial response. The use of this term to describe their feelings suggests an awareness of the significance of the physical body in the case of Japanese American internment.

2 For more discussion of this exclusion, see also Eric L. Muller, *Free to Die for Their Country: The Story of the Japanese American Draft Resisters in World War II* (Chicago: University of Chicago Press, 2001), 22–25; and Ronald T. Takaki, *Strangers from a Distant Shore: A History of Asian Americans* (Boston: Little, Brown & Company, 1989), 379–92. There were also

economic reasons for the decision to exclude people of Japanese ancestry from the West Coast.

3 Lawson Fusao Inada, ed., *Only What We Could Carry: The Japanese American Internment Experience* (Berkeley, Calif.: Heyday Books; San Francisco: California Historical Society, 2000), 401. See also United States, Commission on Wartime Relocation and Internment of Civilians, *Personal Justice Denied: Report of the Commission on Wartime Relocation and Internment of Civilians* (Washington, D.C.: Civil Liberties Public Education Fund; Seattle: University of Washington Press, 1997), 47–92 (hereafter *Personal Justice Denied*).

4 See Inada, *Only What We Could Carry*, 8.

5 David Palumbo-Liu, *Asian/American: Historical Crossings of a Racial Frontier* (Palo Alto, Calif.: Stanford University Press, 1999), 86.

6 R. E. Park, "Racial Assimilation in Secondary Groups," *Publications of the American Sociological Association* 8 (1914): 71. Quoted in R. E. Park, *Race and Culture* (Glencoe, Ill.: Free Press, 1950), 353; cited in Palumbo-Liu, *Asian/American*, 86.

7 Memo, Major C. O. Garver to De Witt, Jan. 8, 1942. National Archives and Records Service, Washington, D.C., Record Group 338 (CWRIC 3122-25); cited in *Personal Justice Denied*, 64.

8 United States Department of War, *Final Report: Japanese Evacuation from the West Coast*, 33; cited in Palumbo-Liu, *Asian/American*, 223.

9 9. *Internment of Japanese Americans: Documents from the National Archives*, Educational Resources Information Center, ED395852, Document 9: 29.

10 On April 13, 1943, DeWitt testified before the House Naval Affairs Subcommittee in San Francisco: "A Jap's a Jap. You can't change him by giving him a piece of paper." Cited in *Americans of Japanese Ancestry and the United States Constitution: 1787–1987* (San Francisco: National Japanese American Historical Society, 1987), 54.

11 Okubo, *Citizen 13660*, 10.

12 Ibid., 124.

13 13. *Internment of Japanese Americans*, ED395852, Document 9: 29.

14 Okubo, *Citizen 13660*, 153.

15 Traise Yamamoto, *Masking Selves, Making Subjects: Japanese American Women, Identity, and the Body* (Berkeley: University of California Press, 1999), 103. A Nisei is a second-generation Japanese American.

16 Okubo, *Citizen 13660*, 110, 23.

17 Yamamoto, *Masking Selves, Making Subjects*, 103.

18 Ibid., 103–4.

19 Shirley Sun, *Miné Okubo: An American Experience*, exh. cat. (San Francisco: East Wind Printers, 1972), 32.

20 Okubo, *Citizen 13660*, 89, 143.

21 Ibid., 190.

22 Ibid., 62.

23 Ibid., 37, 56, 123, 127, 182, 183, 184.

24 Ibid., 78, 185.

25 Ibid., 38, 67.

26 Ibid., 117, 120.

27 Ibid., 72, 74.

28 Ibid., 89, 143, 92.

29 Ibid., 59.

30 Ibid., 50, 51, 98, 100.

31 Ibid., 137, 141.

32 Ibid., 166.

33 Ibid., 169, 180–81.

34 Ibid., 177, 175–76.

35 This stance is in part responsible for the limited amount of literature on Nisei draft resisters during World War II. For further discussion, see Gary Y. Okihiro, "Japanese Resistance in America's Concentration Camps," *Amerasia Journal* 2, no. 1 (Fall 1973): 20–34. See also the documentary film by Frank Abe, *Conscience and the Constitution* (Independent Television Service and Civil Liberties Education Fund, 2000); and Muller, *Free to Die for Their Country*. I would also like to acknowledge Etsuko Kubo's unpublished essay "100% American: Japanese American Draft Resisters during World War II." In July 2000, the Japanese American Citizens League (JACL), a group that preached complete compliance with U.S. governmental policies during World War II, passed a resolution apologizing to the resisters. In the December 15, 2001, issue of *Hokubei Mainichi*, sixteen Nisei veterans' organizations jointly opposed an apology to the resisters, stating: "The actions of the resisters accomplished nothing." Attitudes toward these resisters remain strong and divided.

36 Okubo, *Citizen 13660*, 60, 83, 82.

37 Ibid., 196–97.

38 Vivian Gornick, *The Situation and the Story: The Art of Personal Narrative* (New York: Farrar, Straus & Giroux, 2001), 91.

39 Yamamoto, *Masking Selves, Making Subjects*, 106.

40 Okubo, *Citizen 13660*, 53, 206.

41 *Personal Justice Denied*, xv.

42 *Internment of Japanese Americans*, ED395852, Document 8: 23.

43 Muller, *Free to Die for Their Country*, 26.

44 Paul Ricoeur, *Oneself as Another*, translated by Kathleen Blamey (Chicago: University of Chicago Press, 1992), 154.

45 Okubo, *Citizen 13660*, xii.

46 Stan Yogi, "Japanese American Literature," in *An Interethnic Companion to Asian American Literature*, ed. King-Kok Cheung (New York: Cambridge University Press, 1997).

47 Sun, *Miné Okubo*, 48.

8

MINÉ OKUBO'S WAR

CITIZEN 13660'S ATTACK ON GOVERNMENT PROPAGANDA

HEATHER FRYER

On September 3, 1939, Miné Okubo was in a horrible predicament. The young American art student was traveling in Europe on a yearlong fellowship when she was stranded in Switzerland after France and Britain declared war on Germany. Her temporary home and belongings were in Paris behind a closed border. Short of money and even shorter on options, Okubo settled in with friends on a farm near Berne, where she watched the war spread. Her friends advised her to return home. After all, if the Nazis invaded Switzerland as many feared, Okubo risked persecution as an enemy alien. News of her mother's death hastened Okubo toward taking her friends' advice. Derailed from her chosen path, she was soon on a boat full of American refugees, all headed toward the safety of home and the full protections of citizenship.[1]

Yet as anyone familiar with the history of the ethnic Japanese in America might guess, Okubo's experience of life on the American home front would not be one of unfettered freedom and national unity. On her return to California, she briefly resumed her normal life, living with her brother and working as an artist for the Federal Arts Project painting murals on federal buildings. When the Empire of Japan bombed Pearl Harbor on December 7, 1941, Okubo—along with the rest of the Japanese American community—found herself once again in a horrible predicament. The young American who was an "enemy alien" in occupied Europe suddenly became an "enemy Jap" to her fellow Californians. The FBI took her father into custody without charges, her home was ransacked, and racial slurs resounded on the street and in the press.[2]

In February 1942, President Franklin D. Roosevelt issued Executive Order 9066, restricting all persons of Japanese ancestry from the coastal states and laying the groundwork for their mass evacuation to "relocation centers" in the interior west. The question of how to summarily intern an entire ethnic group without due process caused considerable conflict among federal officials in Washington, D.C., Attorney General Francis Biddle protested removing the Japanese without cause and reminded the American public that "the question of loyalty [is] personal" and not racially determined. Even J. Edgar Hoover expressed discomfort at the civil rights violations sure to spring from the hastily devised security protocols. This feeling became all the more acute as FBI investigators filed report after report of their failure to find evidence of Japanese American involvement in the Pearl Harbor bombing. Although evacuation proceeded with almost no organized resistance among non-Japanese (the American Civil Liberties Union being the notable exception), federal officials were pressed to reconcile the impending roundup with the ideals of freedom that drove the Allied war effort.[3]

The government's official explanation for removing its Japanese citizens from the mainstream was twofold: to protect the West Coast from the handful of Japanese presumed to be saboteurs, and to shield the loyal majority of Japanese Americans from retaliation from hostile whites. The first point was most famously articulated by Lieutenant General John L. DeWitt, who was in charge of the evacuation. Amplifying the long-prevalent belief that Asians were unassimilable and therefore dangerous, DeWitt asserted, "the Japanese race is the enemy race and while many second and third generation Japanese are born on United States soil, possessed of United States citizenship, the racial strains are undiluted. . . . American citizenship does not necessarily determine loyalty." A *Los Angeles Times* editorial put it more succinctly: "a viper is a viper nonetheless, no matter where the egg is hatched—so a Japanese American, born of Japanese parents, grows up to be a Japanese, not an American."[4]

Most Americans shared DeWitt's general assessment, though most believed that the vast majority of the Japanese community was loyal to the United States and that there was unquestionably an unknown number of "vipers" among them. The mainstream view, based on the long-standing stereotypes of Asians as innately treacherous and inscrutable, held that national security could be assured only by casting a wide net—even if it meant that innocent individuals or the integrity of the Constitution might suffer. In official documents and the popular media, the Office of War Information (OWI) promoted the camps as an ingenious method of catching any saboteurs while preventing acts of vigilantism against the loyal Japanese majority. Informational pamphlets for Japanese and non-Japanese alike dissuaded the public from using terms like "concentration camp" and to think of the camps instead as small towns or exclusive communities where the safety of the residents (not "internees") would be the highest priority. Most of the American public took comfort in the conceptual inconsistency that dangerous Japanese needed special government protection, and the Japanese themselves were in no position to challenge these tightly interwoven untruths.[5]

Okubo, like several interned artists and writers, staged effective protests nonetheless. Throughout her internment at the Tanforan Assembly Center and the Central Utah Relocation Center, she kept a record of day-to-day life, a chronicle of cartoonlike sketches and matter-of-fact captions. The title, *Citizen 13660*, ironically identified the work, like Okubo herself, by the serial number the government assigned to her family. Okubo drew the pictures as a gift for her friends outside the camp with an eye toward future exhibition. With the intent of capturing the "humor and pathos" of camp life, Okubo sketched seemingly simple scenes depicting the oddities of life inside barbed wire, including masterful self-portraits whose facial expressions said more than the captions.[6]

This multilayered, multifaceted work is far from the "simple" work of "objective reporting" early reviewers would describe it to be. Through what is shown and hidden, and what is said and unsaid, *Citizen 13660* exposes the "ingeniousness" of the camps as a great hypocrisy. When the government spoke of forced migration as pioneering, Okubo portrayed a dead-end journey. When the government cast the internment as "protective custody," Okubo showed the injuries inflicted within these so-called safe havens. And when the government touted its hasty resettlement of internees from the camps as a triumph for freedom, Okubo wrote frankly about how deeply and indelibly internees had internalized their imprisonment. By pulling back the facade the OWI constructed around the camps, Okubo reveals the "insanity" of a racist policy that appeared rational to even the most astute American progressives.[7]

Beyond exposing the reality behind the official rhetoric of the internment, Okubo's mission of documentation and self-expression was, in and of itself, a subversive act in a setting in which government agencies sought to control the images of the camps and the Americans who inhabited them. Photographic equipment was forbidden, printed material was censored, and the OWI staged and edited its images to make the camps appear consistent with American values and Allied war aims. Just as Japanese bodies were isolated from the American body politic, Japanese voices were cut off from American political discourse and replaced with government propaganda. Miné Okubo continued to speak for herself throughout her internment, and she challenged readers to see it from her complex perspective when the war was over.[8]

Citizen 13660 is a much more confrontational expression of dissent than non-Japanese readers acknowledged in 1946. The ways in which Okubo represents both the conditions of the camps *and* the condition of her spirit speak directly to the most misleading content in the government's pro-internment propaganda. Her subtle and deeply personal accounting of the internment's human cost left no room to argue that the camps were protective havens or staging areas for new opportunities for the Japanese community, as the government led people to believe. Okubo's early reviewers, writing in the midst of American's collective embarrassment about the internment, were readily able to share Okubo's view of the camps but not of Okubo herself. Their readings of *Citizen 13660* blocked out the arresting emotional honesty in Okubo's self-portraits and remade her into an "objective," "unbiased," "unemotional," and "forgiving" representative of the Japanese American community. Approaching *Citizen 13660* as one side of an ongoing political discourse brings to the fore a struggle over image and representation that has implications well beyond the context of the internment itself.

IN SEARCH OF THE BIG PIONEER LIFE

As the evacuation began in early 1942, the OWI produced a short film, *The Japanese Relocation*, to sell the public on the internment. The film is a pioneer story of sorts that begins with a warning from Milton Eisenhower, director of the War Relocation Authority (WRA), that the western states make up a potential combat zone, inhabited by Japanese who live near sensitive military targets (especially railroad tracks, telephone lines, and sewer lines). The safety of the western states could therefore not be assured unless every person of Japanese ancestry is removed. While this would surely cause hardship, the Japanese community would be protected within the safe haven of new "pioneer communities" located on "federally owned land . . . with opportunities to work and more space in which to live," where they would "reclaim the desert" of the interior west and live happily for the duration.[9]

The pioneer may have seemed an odd figure, but it was the one the federal government used to promote all of its wartime migrations, from shipyard labor to the Manhattan Project. Though traditionally depicted as a white westerner in a Conestoga wagon, the pioneer's footsteps could be filled by any group of migrants fulfilling some sort of patriotic mission. The Japanese just had to overlook the fact that for the nineteenth-century pioneers, the trip west was only the beginning. The real venture had been forging an independent life on the land. For internee "pioneers," however, there was no chance for the prosperity and independence that drove white settlers west—the Japanese had already made their hard-earned gains as successful immigrants. These realities aside, the pioneer still held the allure of adventure, and Okubo recalled years later that she had grown weary of life among "all the intellectual decadents" of Berkeley and somewhat relished the idea of "a big pioneer life."[10]

Okubo documents her pioneer life early in *Citizen 13660* by presenting an official notice to "bring work clothes suited to pioneer life" and portraying her search for boots and jeans that would presumably be appropriate for the experience. In the image, other families follow suit, sporting wide-brimmed hats and clunky footwear. Several Japanese then proceed to an information station dressed for pioneering, only to be addressed as internees, not trailblazers. The realization of their true status becomes greater as Okubo prepares for evacuation, though she seems to hold onto hope as she and her brother depart, their names changed to "Family 13660" by government bureaucrats. Okubo looks toward the horizon as if anticipating adventure on the trail; her brother, by contrast, is slumped forward in a pose recalling the defeated Indian warrior in James Earle Fraser's sculpture *The End of the Trail*. Traces of Okubo's pioneer spirit remain as she boards the bus but dissolve as she is reminded of "stories told on shipboard by European refugees to America." Even the college boys who merrily sang their old songs fell silent as they cross the Bay Bridge, she writes. When the singing ends, so, too, does the shared sense that a great adventure is at hand. The Promised Land, it turns out, would be a tiny barrack behind barbed wire, under armed guard.[11]

Okubo's image depicting her and her fellow travelers filing out of the bus is almost identical to the documentary footage of new arrivals in the OWI film *The Japanese Relocation*. In both image and film, bewildered Japanese file out of buses into racetracks and fairgrounds guarded by soldiers with rifles. The film's voice-over attributes the bewilderment of the new arrivals—particularly that of a young boy—to their awe at the possibilities of claiming a land that was untamed and "full of possibility." Okubo's caption reads simply, "The soldier got out and opened the door and we filed out past him" and could well apply to either image.[12]

Okubo, however, then ventures outside the boundaries of the film to show aspects of these "pioneers" arriving that the OWI did not. There was no distribution of homesteads at Tanforan. Instead, the "pioneers" were searched for contraband, stripped for medical exams, and escorted to freshly painted horse stalls along a muddy path. As Okubo is escorted to her barrack she turns to look directly at the reader, making him/her a witness as she crosses the final threshold into the camp. The hard gaze seems to ask whether the reader really still believed in pioneering or protective custody, as Okubo clearly could not. A small tear runs down Okubo's cheek a few pages later as she realizes that her "big pioneer life" involved confinement in a tiny stall.[13]

The productivity of America's new pioneers was one of the OWI's great selling points for the internment. Instead of sitting idle for the duration, the pioneers in *The Japanese Relocation* grow guayule, a source of rubber, and make nets for the military. They raise food and aid with community improvements. In the final frames of the film, the narrator speculates that the Japanese pioneers would transform desolate deserts into verdant farmlands, making the camps a sort of staging area from which the Japanese would discover the American dream. Okubo shows herself and her campmates laboring constantly for the first month, making scrap lumber into furniture and transforming the unfinished camp into a semblance of home and community. She appears focused within a chaotic arrangement of nails and boards, with an intensity that would have pleased the OWI. But Okubo puts labor into a completely different context when she notes, "[m]any of the discomforts of the camp were forgotten in this activity," suggesting that there was much more complexity to the choices internees made in conducting their lives in camp. Unlike the government's voiceless, two-dimensional pioneers, Okubo pioneers to distract herself from her surroundings. For her, hard work was a measure not of optimism but of pain, fear, and her steadfast refusal to succumb to them.[14]

RELOCATION: CITIZEN 13660 IN PROTECTIVE CUSTODY

While the government's pioneering metaphor became widely familiar, federal officials most often used the concept of "protective custody" to make the internment ethically and constitutionally palatable. Orientation materials for new internees described their new surroundings as "a pioneer community, with basic housing and protective services provided by the Federal Government, for occupancy by evacuees for the duration of the war."[15] What, exactly, the government was protecting the internees from was ambiguous at best, especially since the sentries' gun barrels pointed inward toward the Japanese and away from intruding vigilantes. At least one observer went so far as to describe the camps as "barbed-wire democracies" because the WRA made it clear that its agents were fully in charge.[16]

Okubo takes on the protective custody myth toward the middle of the book, as she settles in at Tanforan. Taking on the role of observer, she watches internees standing in endless lines, cars being searched by armed sentries, and women with rounded shoulders standing together in patched dungarees. Okubo's detachment and objectivity dissipate as she confronts the loss of life, liberty, privacy, and even faith as a result of camp life. Her face registers sorrow at the presence of a rickety hearse ready to transfer a fellow internee to his last resting place under armed guard. No longer an observer, Okubo grapples with the realization that not everyone would survive "protective custody" and that some old men lost interest in trying. Okubo's sadness turns to defiance on the next page, as she sticks her tongue out at the man doing the twice-daily roll call and spies on a Caucasian policeman who is spying on Japanese men playing cards in a barrack.[17]

This sequence might appear disjointed and even whimsical at first glance, until Okubo sets these fragments before the backdrop of letters she received from her friends in Europe, who "told me how lucky I was to be free and safe at home." Internees, she has shown us, were neither lucky, free, nor safe. And they were not really at home either. But perhaps the greatest injustice was that America's Japanese community had been utterly silenced, its voices replaced by government propaganda. Okubo not only lost the right to represent her experiences to the general public; she could not even convey the most basic realities of her life to the people who knew her best. Clearly the fight was on for Okubo, whether camp officials were aware of it or not. Each subsequent page of *Citizen 13660* delivers a blow to the system that sought not only to control her but to control how people would understand her experience as an internee.[18]

One arena in which freedom remained intact was that of religious worship, but the exercise of this single freedom brings Okubo spiritual unease. She portrays herself singing hymns with a small congregation, with a caption that reads "[c]hurches were early established to bolster the morale of the bewildered and humiliated people. There were Protestant, Catholic, Seventh-Day Adventist, and Buddhist groups." At first glance, the drawing is unremarkable, and even resembles images in OWI photographs. But Okubo's image of herself amid the crowd of worshipers is cropped at the top so that her face begins with her eyes, which are fixed on other congregants rather than on the minister. Her participation seems tentative and half-hearted, leaving the impression that the internment not only constrained her freedom—it shook her faith. As living with open sewer lines, dust storms, and constant surveillance compounded her misery, Okubo's eyes appear notably more weary. She continues to be observant of other people but interacts with them less, as if withdrawing from her overwhelming surroundings until she can fully make sense of them.[19]

Emotional distance and physical distance become intertwined as Okubo contemplates the distances and proximities marked out by the fence. She sees friends from outside lined up to visit at Tanforan but feels the distance between the worlds inside and outside the gate, stating, "we were close to freedom and yet far from it." She discourages friends from coming to Tanforan to visit and nails a "quarantine" sign to her barrack to keep people away. The camp distances her from others, and then she distances herself. In a sense, she puts herself in her own protective custody, but it is not the sort that preserves freedom or allows her to resume normal life in exile. The greatest blow came when the residents of Tanforan were transferred to their more permanent settlement at Topaz, where they were instructed to build their own fences behind which to confine themselves. Yet by that time, such a task seemed unremarkable. That in and of itself says much about the state of freedom within the protective embrace of government-issued barbed wire.[20]

As with her treatment of pioneering, Okubo's portrayal of Tanforan and Topaz as "barbed-wire democracies" was not simple opposition to government rhetoric. Community life truly did exist in the camps, and while this was due in some part to the WRA's interest in providing institutions for education, self-government, and socialization, Okubo reapportions credit for the success of the camps from the government to the internees themselves. She draws a glimmer of happiness into her

facial expressions as she watches campaign rallies for Community Council candi-
dates, though the caption tells us that the Tanforan Community Council was dis-
mantled by the WRA in the wake of political unrest at another center. Instead of delv-
ing into the loss of the councils, Okubo depicts herself teaching art to unruly children
and draws a series of portraits honoring others' contributions to community life.
Some planted victory gardens, some maintained the community grapevine, some
ran the library, and some started sports teams. Others put on talent shows, worked
on the landscaping, and knit sweaters for soldiers. Some internees, such as the sleep-
ing man laid out like a corpse as he slept in the grandstand in the middle of the day,
did not escape the cynicism and despair that came from idleness, but on the whole
internees pulled together to preserve whatever semblance of normal life they could.
Taken together, Okubo's community scenes demonstrate that it was the internees
who protected themselves and one another, not the barbed wire, guard towers, and
programmatic lifestyle imposed by the WRA.[21]

   This point became abundantly clear in April 1943 when a military policeman
fatally shot sixty-three-year-old James Wakasa, who was taking an evening stroll near
the fence. The sentry testified before the WRA and the War Department's joint board
of inquiry that he ordered Wakasa to halt three times, but Wakasa would not obey.
The board of inquiry, composed of WRA and War Department officials, ruled that
the MP had followed procedure, but the county coroner's report showed that Wakasa
was shot in the front and fell backward, which proved he had been facing the guard
tower and not running from it. The Wakasa shooting shattered the "protective custody" myth for Topazians. Okubo reports the event in words while depicting an out-
pouring of collective grief as the camp gathers en masse. Okubo, who stands out in
the crowd because she faces the reader in three-quarter profile, grimaces with what
appears to be rage. Okubo shows that even as the WRA was scrambling to cover up
the details of the shooting, older women had gathered to make massive tissue paper
wreaths for Wakasa, who had no family at Topaz and, like them, had no meaningful
protections, despite all statements to the contrary.[22]

RESETTLEMENT: FREEDOM BOUND IN RED TAPE

By early 1943—months before the Wakasa shooting—it became clear to both the
general public and the War Relocation Authority that its camps were anything but
pioneer communities or safe havens. After only one year of operation, officials concluded that "relocation centers were for many reasons not socially sound or healthy
communities [and] that there was little chance of any danger being done to the war
effort by any of the evacuees. Furthermore we were convinced that much was to be
gained in behalf of the war effort by bringing the evacuees out of centers and into

normal communities when then could make a real contribution."[23] Officials issued warnings that if the industrious Japanese were left to languish in the camps, they could fall into the dependency that plagued the once self-sufficient Native American tribes who had inhabited the area.[24]

A few internees let their complaints be known, as did Axis propagandists quick to point out that the United States had yet again fallen short of its democratic ideals where racial minorities were concerned. Strikes, demonstrations, and acts of violence grew more frequent and more widespread. Civil libertarians—both within and outside California—found their fears subsiding and their steadfast belief in multi-ethnic democracy resurfacing, along with deep shame for having abandoned their principles. Within a year of their creation, the relocation centers threatened the integrity of America's democratic message, which potentially could create new national security risks as well as domestic dissent.[25]

In a stunning turnabout, the WRA changed its policy from relocation to resettlement. The new program began with extensive screenings to determine which internees were "truly loyal" and to segregate those whose loyalties were suspect. Under the scrutiny of newly activated white liberals, the WRA was all the more eager to take the majority of the 110,000 internees who had never shown signs of disloyalty and disperse them to eastern cities (the West Coast remained a restricted military zone off-limits to all persons of Japanese descent).[26] The problem was that the mainstream public had recently been convinced of the necessity of separating the Japanese from other Americans. Anyone who had seen the government's film *The Japanese Relocation* surely believed that the Japanese were enjoying new opportunities as pioneers reclaiming western lands and that keeping them at a distance promised security for all.

The OWI immediately refashioned its images of Japanese Americans, making them closer to reality but racist nonetheless. Anthropologists for the WRA were assigned to gather data on the extent to which young Japanese Americans were "Americanized" in order to encourage the public to embrace them as fellow citizens (or at least not impede the progress of resettlement). Analysts were fully aware that most Nisei had never even visited Japan, yet they were pleased to report that they wore Western clothes, greeted people with a handshake instead of a bow, played basketball, attended church, were ambitious students, preferred forks to chopsticks, and spoke Japanese badly.[27]

To aid the resettlement effort, young Nisei internees were drafted from the camps into the 442nd Regimental Combat Team and, by extension, into the American mainstream (their units were segregated, but this was rarely mentioned in the press). Their outstanding service record was hailed as exemplary of what assimilated Japanese Americans could accomplish for the nation. Progressive leaders in local communities eagerly aided the WRA in arranging housing and jobs for Japanese college students, young married couples, and industrial workers in the hope of righting the wrongs of the internment and rehabilitating America's image as a beacon for multi-ethnic democracy. The WRA ran regular columns in camp newspapers applauding residents for "earning" their freedom though their wartime sacrifice and definitive proof of their loyalty and urging them to apply for resettlement as soon as possible. To the WRA, both the internment program and the internees were on the brink of a great wartime triumph.[28]

Okubo's treatment of resettlement is very brief, spanning only the last five pages of *Citizen 13660*. Although she also sees resettlement as the best chance for young Nisei like herself to resume a normal life, the path to liberation was not as swift, smooth, or joyous as the WRA seemed to believe. Among her friends, some were prepared to "risk anything to get away," while "others feared to leave the protection of the camp." As Okubo demonstrates in her concluding pages, this contradiction existed within her own mind as she made the decision to depart for New York to work as an illustrator for *Fortune* magazine. One of the last pages of the book shows Okubo looking past the reader with one hand barely managing a stack of forms while the other is being fingerprinted. The caption describes the red tape involved, which included taking a loyalty oath, having job sites and destination residences checked, and attending sessions titled "How to Make Friends" and "How to Behave in the Out-side World." She penned her most poignant line at the end of the process: "I was pho-tographed." On the page, Okubo shows herself having a mug shot taken through a small frame with a new number across the bottom; she was transformed from Citi-zen *13660* to Citizen 44367. The number is barely visible, but the question it raises is evident nonetheless: How would life as a resettled internee differ from life inside the fence? Government officials saw a dramatic transformation, while Okubo antici-pated far subtler changes.[29]

In the panel, Okubo sheds her first tear as she says good-bye to her fellow Topazians, which is surprising, given her many moments of despair during her years among them. Her mixed emotions become clearer in the last captions, in which she extols her freedom on one page, only to confess on the next that "fear had chained me to the camp." Given what Okubo has shown readers about Topaz, her tentative steps toward the gate are fully understandable. Topaz may not have been a real Amer-ican town, but it was the Topazians' only community as long as California remained off-limits. The internment may not have been designed with protective custody as its foremost aim, but its stigma made Japanese Americans extremely vulnerable when they ventured out of the camps. As Okubo boards the bus that will take her to New York, she exposes one of the most difficult truths of the internment for Japa-nese and non-Japanese alike: the injustice of the "protective custody" myth was not that it was largely untrue but that, as internees internalized government propaganda, the myth took on substance, robbing them of their freedom and self-determination long after they had departed the "barbed-wire democracies."[30]

EPILOGUE: READING OKUBO IN 1946

Citizen 13660 received its first reviews after its initial publication in 1946. Most of those who were asked to comment—journalists, bureaucrats, and academics—had been close observers of, if not participants in implementing, the internment and resettlement programs. Their responses to the book suggest the degree to which wartime perceptions remained in force, even after the Supreme Court declared the detention of loyal citizens unconstitutional and the press denounced the internment as America's "worst wartime mistake." The greater share of their comments on *Citizen 13660*, though laudatory, focus almost solely on the conditions of the camps, a perceived "objectivity" that ignores the humanity of Okubo's self-portrayal, and the characteristics of the book that make Okubo more or less "American" in their view.[31]

A survey of excerpts from early reviewers shows three general trends in the initial reception of Okubo's works by mainstream readers. The first, as mentioned earlier, is the tendency to see *Citizen 13660* as a piece of "objective reporting." Okubo's "detachment" is read as a sign of fidelity to an objective truth about the internment rather than as an indication of the damage done to her over the course of her incarceration. The *New York Times Book Review* described the illustrations as "dramatic," "detailed," and "vivid," while characterizing her process as "recording all that she saw, objectively, yet with a warmth of understanding." Joseph Henry Jackson of the *San Francisco Chronicle* added that Okubo's evident strength of character "enabled the artist-author to go beyond her personal feelings and record the story as it was, without bias."[32]

Perceptions of objectivity range as far as that of Harry Hansen's open letter to Okubo in the *New York World Telegram* in which he expresses appreciation for *Citizen 13660* because it has "[given] me a great deal of precise information and has taught me something about making a point with deadpan irony." Oddly, *Citizen 13660* presents very little precise or factual information about the internment beyond Okubo's chronology of personal events. here are no maps and only scant facts, figures, and dates. Read *Citizen 13660* as objective documentary, and the Okubo figure is no different from the two-dimensional figures the OWI presented in *The Japanese Relocation*. When internees are reduced to "pioneers" or "crack reporters," their stories disappear into the background, and the depth of the harm perpetrated against them could never come fully to the fore.[33]

A second prevailing trend among reviewers was to attribute the more striking characteristics of Okubo's work to her ethnicity or nationality, without dealing with the content of the work itself. The *New Yorker* said of this, "Miss Okubo, who considers herself completely American, tells her story with ingenuousness, but there is a certain Oriental subtlety in the illustrations. The captions are written with restraint and humor and seem to depreciate the inconveniences of the camps: the drawings themselves do not minimize them at all." The *Book-of-the-Month Club News*, by contrast, identified Okubo as a California-born "highly gifted young artist." Other writers presented their own calculations of how "American" or "Japanese" Okubo showed herself to be, with the subtlety of her artistry and political message a Japanese trait and her objectivity an American one. This process brought most reviewers to the conclusion that, on the whole, Okubo was more American than Japanese—a point that, to them, made the internment so egregious.[34]

This calculus did not come from Okubo: *Citizen 13660* does not contemplate the degree to which she or any internee was "American" or "Japanese." It is the scheme by which the WRA presented and re-presented internees. During the evacuation phase, they were "too Japanese" to be fully loyal to the United States. During resettlement, they were, on balance, more American than Japanese. The most interesting use of this framework is found in the remarks of NBC radio journalist John W. Vandercook, known for his reports on the Normandy invasion and his books on Pacific island and Caribbean history. His vehement denunciation of the racist frenzy that fueled the internment contains the embedded assumption that Japanese Americans were fundamentally foreigners. After asserting that "the hysterical roundup and imprisonment of American citizens of Japanese ancestry [would] one day be unanimously agreed [to be] a shameful stain upon the American record." Vandercook expresses "delight" that Okubo and other Japanese Americans have "found it in their hearts to forgive us, and do us the honor still to regard themselves as our fellow citizens." While Okubo does not pour forth her rancor, she also does not mention forgiveness. In his deep desire for absolution of his liberal guilt, Vandercook recasts Okubo as an outsider whose nationality was more a matter of choice than the usual accident of birth.[35]

In addition to portraying Okubo as a two-dimensional figure instead of a complex human being, the vast majority of the reviews erased the federal government's role as the agent of Okubo's oppression. Even to those most centrally involved in the internment, it was as though the internment policies had been made by "war hysteria," not by individuals within the government. This is especially noticeable in reviews by Dillon Myer, director of the WRA, and Harold Ickes, head of the Interior Department, which oversaw WRA operations. Ickes urges "those who are disposed to be indifferent about our treatment of alien strains" to read *Citizen 13660* in order to "understand just what we did to many thousands of our fellow Americans." One wonders why, if Ickes wanted to shed light on the motives behind the internment, he did not offer his own explanation of what he and his colleagues hoped to achieve by it.[36]

Myer similarly praises the book as a "reproof to those who would malign any racial minority, and it should help to forestall any future mass movements of the type she portrays." Both express surprise at Okubo's absence of "rancor" and affirm that her account is a faithful portrayal of Japanese Americans' "wartime exile." Yet they write as though someone else was responsible for the internment—or perhaps that no one was. For those closest to the internment, it was perhaps easier to read *Citizen 13660* as an account of a destructive phenomenon, presented as a reporter might describe a hurricane.[37]

The belief that the internment was "a sad chapter from the past," "a failure to recognize the Americanness of Japanese people," and a series of "inconveniences" that unduly burdened internees created little impetus to tally its human cost. The assumption that the camps were gone and Americans would never make the same mistake twice served to make Okubo and her fellow internees invisible yet again. And perhaps more important for some, focusing on the camps instead of the humanity of the occupants allowed them to avoid seeing their part in the story of *Citizen 13660.*[38]

Taken together, these early responses to Okubo and her work suggest that the pattern of dealing with racial anxiety by making Japanese people invisible to the mainstream was still firmly in place, and Okubo's feat in making herself seen and heard to some 1946 readers was remarkable indeed. H. V. Kaltenborn of CBS radio, one of the most forthright commentators, characterizes *Citizen 13660* as a "human document" embodying both humor and tragedy. While he found the drawings "delightful," Kaltenborn was left with "a sense of shame that we showed so little discrimination" in response to wartime anxieties.[39]

M. M. Tozier of the Bureau of Indian Affairs described "a strong sense of participation in the evacuation and relocation center experience. She makes you feel that this actually happened, that it might have happened to you, and that it should never happen again. . . . I felt that I knew for the first time what camp life looked like, smelled like, and felt like to the evacuated people." The *Pasadena Star-News* marveled at Okubo's refusal to "engage in argument" about the internment in favor of telling "an authentic, moving tale," while the progressive magazine *PM* praised the "stoical humor" with which Okubo "describes her wartime experiences in 'protective custody.'" Such comments prove that Okubo's message was clear and discernible, but readers had to be willing to absorb it instead of resisting its content and its implications.[40]

In an open letter to Miné Okubo in 1946, University of California vice president Monroe B. Deutsch reflected on *Citizen 13660* in light of his last conversation with Okubo in his office as she prepared for the evacuation. He praised her for "[keeping her] sense of humor and portraying the amusing incidents in [her] life at Tanforan and Topaz," as he had asked her to do. He also made special acknowledgment that "the undercurrent of tragedy is clearly to be seen" in her brilliantly wrought presentation. In publishing *Citizen 13660*, Okubo had "done something really important" by having "set forth clearly but without passion what you and others had to endure."[41]

Okubo continued this important work throughout her life by retelling her story to scholars, journalists, artists, and activists and by testifying before the Commission on Wartime Relocation and Internment of Civilians in the 1980s. As part of her testimony, Okubo presented Congress with a copy of *Citizen 13660*, and her passage on the Wakasa shooting (without illustration) was written into the official record. Readers, now a generation removed from the war, acknowledged some of the enduring costs of the internment and were persuaded to offer compensation (albeit quite small) and a formal apology to former internees. After four decades, Okubo became visible to the government that had sought to make her disappear from plain sight. With Miné Okubo's passing in 2001, students of America's racial history lost a great teacher. The genius of *Citizen 13660*, however, is that its many layers remain rich with untapped insights and questions yet to be fully examined. The more closely we look at her, the more we may come to understand exactly what the internment was, and what it really means for Americans on both sides of the fence—both then and now.[42]

NOTES

1 Miné Okubo, *Citizen 13660* (New York: Columbia University Press, 1946), 3–5; Miné Okubo, interview by Sandra Taylor, October 4, 1987, University of Utah Special Collections.

2 Okubo, *Citizen 13660*, 8–11; Miné Okubo, interview by Sandra Taylor.

3 Francis Biddle, "The Question of Loyalty is Personal," *San Francisco Chronicle*, January 20, 1942, 12; Paul S. Taylor, "Our Stakes in the Japanese Exodus," *Survey Graphic* 31 (September 1942): 423; United States War Relocation Authority, *Wartime Exile: The Exclusion of Japanese-Americans from the West Coast* (Washington, D.C.: U.S. Government Printing Office, 1945), 70–71; Jacobus tenBroek, Edward N. Barnhardt, and Floyd W. Matson, *Prejudice, War, and the Constitution* (Berkeley: University of California Press, 1968) 235–38; Greg Robinson, *By Order of the President: FDR and the Internment of Japanese Americans* (Cambridge, Mass.: Harvard University Press, 2001), 3, 110; and Morton Grodzins, *Americans Betrayed: Politics and the Japanese Evacuation* (Chicago: University of Chicago Press, 1949), 133–34.

4 Quoted in Frank H. Wu, *Yellow: Race in America beyond Black and White* (New York: Basic Books, 2002), 96.

5 United States War Relocation Authority, "Questions and Answers for Evacuees: Information Regarding the Relocation Program" (Washington, D.C.: U.S. Government Printing Office, 1942).

6 *Citizen 13660* is only part of a large wartime oeuvre that includes sketches, paintings, gouaches, and illustrations for the Topaz literary magazine *Trek*. It is also quite different from the vast majority of Okubo's work, which is generally classed as modern urban landscape, genre painting, or abstract. To examine the breadth of her work, see Shirley Sun, *Miné Okubo: An American Experience*, exh. cat. (San Francisco: East Wind Printers, 1972); Charleen Touche, ed., *Women's Caucus for Art Honor Awards for Outstanding Achievement in the Visual Arts* (Washington, D.C.: National Women's Caucus for Art, 1991); *Persistent Women Artists: Pablita Velarde, Mine Okubo, Lois Mailou Jones*, presented by Betty LaDuke (Botsford, Conn.: Reading & O'Reilly, 1996); and Deborah Gesensway and Mindy Roseman, *Beyond Words: Images from America's Concentration Camps* (Ithaca, N.Y.: Cornell University Press, 1987).

7 Okubo frequently referred to the internment as being "crazy" or "insane," as in this interview for the exhibition *Beyond Words*: "After being uprooted, everything seemed ridiculous, insane and stupid. There we were in an unfinished camp, with snow and cold. The evacuees helped sheetrock the walls for warmth and built the barbed wire fence to fence themselves in. We had to sing 'God Bless America' many times with a flag. Guards all around with shotguns, you're not going to walk out. I mean . . . what could you do? So many crazy things happened in the camp. So the joke and humor I saw in the camp was not in a joyful sense, but ridiculous and insane." In Gesensway and Roseman, *Beyond Words*, 71.

8 For a fuller examination of image-making during and after the internment, see Elena Tajima Creef, *Imaging Japanese America: The Visual Construction of Citizenship, Nation, and the Body* (New York: New York University Press, 2004), especially chapter 1, which compares the internment photographs of Ansel Adams, Dorothea Lange, and Toyo Miyatake and explores the differences between the way the FSA and internee photographers represented both the Japanese and the internment generally.

9 United States Office of War Information, *The Japanese Relocation* (1942; Chicago: International Historic Films, 1984). Topaz residents were also handed brochures on arrival describing their new surroundings as a "pioneer community, with basic housing and protective services provided by the Federal Government, for occupancy by evacuees for the duration of the war." See United States War Relocation Authority, "Questions and Answers for Evacuees."

10 Ronald Takaki, *Strangers from a Different Shore: A History of Asian Americans* (Boston: Back Bay Books, 1989). For more on the government's use of the pioneer metaphor for war migration, see Heather Fryer, "Pioneers All: Civic Symbolism and Social Change in War-Boom Portland," *Journal of the West* 39, no. 2 (2000): 62–68.

11 Okubo, *Citizen 13660*, 15–17, 22–26.

12 United States Office of War Information, *The Japanese Relocation*.

13 Okubo, *Citizen 13660*, 30–37. The illustration in which Okubo gazes directly at the reader is on page 33.

14 Ibid., 48–51.

15 "Questions and Answers for Evacuees: Information Regarding the Relocation Program," (Washington, D.C.: U.S. Government Printing Office, 1942). For a history of the internment generally and of Topaz in particular, see Roger Daniels, *American Concentration*

Camps (New York: Garland Press, 1989); and Sandra Taylor, *Jewel of the Desert: Japanese-American Internment at Topaz* (Berkeley: University of California Press, 1993).

16 Taylor, *Jewel of the Desert*, 112.

17 Okubo, *Citizen 13660*, 52–53.

18 Ibid., 61.

19 Ibid., 62–79. The church service is pictured on page 62.

20 Ibid., 79–83.

21 Ibid., 164–74. Federal officials began to question the wisdom of community governments after a series of strikes by workers who were not being compensated for their labor and protests from internees after the FBI made a series of arrests without cause during sweeps of the camps.

22 Taylor, *Jewel of the Desert*, 137–39; R. A. Bankson, Central Utah Relocation Center Project Reports Division, Historical Section, "The Wakasa Incident," May 10, 1943, WRA Collection, University of Washington Special Collections; and Okubo, *Citizen 13660*, 180–81.

23 Dillon S. Myer, *Uprooted Americans: The Japanese Americans and the War Relocation Authority during World War II* (Tucson: University of Arizona Press, 1971), 157.

24 Heather Fryer, *Enclosed Worlds in Open Space: Federal Communities and Social Experience in the American West*, Ph.D. diss., 2002, 99–102. A WRA community analyst's report warned, "Remember, the Crow and Blackfoot Indians whose cultures stressed individual initiative and personal bravery and what has happened to the brilliant warriors under Reservation conditions . . . many are today lacking in individual initiative and possessed of a typical wards-of-the-government outlook on life." John F. Embree, "Community Analysis Report No. 1: Dealing with Japanese Americans," Washington, D.C., War Relocation Authority Documents Section, Office of Reports, 1942 (unpublished typescript, University of Washington Special Collections).

25 Propaganda about conditions in the camps was being beamed to Latin America to ignite old resentments of American imperialism and to forge an alliance between non-white peoples. A November 8, 1943, broadcast (intercepted and translated by the OWI) stated simply, "North America mistreats the Japanese in concentration camps. A dispatch from San Francisco informs us that the United States Authorities on the Evening of November Fourth imprisoned some fifty Japanese in the concentration camp of Tule Lake in the State of California. They were conducted by elements of the North American army provided with machine guns and rifles with bayonet attached. The news caused great indignation to the Japanese people." See Office of War Information Alpha file (Tu–Un), Truman Presidential Library; and WRA, *A Voice That Must Be Heard* (Washington, D.C.: U.S. Government Printing Office, 1943), 1.

26 The screening process generated some of the worst controversy and criticism because it asked noncitizens to renounce all ties of loyalty to the Empire of Japan. Ineligible for citizenship in the United States, these older Japanese were asked to make themselves stateless in order to regain their freedom. Citizens, for their part, resented having their loyalty questioned and being asked to choose separate loyalties from their families. Okubo wrote of this in *Citizen 13660*: "Whatever decision was made, families suffered deeply."

27 United States War Relocation Authority, Report #6, "Nisei Assimilation," July 21, 1943, in

Reports of the War Relocation Authority (Washington, D.C.: U.S. Government Printing Office, 1946); and Dillon S. Myer, "Remarks for The March of Time," June 24, 1943, Dillon S. Myer Papers, Truman Presidential Library.

28 United States War Relocation Authority, *Nisei in Uniform* (Washington, D.C.: U.S. Government Printing Office, 1945); and Robert W. O'Brien, *The College Nisei* (Palo Alto, Calif.: Pacific Books, 1949).

29 Okubo, *Citizen 13660*, 139, 205–7; Miné Okubo, interview by Sandra Taylor.

30 Okubo, *Citizen 13660*, 175.

31 Eugene V. Rostow, "Our Worst Wartime Mistake," *Harper's* 191, November 1944, 193–201; *Ex Parte Mitsuye Endo* 323 U.S. 283 (1944).

32 Columbia University Press, "Excerpts from Comments on 'Citizen 13660,'" unpublished typescript, September 1946, 1–2, private collection of Aiko Yoshinaga-Herzig (hereafter "Excerpts").

33 Ibid., 3.

34 Ibid., 1, 6.

35 Ibid., 5. John Dower documents the process by which specific characteristics were racialized and categorized as "safe" or "dangerous" and assigned to Asians and non-Asians and Chinese and Japanese at home and abroad. See John Dower, *War Without Mercy: Race and Power in the Pacific War* (New York: Pantheon Books, 1986), 15–33. See also Robert G. Lee, *Orientals: Asian Americans in Popular Culture* (Philadelphia: Temple University Press, 1999), for an analysis of how racial stereotyping in wartime influenced U.S. policy toward Asian communities—most notably, lifting the Chinese Exclusion Act in 1943 while the internment was well under way.

36 "Excerpts," 1.

37 Ibid., 4; and Speeches and Press Releases File, Dillon S. Myer Papers, Truman Presidential Library.

38 "Excerpts," 1–2.

39 Ibid., 4.

40 Ibid., 4–5.

41 Ibid., 6.

42 United States, Commission on the Wartime Internment of Civilians, *Personal Justice Denied* (Washington, D.C.: U.S. Government Printing Office, 1982), 175–76.

9

TO KEEP A RECORD OF LIFE

MINÉ OKUBO'S AUTOGRAPHIC
MANGA AND WARTIME HISTORY

KIMBERLEY L. PHILLIPS

In the camps, . . . I had the opportunity to study the human race from the cradle to the grave, and to see what happens to people when reduced to one status and one condition. Cameras and photographs were not permitted in the camps, so I recorded everything in sketches, drawings, and paintings.

—MINÉ OKUBO, *CITIZEN 13660*

Just a few pages into *Citizen 13660*, Miné Okubo presents a startling image of herself as she waits to register for the forced evacuation and incarceration of Japanese Americans. She sits in the foreground, reading the "funnies" while squeezed between a soldier holding a gun and a man clutching his face. The juxtapositions in the accompanying text equally startle:

A woman seated near the entrance gave me a card with No. 7 printed on it and told me to go inside and wait. I read the "funnies" until my number was called and I was interviewed. The woman in charge asked me many questions and filled in several printed forms as I answered. As a result of the interview, my family name was reduced to No. 13660. I was given several tags bearing the family number, and was then dismissed. At another desk I made the necessary arrangements to have my household property stored by the government.[1]

Her compliance with the evacuation order and her patient reading of the "funnies" did not prevent her from losing her family's name and household property. Struck homeless, property-less, and nameless by her own government, Okubo and her brother were assigned to Tanforan Assembly Center, the former Tanforan Race Track located just miles south of San Francisco.

Okubo's seemingly calm perusal of the comic pages floats as her silent rebellion against the aggressive martial response to Japanese Americans' presence in the United States, her action an ironic engagement with a quintessentially American activity, and a humorous intervention into the dehumanizing experience of relocation.[2] Throughout the panels in *Citizen 13660*, Okubo composes danger and resistance alongside playful poses, gestures, and settings.

Other Japanese Americans recorded their internment experiences through art, but Okubo's sequential and richly detailed pictures, accompanied by direct and spare prose, turned her graphic autobiography into a subversive comic book about Japanese Americans' imprisonment during World War II. While the visual vocabulary of Okubo's *Citizen 13660* drew on the long tradition of a transpacific comic-book tradition loosely termed *manga*, she also gave the genre of comic books in the United States a new and challenging aesthetic through her use of social commentary that fused Japanese immigrant print culture—art and text—with the radical political dissent of 1930s public art in the Americas. In doing so, Okubo took on the wartime "funny pages," a site where American anxieties about the war and race, particularly anti-Japanese attitudes and behaviors, were represented. *Citizen 13660* combines the comic book with memoir to create an autographic social criticism about a horrific personal and group experience, a combination not seen again until Art Spiegelman's *Maus* in 1986.[3]

◆◆◆

Artists' use of the comic form to tell a visual, textual, critical, and sometimes "humorous" story has a long and varied history, especially in Asia. This combination of humorous, sometimes subversive, storytelling through art took specific shape in Japan between 1100 and 1700. By the twelfth century, narrative picture scrolls appeared in sacred and secular forms, the latter typically erotic. In 1702, artist Ooka Shimboku, whose woodblock prints were known as ukiyo-e (translated as "floating world"), "bound together some prints and created *Tobae Sankokushi* [and] Japan had its (and perhaps the world's) first cartoon book."[4]

Over the next two centuries, this comic art took various forms. Ukiyo-e were "lively, topical, cheap, entertaining, and playful." Many tended toward the "macabre and the erotic."[5] Beginning in the eighteenth century, booklets called *kibyoshi* ("yellowbacks," because of their yellow covers), presented satiric, parodic, and topical subjects with strong story lines for an adult audience, expanding on the illustrated fables printed for children. These booklets used monochrome prints and captions in equal proportions, filling each page with images and dialogue. Authorities occasionally banned *kibyoshi* when the satire, ironic parodies and "grotesque allegories" of the manners and morals of elites became too critical. By the early nineteenth century, these indigenous cartoons all but vanished under the repressions of the Tokugawa period (1600–1868). During the Meiji period (1868–1912), European and American comics, some produced by expatriate artists, appeared in urban newspapers, journals, and magazines. These imports accelerated the use of new printing techniques, bilingual word balloons, and sequential panels in Japanese-produced comics.[6]

Japanese artists began to include social commentary and subversive politics in their comics and cartoons, but those who parodied Japanese authorities did so with grave consequences. Illustrated periodicals such as *Kokkei shimbun* (Humor newspaper) and *Ehagaki sekai* (World of picture postcards) created a milieu for subversive politics in turn-of-the-century Japanese mass-circulation print culture. While these two publications were short-lived, other venues for humor flourished for short periods of time. In the late Meiji period, for example, journalist Miyatake Gaikotsu edited several satirical illustrated periodicals. His efforts, however, were halted when he faced prison terms, suspension of his publications, and frequent fines. Other artists, too, conveyed opaque social and subversive commentary through postcards, comic strips, and comic books to a wide audience that included women, children, and émigrés.[7]

Hardly confined to Asia, comic art, which included comic strips in Europe and the United States, began cross-fertilizing within the context of a massive worldwide movement of texts and people. By the early twentieth century, newspapers in Japan, China, and India were publishing some "nonsensical" and generally farcical American comic strips, which influenced versions in Asia. Some publications literally translated European and American titles into Japanese. Newspaper cartoon strips and cartoon books shaped and were shaped by the growth of mass production, visual culture, and the mass-circulation press in Japan.[8] Carried and transmitted across the Pacific from Japan to the United States, and sometimes circulating back into Japan again, this complex transmission of cartoon-making influenced the art and storytelling practices of Japanese immigrants and their American-born children in the United States.

At the start of the twentieth century, a Japanese emigrant returned to Japan and published his *manga* in book form.[9] In 1904, nineteen-year-old Yoshitaka Henry Kiyama emigrated to San Francisco to study and work. Kiyama joined an increasing population of Japanese male emigrants with similar aspirations, many laboring as domestic servants in Anglo-Californian households during the day and attending school at night. Kiyama enrolled at the San Francisco Art Institute, won several prestigious awards, and exhibited his work. Known as a "fine" artist, Kiyama drew and displayed dozens of cartoons in early 1927. *The Japanese American News* reported that "the exhibit consists of 52 pieces dealing historically with the life of Japanese residents here. It is extremely interesting, and has proved to be very popular." A columnist for the newspaper noted that the work, *Manga hokubei iminshi* (A *manga* North American immigrant history), was too immediate for serious art and better suited to the weekly comics.[10]

Kiyama eventually self-published his graphic autobiography of fifty-two cartoon strips, each made up of twelve panels, but not in the United States. In 1927, he returned to Japan and self-published *Manga yonin shosei* (The four students comic). Focused on the lives of four young Japanese men who come to San Francisco to live and work in the United States, Kiyama's comic-book narrative found a small and appreciative audience. When he returned to San Francisco in 1931, he republished *Manga yonin shosei*. How Kiyama adapted his panels into a comic book that was also a transpacific text is worth some consideration, but such exploration is beyond the scope of this essay.

Hardly immune to the racial and ethnic stereotypes of African Americans and Chinese Americans, especially those deployed in visual form, *Manga yonin shosei* nonetheless emerges as a complex narrative of Issei experience specifically written for an audience of Issei and potential emigrants in Japan. The four young men struggle to find work, encounter a lynch mob, and survive the 1906 San Francisco earthquake and the influenza outbreak of 1918. Events in their personal lives include seeking a picture bride and surviving rejections of their efforts to acquire citizenship. These sequences written in Japanese and English simultaneously challenge and make comic the four men's efforts to succeed in spite of their frequent encounters with racial prejudice, bigotry, and U.S. exclusion policies. In the final sequence of panels, the men meet again after some time. Two returned to Japan and two stayed in the United States, a reminder that emigration and the immigrant experience were unstable and ambiguous.

Why Kiyama's strips were not published in the Japanese newspapers in the United States remains something of a mystery.[11] The Japanese immigrant press in the United States grew slowly, but it was in its "golden era" by the interwar years, according to David K. Yoo.[12] Initially intended for distribution in Japan in order to encourage emigration at the beginning of the twentieth century, newspapers such as *Soko Shimbun* (San Francisco News), founded in 1906, and *Rafu Shimpo* (Los Angeles Japanese Daily News), shifted their content to serve the growing American-born population of Japanese communities. These and other papers published both Japanese- and English-language editions after World War I. Starting in 1928, the *Japanese American Courier* published English-only texts for the Nisei, who were navigating and negotiating complex citizenship, social, and racial identities within a larger context of legal, political, and economic restrictions. Editors considered the aspirations of this American-born generation, along with racial formations they faced in the interwar years, as different from the concerns and experiences of earlier generations of people of Japanese descent in America. By the 1920s, U.S. publications reached an audience of Nisei with diverse and broad reading interests; most read little Japanese. Alongside Japanese-language newspapers based in the United States, the Issei frequently read English texts in translation.[13]

Perhaps Kiyama's bilingual text and Japanese orientation were not ideally suited for an audience of younger readers with little skill in reading Japanese. More likely, its sequential and documentary character made it unusual for an audience schooled in the American comic strip; as well, the American comic book had yet to appear, making its unsteady debut in 1933.[14]

Harsh legal restrictions, racism, and an anti-Japanese visual culture were the backdrop for Kiyama's sympathetic rendering of Japanese immigrant life. American cartoon art in the mainstream press included racist dialogue and violent action that encoded ethnic and racial stereotypes of Asians generally. In West Coast newspapers, these cartoons appeared alongside virulent expressions of anti-Japanese prejudices. These visual codes enfolded anti-immigrant and anti-black images and attitudes into the particularized anti-Japanese images. The images, for example, tended to portray all non-whites as "swarthy" and Japanese characters as "swarthy," sinister, arrogant, duplicitous, and animal-like.[15] These racial stereotypes, fueled by social, cultural, and political developments such as segregation and anti-Asian immigration laws, were deployed in popular songs and in the newer technologies of film, radio, and print, especially advertisements.[16]

Japan's bombing of Pearl Harbor in late 1941 further fueled extreme anti-Japanese images in films, newspaper stories, and poster campaigns. Alongside these media, editorial cartoons, such as those drawn by Theodore Geisel—popularly known as Dr. Seuss—seared depictions of the Japanese as dangerous and grotesque into a common visual vocabulary.[17] As Gordon Chang reminds us, in the wartime comics, "the Pacific War received much greater attention than the war in Europe." The pages of comic strips and comic books displayed "the grotesquely racist caricatures of the Japanese," depicted "routinely as vermin, sub-human or simian." Such images, he concludes, "were as simple and unproblematic as the American patriotism that was promoted."[18] Such widespread verbal, visual, and editorial assaults had extreme consequences for the Japanese in America. Editorials argued that Japanese Americans could only demonstrate loyalty, ease public hysteria, and redeem themselves as citizens by submitting to internment without rights.[19] With few Japanese Americans in positions of political and cultural authority, "the wheels of injustice" forced the majority into prison camps.[20]

Writers and artists committed to the anti-fascist agenda of the war challenged these images and associations, but the federal government made few, if any, efforts to stipulate appropriate content in the mass media and certainly not in comic strips during the period. The *Superman* story line that ran for eight weeks from June 28, 1943, to August 21, 1943, for example, depicted Superman visiting the relocation camps, uncovering plots for sabotage by subversive and disloyal Japanese, and preventing similar acts outside the camps. The strip's story line appeared when criticism against the camps became widespread *and* as thousands of Japanese Americans began to leave the camps or enter the military. Warned of the potential damage to these efforts, the Office of War Information neither censored the strip nor insisted on insertions attesting to the loyalty of the Japanese living in the United States.[21]

◆◆◆

When she entered Tanforan Assembly Center on May 1, 1942, Miné Okubo expanded her drawings, which she had decided to make for friends, to include documentation of the entire experience as a public record.[22] Her panels provide pungent insight into the horrific stench, the rats, the intrusions of officials, and the separation from the outside world that Japanese Americans confronted repeatedly. Elena Tajima Creef argues that Okubo's drawings offered more "fluid and interpretational scenes" than any static photos from a camera could have provided.[23] Okubo had access to private and public scenes that cameras could not and did not record. The black-and-white drawings highlight the pervasive gloom and the endless weariness in the women who find no privacy to tend to the basic needs of the body: showering, using the toilet, bathing a child, or going to sleep. Equally important, Okubo conveyed the conflicting sensibilities of the internees, particularly their everyday resistances alongside their resilient creativity.

Her recording and documenting of camp life in sketches and text take four visual and textual perspectives—personal, communal, cultural, and political—widening and altering the comic-book idiom and narrative in ways that would not be seen again until the late twentieth century. Okubo begins with an account of the internment's impact on her personally, documenting her one-day transition from citizenship to prisoner in twenty-six drawings. In this long sequence, she reverses the story of immigration, beginning with the loss of her "happy home" and ending with her falling asleep, cold and shivering, on a straw mattress. Each drawing in this inversion is one of spectacular "bedlam."[24] Stripped of citizenship and property, by the day's end she is forced to make a home in a horse stall.

This systematic and government-sanctioned assault on the Japanese American body—taken as individuals, families, communities, and citizens—remains a theme as Okubo shifts the visual tone of her drawings away from the more personal account of her arrival at the camp to one of witness to a people's experiences in the camp.

In capturing these common experiences, Okubo highlights art as news. By early 1942, West Coast Japanese American newspapers had ceased publication, and the assembly centers received limited information.[25] Many internees depended on rumors or the *San Francisco Chronicle*, well known for its anti-immigration stance and strong support for mass incarceration of Japanese living in the United States. In other panels, Okubo presents news as rationed.[26] Information from the outside was limited and censored; news about the camps was equally limited and certainly circumscribed.

In contradistinction to this lack of news about the camp, Okubo's panels become documentation of the center's unsavory conditions. Through different vantage points, Okubo exposes the lack of privacy, the pervasive idleness, horrific sanitary conditions, limited space and crowded environment. She includes details that government officials forbade photographers to depict: barbed wire, guard towers, and armed guards. While only nine of the panels in this section show one or more of these restricted images, Okubo's panels portray other disagreeable details excised from official photographs and depictions of the camps. Unlike the cheerful, clean, and happy images in the famous internment photographs of Ansel Adams, Okubo's images capture a range of the internees' responses, depicting sullen, angry, sad, frustrated, discomfited, and resistant visages. All of these varying responses highlight the "harshness and inconvenience of day-to-day living" that is omitted from the photographs in the official record.[27] They also challenge the rhetoric that Japanese Americans posed a danger to the United States. Instead, Okubo's intimate details of the harsh conditions of domestic life implode the arguments about the camps as spaces in which Japanese Americans could demonstrate their loyalty. Okubo's renderings of the assaults on Japanese American women's dignity are overt references to the familiar associations between protection of white women's bodies and defense of the nation.

Okubo layered the "ridiculous and the insane" aspects of humor between the humiliations and discomfort in camp. In one panel, patrols uncover contraband and "suspicious actions," but not the sort that white Americans feared, unless they found gambling or packages ordered from the Sears Catalog harbingers of danger. In another, Okubo displays the confluence of seduction and danger in forced leisure— as in her portrayal of a man asleep with a newspaper over his face, his hands folded suggestively across his groin. In another, a couple jitterbugs, the sexual metaphor amplified by the text: "The incomplete partitions in the stalls and barracks made a single symphony of yours and your neighbors' loves, hates, and joys. One had to get used to snores, baby-crying, family troubles, and even to the jitterbugs."[28] Okubo's record of life becomes as much a record of sound—a cacophony that was part symphony and part dissonance—as it was a visual record. Such noise provides an amplification to the images absent from Ansel Adams's photographs and WRA images. Okubo's citizens gaze and speak.

◆◆◆

Citizen 13660 also introduces us to a female subjectivity about personal and physical danger that is difficult to apprehend in white women's narratives about life in the wartime United States. In contrast, Okubo's memoir, like Ann Petry's short stories about the riots in Harlem, provide insight into the sense of harm that women and communities of color faced during the war. On the one hand, excluded from the simultaneous representations of the violated nation and the protected white female body, Japanese women were cast as dangerous to the nation. On the other, in the visual and textual narratives produced within marginal communities, danger as a result of racialized violence has been typically cast as a male experience. Okubo simultaneously inserts a woman's perspective and offers a challenge to the construction of the dangerous Japanese. In one illustration, authorities allow Okubo, accompanied by a "police guard," to leave the camp and finalize the storage of personal property. We see her under surveillance and with her pockets stuffed with purchases, her desire for liberty reduced to pointing to candy in a shop window. She appears giddy in both her freedom and the absurdity of having a guard watch her as she shops.

If the journey to Tanforan was an inversion of the immigrant narrative, the long train ride from the center in California to Topaz in the Utah desert suspends any reading of the journey as liberatory—as train travel is so often portrayed in American film and song. Okubo depicts it as uncomfortable and dangerous, reflecting the experience she and the other passengers endured, of choking dust, overheated cars, and relentless darkness. A brick was thrown through a window, and many suffered from train sickness. Okubo finds irony in the ritual of departure, when those who remained behind waved large banners bearing the words "bon voyage." Traveling from the West Coast into the interior may have relieved the minds of those who believed Japanese Americans posed a danger, but Okubo underscores in drawing and text that she has become a prisoner in her own country.

Once at Topaz, Okubo rendered the American frontier as taking on a fiendish role, imposing repeated dangers to the health of the prisoners. The swirling dust chokes them and makes them white as they arrive. Water is alternately scarce and contaminated, causing outbreaks of dysentery. In no way presented as humorous or comical, Okubo's drawings instead depict the setting not as a natural obstacle for the internees to conquer but as one of the arbitrary barriers they are forced to construct and endure. Topaz was half finished when they arrived, and everyone had to help complete the building of the camp. One panel depicts Okubo watching as the "evacuees construct fence posts and watch towers . . . to fence themselves in."[29]

Okubo describes the newsroom of the camp paper, the *Topaz Times*, a jumble of bodies doing anything but reporting about the camp. She sketched herself, positioned to the left, eating a sandwich; a man reads behind her, his feet perched precariously on the table. Others yawn, sleep, and read in the background. Launched as a mimeographed sheet, the *Topaz Times* later "became a daily, with a Japanese section and a comic section." Despite its growth, the paper was neither independent nor a challenge to write: "All news passed the censorship of the administration staff." Other newspapers inspired similar disdain because they lacked freedom and were constantly censored.[30] Here Okubo makes a distinction between the censorship of news, story, and image. Within months of the newspaper's start, Okubo and "a small group" bolted to "start a fifty-page art and literary magazine."[31]

Okubo's claim insists, then, that we see *Citizen 13660* as complex and subversive popular art. These panels and the drawings she produced for *Trek* are not substantially different. Anthony W. Lee describes the drawings from this period as substantial and "complex, her compositions more compressed, . . . her tone more biting."[32] Lee argues that Okubo's training with politicized artists and writers during the late 1930s informed her art during her years at Tanforan and Topaz. The last two dozen panels in *Citizen 13660*, for example, demonstrate this "biting tone." When compared to the more intimate and personal early sections, the last panels alternate between depicting the growing and diverse resistance in the camps and noting the seemingly mundane presence of dogs and mosquitoes. Most important, Okubo injects tension into the binary of loyal or disloyal citizen demanded by the United States. After suffering in the camps while at the same time creating victory gardens, organizing bond and scrap-metal drives, and volunteering for the army, Japanese Americans must submit to the WRA's questions for the purpose of determining their loyalty.[33]

In an era when comic books and comic strips served to define enemies and allies, inculcate pro-war sentiments, and promote values associated with American citizenship, Okubo produced reminders that comic-book art could also be subversive and critical of racial prejudice transmitted through mass culture. She captured the daily hardships, indignities, and resilience that official photographs and other forms of popular culture either ignored or refused to depict. While her surname had been changed to 13660, her first name, Miné, with its diacritical mark faintly visible (and possibly re-read as the possessive "mine"), floats across each drawing as vivid evidence of her authority as a citizen eyewitness to the incarceration of tens of thousands of American citizens.

The edgy balance of irony, comedy, nation, and individual in *Citizen 13660* had no equal in the burgeoning mass production of postwar comics in the United States.

Years after its 1946 publication, Okubo recalled the difficulties of getting her auto-graphic account of the internment published. Anything Japanese was considered "rat poison," she noted. Americans' responses to the visual ingenuity and subversive content of *Citizen 13660* need to be assessed. Equally pressing, her text should be considered by the growing literature on the autographic genre within the tradition of comic books. Cultural historians need to do more than incorporate Okubo's achievement in this history. *Citizen 13660* is not simply an antecedent to the work of Art Spiegelman and other writers of graphic histories. Rooted in a long tradition of Japanese and Japanese American art and text, *Citizen 13660* demands that our understandings of the history of comic books, their audiences, and their producers be rethought and rewritten.

NOTES

1 Miné Okubo, *Citizen 13660* (Seattle: University of Washington Press, 1983), 19.

2 Okubo noted years later that "the joke and humor I saw in camp was not a joyful sense, but ridiculous and insane." Quoted in Deborah Gesensway and Mindy Roseman, *Beyond Words: Images from America's Concentration Camps* (Ithaca, N.Y.: Cornell University Press, 1987), 71. She has commented that Japanese Americans did not believe that they, too, would be evacuated along with the Japanese-born. In *Citizen 13660*, Okubo writes of Civilian Exclusion Order No. 19, issued on April 24, 1942, which included the Nisei: "It was a real blow when everyone, regardless of citizenship, was ordered to evacuate" (17). Two panels later, readers, too, feel the blow. At the same time, Okubo's reading of the funnies is reminiscent of Japanese cartoonist Ippei Okamoto's observation in 1922 when he visited the *New York World*: "American comics have become an entertainment equal to baseball, motion pictures, and the presidential elections. Some observers say that comics have replaced alcohol as a solace for workers since prohibition began." Quoted in Frederik L. Schodt, *Manga! Manga!: The World of Japanese Comics* (New York: Kodansha International USA, 1983), 43.

3 Charles McGrath, "Not Funnies," *New York Times Magazine*, July 11, 2004; Joseph Witek, *Comic Books as History: The Narrative Art of Jack Jackson, Art Spiegelman, and Harvey Pakar* (Jackson: University of Mississippi Press, 1989). Neither McGrath nor Witek include Okubo in their overviews of comic books as graphic historical narrative.

4 John A. Lent, "Introduction," in *Illustrating Asia: Comics, Humor Magazines, and Picture Books* (Honolulu: University of Hawaii Press, 2001), 2; Schodt, *Manga! Manga!*, 28.

5 Kendall H. Brown, "Postcards, Commerce, and Creativity in Japan, 1904–1940," in *Art of the Japanese Postcard: The Leonard A. Lauder Collection at the Museum of Fine Arts, Boston*, ed. Anne Nishimura Morse, J. Thomas Rimer, and Kendall H. Brown (Boston: Museum of Fine Arts, 2004), 47–49; Schodt, *Manga! Manga!*, 34–35.

6 Schodt, *Manga! Manga!* 37–43; Howard Hibbett, *The Chrysanthemum and the Fish: Japanese Humor since the Age of the Shoguns* (New York: Kodansha International, 2002), 118–24;

Haruo Shirane, ed., *Early Modern Japanese Literature: An Anthology, 1600–1900* (New York: Columbia University Press, 2002); and Paul Varley, *Japanese Culture,* 4th ed. (Honolulu: University of Hawaii Press, 2000), 197–204.

7 Morse, Rimer, and Brown, *Art of the Japanese Postcard*, 200.

8 Schodt, *Manga! Manga!*; John A. Lent, "Easy-Going Daddy, Kaptayn Barbell, and Unmad: American Influences upon Asian Comics," *Inks* (November 1995): 59–72; and Shimizu Isao, "Red Comic Books: The Origins of Modern Japanese *Manga*," in Lent, *Illustrating Asia*, 137.

9 *Manga* as a term dates from the early nineteenth century and has broad meaning that includes caricature, cartoon, comic strip, comic book, and animation. The word *manga* did not come into wide usage until the early twentieth century. In the last third of the nineteenth century, the term *ponchi-e*, after the imported British magazine *Punch*, was the one commonly used for comics.

10 Quoted in Henry Yoshitaka Kiyama, *The Four Immigrants Manga: A Japanese Experience in San Francisco, 1904–1924* (Berkeley, Calif.: Stone Bridge Press, 1999), 10.

11 Ibid.

12 David K. Yoo, *Growing Up Nisei: Race, Generation, and Culture among Japanese Americans of California, 1924–49* (Urbana: University of Illinois Press, 2000), 70.

13 On the growth of this bilingual press, see Frank Chin, ed., *Born in the USA: The Story of Japanese America, 1889–1947* (Lanham, Md.: Rowman & Littlefield, 2002), 101, 161–64, 177–79. For a specific analytical focus on the Nisei, see Yoo, *Growing Up Nisei*.

14 Bradford W. Wright, *Comic Book Nation: The Transformation of Youth Culture in America* (Baltimore, Md.: The Johns Hopkins University Press, 2001), 1–7.

15 John W. Dower, *War without Mercy: Race and Power in the Pacific War* (New York: Pantheon Books, 1986), 81–93.

16 Ibid., 81.

17 Elena Tajima Creef, *Imaging Japanese America: The Visual Construction of Citizenship, Nation, and the Body* (New York: New York University Press, 2004), 15–16; and Richard H. Minear, *Dr. Seuss Goes to War: The World War II Cartoons of Theodore Seuss Geisel* (New York: New Press, 2000).

18 Gordon H. Chang, 'Superman Is About to Visit the Relocation Centers' and the Limits of Wartime Liberalism," *Amerasia Journal* 19 (Winter 1993): 38.

19 Lawson Fusao Inada, ed., *Only What We Could Carry: The Japanese American Internment Experience* (Berkeley, Calif.: Heyday Books; San Francisco: California Historical Society, 2000), 22–23.

20 Yoo, *Growing Up Nisei*, 95–96.

21 Ibid., 38–56.

22 In *Citizen 13660*, Okubo writes that her response to the confiscation of the evacuees' dignity, privacy, citizenship, and property was to "keep a record of camp life in sketches and drawings" (53). Later, she calls her efforts a "documentary" (206).

23 Creef, *Imaging Japanese America*, 83.

24 Okubo, *Citizen 13660*, 39.

25 Yoo, *Growing Up Nisei*, 124; and James Omura, "Japanese American Journalism during World War II," in *Frontiers of Asian American Studies*, ed. Gail Nomura, Russell Endo,

Stephen H. Sumida, and Russell C. Leong (Pullman: Washington State University Press, 1989), 71–80. While West Coast papers were forced to close, newspapers in Utah and Colorado—some of them transplants from San Francisco—flourished.

26 Okubo, *Citizen 13660*, 94, 84, 91.

27 For a discussion of official photography in the camps, see Creef, *Imaging Japanese America*, 13–67.

28 Okubo, *Citizen 13660*, 60, 96, 66.

29 Ibid., 155.

30 Yoo, *Growing Up Nisei*, 98–99.

31 Okubo, *Citizen 13660*, 134.

32 Anthony W. Lee, *Painting on the Left: Diego Rivera, Radical Politics, and San Francisco's Public Murals* (Berkeley: University of California Press, 1999), 199–200.

33 Okubo, *Citizen 13660*, 175.

10

MINÉ OKUBO'S *CITIZEN 13660* AND HER *TREK* ARTWORK

SPACE, MOVEMENT, IMAGE, TEXT, AND THEIR SITES OF PRODUCTION

LYNNE HORIUCHI

Space and movement are key elements in Miné Okubo's book *Citizen 13660*, and are important in her work as art editor of *Trek*, a literary journal she created with other young Japanese American writers and artists in the Central Utah Relocation Center in Topaz, Utah. We may examine these key elements comparatively in the two sets of artworks in varied ways. We may understand space and movement as stylistic elements in works of art. Or we may understand them as key to the images and narratives of Okubo's confrontation with internment, full of pathos and irony, that portray the physical impacts of the loss of civil liberties and freedom of movement in close proximity to us as viewers.

We must also, however, consider the sites or spaces of production; the prisonlike conditions of the internment camps inflected and constrained artistic production. Under the control of the U.S. government, Okubo created artistic interventions and representations that were complicated by their sites of production, which offered what we might consider an undemocratic and non-normative discursive environment. As Okubo noted of her incarceration, "I was an American citizen, and because of the injustices and contradictions nothing made much sense, making things comical in spite of the misery."[1] Producing images about internment camps for their incarcerated audience as part of an artists' cooperative project and communicating the conditions of that internment to an American art public were very different activities. This exploration of space, movement, image, and text is organized around several topics: (1) spaces of production, (2) a comparative stylistic analysis of

Okubo's representation of space and movement in her artwork, and (3) a detailed analysis of her *Trek* works, which have been less accessible to the general public than those in *Citizen 13660*.

THE SPACES OF PRODUCTION — *CITIZEN 13660* AND *TREK*

The contexts within which Okubo created these works of art were quite dissimilar. *Trek* was produced in an internment camp for the internee population. The U.S. government's Project Reports Division of the War Relocation Authority (WRA) was the official administrative unit that oversaw its production between December 1942 and June 1943.[2] As art editor for *Trek*, Okubo created the majority of its illustrations, which functioned as supporting visual material for the journal's stories and defined its graphic character.[3] The *Trek* writers and artists negotiated in a cooperative effort with the WRA throughout the journal's production processes.

Though incarcerated, the *Trek* staff chose an identity for their literary journal that embodied movement into and out of the internment camps. According to a history of their work, which they published in their last issue in June 1943, the journal name was based on the Webster's dictionary definition of "trek": "A migration, an expedition, especially of a group, to a new home; to make one's way slowly or arduously; also a stage of such a journey. . . ." They explained: "And so it was chosen as the name of the projected publication of the out-standing young writers and artists group of Topaz, as they came eastward from California to this desert settlement in Utah."[4]

They noted that the first issue was a special holiday issue distributed to Topaz internees on Christmas morning 1942, which they designed "with an emphasis on the physical aspects of the city." Its success inspired a second issue reporting on life beyond the internment camp. The last issue set the tone for resettlement and the official "relocation" of the internee population. The task of the young artists was to depict the moods adrift in Topaz and to "show a not-too-grim side of life in camp."[5]

As Jim Yamada reported in his Christmas 1942 *Trek* article "Portrait of an Artist," Okubo had already established herself as an emerging talent.[6] Other contributors such as Toshio Mori and Larry Tajiri were already experienced as writers and would later gain recognition as Japanese American authors. In her capacity as art editor and through her *Trek* illustrations, Okubo created a visual identity for the journal and its articles. The *Trek* cover designs, for example, functioned boldly as nearly independent artworks in themselves; the ornamental use of type for the title became one of the journal's identifiable characteristic. Okubo also created and organized her illustrations for articles following the staff's general direction for that issue so as to convey information about Topaz and its physical environment.

For her book *Citizen 13660*, Okubo drew and annotated her personal journey through the Japanese American internment of World War II with care and incisiveness. The work is in a small-book format with images on each page and personal annotations for each image.[7] Her audience was the post–World War II East Coast art public; according to her friend, Nobuo Kitagaki, she initially had difficulty finding a press to publish the work because it was viewed as "a touchy subject."[8] None of the presses on the West Coast were willing to publish it immediately after World War II.

In *Citizen 13660*, Okubo created drawings that she referred to as "a record of the Evacuation in drawings and sketches."[9] An astute observer, she relied on her drawings to tell the story, since the U.S. government in its initial directives banned possession of cameras within the camps.[10] She responded to her captors by effectively turning her artist's gaze "to study the human race from the cradle to the grave, and to see what happens to people when reduced to one state and condition."[11] Her intimate images and textual representations of camp life are some of the most poignant, uncensored views we have of everyday life during the internment, although she would later caution, "You have to live the camp life to know what it was like."[12]

In contrast to *Citizen 13660*, *Trek* was produced as a group effort, from design and layout through assembly and distribution. Physically, the materials and equipment used to produce the journal were modest, although it was guaranteed a wide distribution among its captive audience of approximately eight thousand.[13] The covers of the three issues of *Trek* appear to have been printed with a multi-lith press on light stock paper. The thirty to forty-five pages inside were mimeographed verso and recto on letter-size paper. Okubo used this format to good advantage by spreading some of the illustrations over two pages. The mimeographed portions were printed by internee staff, who cut stencils, proofread, printed, collated, and stapled the pages into the covers.[14]

The *Trek* staff described their efforts as "the result of many hours . . . creative and physical; a concerted effort of many talents."[15] Assignments apparently overlapped at the newspaper, *Topaz Times*, as Okubo noted of her memoir: "I was always busy. In the daytime, I went around sketching . . . I worked all night at the newspaper. It was lunacy to work all night, going twenty-four hours a day. I was art editor for the daily newspaper and art editor for *Trek* literary magazine."[16] During this period, Okubo produced approximately two thousand drawings, part of an oeuvre of works from which she would create *Citizen 13660*, and concurrently worked on *Trek*.

Throughout its three-issue run, the writers and artists who produced *Trek* struggled with the flux of staff and contributors as people left the semi-permanent internment camp and the WRA directed their energies toward other tasks. An editors' note to readers explained the late publication of the February 1943 issue by noting that the staff had been assigned to work on the WRA's and U.S. War Department's registration program, which was designed to identify internees loyal to the United States and segregate those who were deemed disloyal.[17]

MIGRATIONS IN A LARGER HISTORICAL CONTEXT

The title *Trek* may be taken as the key to the larger historical context for the sites where Okubo produced her artwork. The forced removal of 117,000 people of Japanese ancestry from the West Coast was also a story of the denial of the internees' national belonging. In December 1942, the internees were just beginning to settle into semi-permanent internment camps, or "relocation centers," in isolated corners of the western United States and Arkansas. They had suffered indignities, financial losses, and restrictions. After Pearl Harbor was bombed on December 7, 1941, the FBI arrested many community leaders; bank accounts were frozen; delivery of social security and life insurance benefits ceased; welfare benefits were denied; and a congressional act criminalized any movement out of zones defined by the military. President Franklin D. Roosevelt had authorized the internees' removal, and the courts had upheld it. Japanese American communities were economically crippled.[18]

Most Japanese and Japanese Americans had been unaware of the planning for their incarceration. A wall of hostility and anti-Japanese agitation had opposed their voluntary evacuation in the interior western states. Many expressed shock at discovering that watchtowers, searchlights, and armed guards were omnipresent conditions of their internment. To the internees, the new cities they inhabited were similar to prisons as places of punishment and provided the U.S. public with proof that they were guilty of unnamed criminal acts.[19]

Nothing in their education had prepared the younger generation of Japanese Americans for this sudden event. Cooperating fully with wartime regulations and enlisting in the war effort were some of the ways the Nisei, or second-generation Japanese Americans, thought they could demonstrate their loyalty to the country of their birth. Many of the Issei, or first-generation Japanese immigrants, who were denied naturalized citizenship, had no option other than retaining their Japanese citizenship despite their decades of residence in the United States. For many Nisei, like Okubo, Japan represented a national enemy of the United States as well as the distant homeland of their parents, about which they remained ambivalent.

CENSORSHIP AS A CONDITION OF PRODUCTION

Given the historical conditions of Topaz as an internment site, the WRA exercised a patriarchal direction and surveillance of the *Trek* staff's production and thereby censored their artistic expression. The WRA administrative staff at each internment camp included a Reports Division. The division was in charge of publicity for the camp and exerted control over the internees' publications, such as *Trek*, through editorial direction, review, and censorship. From the WRA perspective, the Reports Division's job was to maintain control over the internees' activities, public spaces, and intimate everyday needs—as Okubo had described it, "from the cradle to the grave."

Censorship may be understood as a means by which the WRA presented itself to the U.S. public as an efficient and capable administration.[20] While it is difficult to estimate from a historic distance the degree of influence the U.S. government exerted in censoring and editing the journal, it is clear that the government did structure the process. It is also difficult to know how the *Trek* staff may have negotiated these restrictions without specific documentation of their activities. *Trek* itself, however, contains references to censorship. Jim Yamada slips a reference to "the fourth of July we spent de-stapling censored papers" into a list of humorous high points of the internees' stay at Tanforan Assembly Center, a racetrack that had been converted into a temporary internment camp. The list also includes housing accommodations and "the admirer of Russia who christened his stable 'Stall Inn.'" The humor lends an air of innocence to the reference to censorship.[21]

The WRA control no doubt functioned as a screen for content in text and images. As the U.S. public remained somewhat hostile to the internees, the WRA was particularly sensitive to accusations that it was coddling the latter. Okubo depicted the celebration of Japanese rituals in *Citizen 13660*, but these may not have been permitted in *Trek* in late 1942 and early 1943, a time when the United States was battling Japan island by island in the Pacific and some members of the *Trek* staff were leaving to fight in the war.[22] The WRA did, however, allow the internees to satirize the internment camp conditions, and the topic was pursued in *Trek*. Jim Yamada, for example, protested that WRA critics were correct regarding the concept of coddling by pointing out that internees were in fact being coddled—like eggs kept just below the boiling point in the desert heat of Poston, Arizona. Such conditions and satire clarify the tensions between words and images in Okubo's work.

WRA censorship of internee newspapers has been reported in other instances. Jack Yamaguchi and his wife, Dorothy, documented one example of the censorship of a visual image submitted to the *Minidoka Irrigator*, the Minidoka Relocation Center's official newspaper; the WRA rejected a photograph that showed suitcases stored under the bed and towels hanging from nails on the wall because the photo would not present the proper image to the general public.[23]

Charles Kikuchi also documented in his diary the continuous struggle with WRA administrators at Tanforan Assembly Center over censorship of the *Tanforan Totalizer*. By July 31, 1942, he noted: "We have to fight for every inch and never have received much cooperation from the administration. We take the censorship in stride, feeling that there is not much use in trying to buck . . . [the WRA administrators] with their Fascist ideas. . . . Taro and the others absolutely refuse to expend more energy under the present setup. And I hardly blame them." He goes on to explain the effects of censorship on the display of national loyalties: "We have sort of developed a policy of subtle Americanization and avoid loud protestations of loyalty, of waving the flag. We minimize things Japanese." [24]

Censorship was one of the real conditions that *Trek* editors had to accommodate in creating their images and text. Their labor must be considered unfree because of their incarceration, and their freedom of speech was curtailed through censorship authorized by the military and administrative powers that enforced the internment.

A STYLISTIC COMPARISON — CHRISTMAS 1942

A comparison of two of Okubo's images of Christmas 1942—one from the narrative *Citizen 13660* and the other the cover for *Trek*—illustrates the difference in style, format, and production between them. In the *Citizen 13660* illustration of Christmas 1942, a family of five—a middle-aged mother and father, a young daughter, two small boys about two and three years old—and a cat are arranged in a circle on the picture plane around a pot-bellied stove crowned with a tea kettle. The pot-bellied stove acts much as a hearth to draw in the family and provides the anchor of activity in the drawing. Only the young daughter is somewhat still; the other family members are busy with Christmas Day activities. The father is entertaining one of the boys with a toy; the smaller boy seems to be playing with comics; the mother is dressed in her apron and is serving tea. Their activities are drawn together by the direction of their gazes as well. The father seems to be speaking or smiling to his son to draw him into a string game, and his elder son reaches for the toy, while the younger gazes distractedly at his brother. The mother directs a solicitous look at the father as if to call his attention to the prepared tea.

In spite of this family interaction, Okubo observed the pathos of that Christmas in her annotation, with a comment on the *Trek* staff:

The first Christmas was sad. The mess halls provided decorated trees and served special dinners but there was a lack of holiday spirit. Some families made a brave attempt to hold their usual celebrations.

The *Trek* staff held a party. We concocted a drink of grape jam and lemons and pretended it was the real stuff. Dancing and games made the party a noisy affair.[25]

The first Christmas was sad. The mess halls provided decorated trees and served special dinners but there was a lack
of holiday spirit. Some families made a brave attempt to hold
their usual celebrations.

The *Trek* staff held a party. We concocted a drink of grape
jam and lemons and pretended that it was the real stuff.
Dancing and games made the party a noisy affair.

Fig. 10.1   Miné Okubo, "Christmas 1942," *Citizen 13660*

From the annotation, we understand that this first Christmas at Topaz is tinged
with melancholy and real deprivations that the special dinners could not assuage.
The family scene appears tranquil enough; however, Okubo's comments reveal the
forced quality of the celebration. She intimates that the *Trek* staff's attempt at mer-
riment could not overcome their sense of futility at trying to create a normal festive
occasion within the internment camp.

Yet, *Citizen 13660* is a narrative, and in the drawing on the next page, Okubo illustrates the gaiety of *mochi*-making, a Japanese new year's ritual, which relieved the
sadness of the first Christmas in Topaz. As Okubo described it: "*Mochi*-making
added a little more gaiety on New Year's Day. *Mochi* is made to celebrate the traditional Japanese New Year. To make it, a special kind of rice is boiled and pounded
with wooden mallets into a sticky mass from which round cakes are molded. Much

Mochi-making added a little more gaiety on New Year's Day. *Mochi* is made to celebrate the traditional Japanese New Year. To make it, a special kind of rice is boiled and pounded with wooden mallets into a sticky mass from which round cakes are molded. Much jovial ceremony is connected with *mochi*-making.

Fig. 10.2   Miné Okubo, "*Mochi*-making," *Citizen 13660*

jovial ceremony is connected with *mochi*-making."[26] She has chosen to showcase the most physical part of the celebration, illustrating the intense activity required as the onlookers and the finished rice cakes frame the scene. The New Year's festival signaled auspicious felicitous wishes for the immediate future, as it does in most cultures. *Mochi* was also a celebratory ritual food closely associated with the internees' Japanese heritage and homeland—served in steaming bowls of homemade soup and offered to ancestors, part of a celebration of purity, happiness, and longevity.[27] The drawing illustrates one of the ways in which the internees maintained some continuity with their prewar lives in the internment camps, which abounded with such displays of their Japanese homeland despite the questions over their loyalty.

The *Trek* cover depicting Christmas 1942 in Topaz contains elements similar to those in the *Citizen 13660* drawing. The image occupies 85 percent of the picture plane, with the rest taken up by the title, its four letters spread across the bottom of the cover. The representational space in the drawing is abstract and geometrically organized in sets of planes. In the foreground, two small children gather around a table bearing Christmas bundles and a bare tree in a pot; mother, father, and a young boy occupy the middle ground. The background, in which the pot-bellied stove stands, is strongly delineated by a rope, hung with laundry and Christmas stockings, stretched horizontally across the room.

Although Okubo's figures do not generally smile broadly or have their mouths open in laughter, this gathering seems especially somber. The family group is comparatively still and formal, and its members don't appear to be looking directly at one another. The mother's raised hand seems to have arrested the group's movement. The father, dressed as Santa Claus, exhibits none of the merriness his assigned role would suggest, and the figure lacks the wit and whimsy of depictions in *Citizen 13660*.

Okubo uses two different modes of telling a story in text and images. In *Citizen 13660*, the text modifies the drawn image, and we are permitted access to the artist's private thoughts through the textual and pictorial narrative. The text alters our impulse to accept the Christmas party as a joyous event. Okubo's absence from this private gathering underscores the importance of her testimony informing us that the internees struggled to maintain Christmas cheer in Topaz in 1942.

Okubo's annotation in *Citizen 13660* alerts us to the sadness that seems to be present in this Christmas celebration at Topaz. In the case of *Trek*, however, the connection between the art object and the meaning of the event is direct and immediate. Publication of *Trek*'s first issue coincided with Christmas 1942. It was created as a gift for its audience and was delivered on Christmas Day. Okubo's image of a somber Christmas must have resonated with the internees at that historic moment.

SPACE AND MOVEMENT IN *CITIZEN 13660*

Okubo created space and movement in *Citizen 13660* and *Trek* using different modes to communicate similar messages. In *Citizen 13660*, she depicts her personal journey through a series of annotated drawings. She places herself as the artist and a participating witness by appearing in nearly every frame. The principal spaces and activities she represents are often in the foreground, within a few steps of her viewing distance within the frames. This places her in close proximity to her observations of what Traise Yamamoto and Elena Tajima Creef have described as "the manipulation and disciplining of the Japanese American body" that are central to representations of internment.[28] With the foreground as a kind of stage, Okubo created depth, extending activities into the background and often showing the barracks, barbed wire fences, and guards from within the internment camps. Her annotations elucidate the contents of the drawings, creating more elaborate and richer meanings with humor, drama, defiance, and angst.

Okubo's relocation from her place of residence in Berkeley, California, to an urban Civil Control Station, and then to the Tanforan Assembly Center across San Francisco Bay is documented and illustrated in *Citizen 13660*. She annotated the drawing depicting her bus journey across the Oakland Bay Bridge:

> The military police opened the bus door and we stepped into the bus as our family number was called. Many spectators stood around. At that moment I recalled the stories told on shipboard by European refugees bound for America.
>
> We were silent on the trip except for a group of four University of California boys who were singing college songs. The bus crossed the Bay Bridge. Everyone stared at the beautiful view as if for the last time. The singing stopped.[29]

Okubo contextualized her illustrations and text through references to the University of California, the Bay Bridge, and European immigration. She chose movement toward the United States in her reference. The spectators remind her of European immigrants on shipboard, embarking on their diasporas; then she abruptly halts the feeling of movement and catapults it into an extended interregnum as the "singing stopped."

Upon arriving at the Tanforan Assembly Center, Okubo found Stall 50, her new home, recently vacated by horses. Her annotation provides us with specific details about the space:

> The guide left us at the door of Stall 50. We walked in and dropped our things inside the entrance. The place was in semidarkness; light barely came through the dirty window on either side of the entrance. A swinging half-door divided the 20 by 9 ft. stall into two rooms. The roof sloped down from a height of twelve feet in the rear room to seven feet in the front room; below the rafters an open space extended the full length of the stable. The rear room had housed the horse and the front room the fodder. Both rooms showed signs of a hurried whitewashing. Spider webs, horse hair, and hay had been whitewashed with the walls. Huge spikes and nails stuck out all over the walls. A two-inch layer of dust covered the floor, but on removing it we discovered that linoleum the color of redwood had been placed over the rough manure-covered boards.[30]

In *Citizen 13660*, Okubo presents a powerful ethnographic survey with specific information about the spaces of internment. Unlike the disinterested reporting of a participant observer trained in the social sciences, her self-presentation and observa-

The military police opened the bus door and we stepped into the bus as our family number was called. Many spectators stood around. At that moment I recalled some of the stories told on shipboard by European refugees bound for America.

We were silent on the trip except for a group of four University of California boys who were singing college songs. The bus crossed the Bay Bridge. Everyone stared at the beautiful view as if for the last time. The singing stopped.

Fig. 10.3   Miné Okubo, "The Bus from Berkeley to Tanforan," *Citizen 13660*

tions of behavior convey physical and cognitive information that is emotionally loaded. We can sense the atmosphere of the silent bus and nearly touch the horsehair and nails on the stall walls.

TREK AND "THE PHYSICAL ASPECTS OF THE CITY"

In *Trek*, Okubo created a sense of place for the internees through her graphic designs and illustrations. Her illustrations reflected the staff's editorial direction depicting "the physical aspects of the city" at Topaz. She used a number of graphic techniques to do this: cityscapes, landscapes, illustrated maps, humorous drawings, and references to places the internees called home before their internment.

The guide left us at the door of Stall 50. We walked in and dropped our things inside the entrance. The place was in semidarkness; light barely came through the dirty window on either side of the entrance. A swinging half-door divided the 20 by 9 ft. stall into two rooms. The roof sloped down from a height of twelve feet in the rear room to seven feet in the front room; below the rafters an open space extended the full length of the stable. The rear room had housed the horse and the front room the fodder. Both rooms showed signs of a hurried whitewashing. Spider webs, horse hair, and hay had been whitewashed with the walls. Huge spikes and nails stuck out all over the walls. A two-inch layer of dust covered the floor, but on removing it we discovered that linoleum the color of redwood had been placed over the rough manure-covered boards.

[35]

Fig. 10.4   Miné Okubo, "Tanforan Housing Unit in a Stable"

The landscapes often extended over the fold and created images that are impressive graphically. Okubo created two for Taro Katayama's lead article "State of the City." While the article provides a sociological and physical description of the "infant city" of Topaz, Okubo's lead drawing, extending over pages 2 and 3, depicts the internees heroically transplanting a large tree.[31] They grapple with and arrange pulley systems while moving a tree whose size appears to overwhelm them. The drama and activity in this cityscape contrasts with the dry, descriptive writing style of edi-

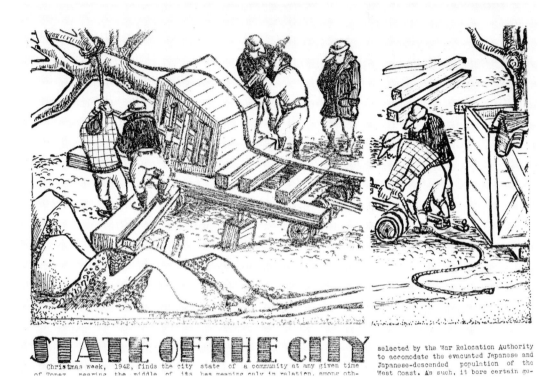

Fig. 10.5 Miné Okubo, illustration for Taro Katayama's "State of the City"

tor and author Taro Katayama, who strove for balance and objectivity in reporting facts about the city to the citizens of Topaz. The second illustration for this article shows a corner streetscape near the entrance gate, including the barracks and an administration building with open ditches along the street, a newly installed fireplug, and people scavenging for lumber.[32] It reflects the article's general and neutral message that the evolutionary development of the city was inevitable. Generally, the illustrations convey the sense of a city settling into its normal functions, although armed guards control the gate in the background.

Okubo and *Trek*'s contributing artists used maps to orient the internees geographically in their illustrations. They provided geographic, geologic, and historical information about the local area with articles by Frank Beckwith, Sr., publisher of the *Millard County Chronicle*, and Jim Yamada. Beckwith's article, "Landmarks of Pahvant Valley," published in the inaugural December 1942 issue, included an unsigned, hand-illustrated topographical map titled "Topaz and Surrounding Areas." It introduced internees to interesting local features of the Utah landscape in Millard County, such as mountain ranges, hot springs, Native American sites, local towns, and game preserves, drawn with the whimsy of a tourist map.

Fig. 10.6   Miné Okubo, illustration for Taro Katayama's "State of the City"

Okubo drew a map of Topaz for the last issue of *Trek* in June 1943.[33] Modeled on the government's plot plans of the internment site, which include a typical block plan, Okubo's map provides a guide to key community services such as schools, libraries, administrative areas, and recreational areas in the "City of Topaz." Unlike its government model, satirical notes dot the map, pointing out annoying features such as sewer odor and mud. The map is framed by barbed wire with the guard tower sites identified, and the guardhouses are included in the map's legend.

OKUBO'S *TREK* ILLUSTRATIONS AND THE SPATIAL MARKERS OF INCARCERATION

In Okubo's *Trek* illustrations, the spatial markers of incarceration—guard towers, gates, armed guards, barbed wire, and fences—recur as themes. A guard and guardhouse often appear in her illustrations for the lead stories. Miniature guard towers and armed guards insistently reappear, as they did in the map of the City of Topaz. She drew a guard tower and barracks in the foreground of a night landscape illustrating Toshio Mori's essay "Topaz Station" and another guard tower as an ornament for a page of text.

Her drawings for Taro Katayama's article "Beyond the Gate," in *Trek*'s second issue, of February 1943, illustrate her interest in the spaces of internment. Katayama delicately assessed the WRA program to send many of the internees "back to free and normal ways of living," or, as he noted with irony, "back to America." He reported on favorable conditions beyond the gate and advocated for the WRA's assimilation and resettlement policies. Instead of looking beyond the gate, Okubo illustrated this article by portraying the oppressive conditions within the City of Topaz. Four of the five drawings look inward toward the internment camp: a streetscape, an abstract of two men shielding themselves from a fierce duststorm, a miniature guard tower, and a view of Topaz past the armed guard and entrance gate. Her drawing of the two men in a duststorm curiously illustrates a comment Katayama made in his lead story, "State of the City," in the first issue of *Trek*.[34] He had noted, "Asked what the infant city was like, those first residents might have, with some justice, summed it up with one word—dust."[35] One of her "Beyond the Gate" illustrations shows the guard standing prominently in front of the gate and his guardhouse. Her depiction of the guard may be characterized as bland and relatively benign compared to characters in *Citizen 13660*, yet rather than looking beyond the gate from the vantage point inside the camp, Okubo redirects the view so that it looks in from the outside, toward the camp's oppressive conditions, with the barracks in the middle ground. This example of the lack of synchronization between Okubo's *Trek* illustrations and Katayama's "Beyond the Gate" contrasts with her effective links between image and text in *Citizen 13660*.

This is not a general pattern, however, and Okubo's illustrations for fictional pieces by Toshio Mori and Jim Yamada dramatically enliven their stories. For *Trek*'s last lead story, "Relocation," by Larry Tajiri, Okubo illustrated another view looking into Topaz at the gate. In this drawing, she conveys the excitement of departure

Fig. 10.7   Miné Okubo, "Map of the City of Topaz"

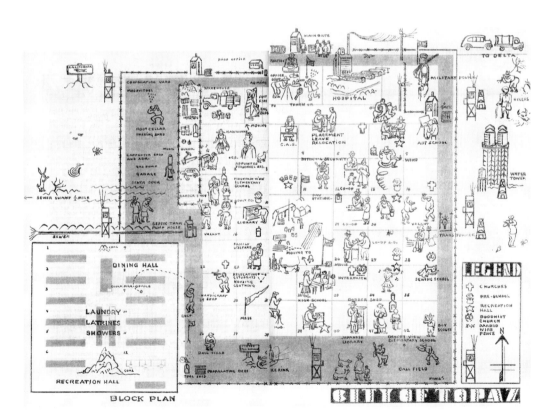

Fig. 10.8 Miné Okubo, illustration for Taro Katayama's "Beyond the Gate"

among a crowd of internees, the ever present guard, and his guardhouse, exhibiting some of the wry wit and liveliness of her *Citizen 13660* drawings.[36]

REMEMBERING CALIFORNIA AND JAPAN —
CONTINUITY WITH THE PAST

Through place markers, Okubo reconnected many members of two generations to their former homes. She often chose to depict references to California and her alma mater, the University of California at Berkeley, in her *Trek* drawings. In the Topaz map, she included a signpost pointing to California. For Jim Yamada's story, "The Dance They Saved for John," about Nisei social alienation at the university, she illus-

Fig. 10.9   Miné Okubo, illustration for Larry Tajiri's "Relocation"

trated his character John fixing his bowtie for the dance and drew a school pennant
with "California" written on it in the background. To illustrate a related Yamada story
about John's discomfort with his immigrant father's lack of sophistication, Okubo
drew the father and son together, contemplating the university's Sather Gate and
examining John's diploma, with Sather Tower in the background.[37]

For the Issei, she illustrated the Japanese translation of Toshio Mori's story
"Tomorrow Is Coming, Children" with an Issei bride in kimono waving good-bye as
she sails away aboard a ship with Mount Fuji in the background.[38] Okubo must have
intentionally included Mount Fuji, with its centuries of meaning associated with Japanese identity and religion, as a reference to their national affiliations and the diasporic history of their lives. It did not, however, carry the nationalist political associations that could justify the U.S. government's incarceration of the Issei and their
descendants as potential saboteurs or spies.

CONCLUSION

Through Okubo's illustrations in *Trek*, we can trace some of her resistance to the
WRA's autocratic and patriarchal governance of publications within the internment
camp, particularly in her illustrations of guards and guardhouses. In her cooperative

Fig. 10.10 Miné Okubo, illustration for Toshio Mori's "Tomorrow Is Coming, Children"

efforts with the *Trek* staff, her illustrations may also be seen as service to the community, providing information about the "physical aspects of the city," and as a Christmas gift, with the first issue presented on December 25, 1942.

In representing space and movement in image and text, Okubo has provided invaluable documentation of the physical spaces of internment and the internees' movement through it. She leads us into her personal space through her self-presentation so we may vicariously understand the cognitive impact of these spaces. She observed, recorded, and illustrated with humor—as she explained it, "not in a joyful sense, but ridiculous and insane." Through Okubo's art, we understand the importance and contrast of the spaces of production inside and outside the internment camps. In her work for *Trek,* she illustrated the camp conditions for internees, ironically including the spatial markers of their confinement while negotiating WRA censorship and control.

The larger historical context of the injustice of internment and the forced movement of 117,000 people created the tensions and ironies in Okubo's work. This in turn lent specific meanings to her images and text as political interventions in the ways she depicted spatial confinement, its markers, and the internees' homelands in *Citizen 13660* and in *Trek.* These historical social and political relationships enrich our understanding of Miné Okubo's artwork and its functions.

NOTES

1   Miné Okubo, *Citizen 13660* (Seattle: University of Washington Press, 1983), ix. *Citizen 13660* was first published by Columbia University Press in 1946.

2   The title page of each of the three issues of *Trek* (December 1942, February 1943, and June 1943) notes that it was a special publication of the Project Reports Division of the Central Utah Relocation Center.

3   Miné Okubo is listed as the art editor for each *Trek* issue.

4   The Staff, "Trek," *Trek* 1, no. 3 (June 1943): 37.

5   Ibid.

6   Jim Yamada, "Portrait of an Artist," *Trek* 1, no. 1 (December 1942): 21–22.

7   Elena Tajima Creef, *Imaging Japanese America: The Visual Construction of Citizenship, Nation, and the Body* (New York: New York University Press, 2004), 77.

8   Cited in Shirley Sun, *Miné Okubo: An American Experience,* exh. cat. (San Francisco: East Wind Printers, 1972), 29.

9   Ibid.

10 Creef, *Imaging Japanese America,* 79. Creef discusses the communicative capabilities of Okubo's drawings compared to photography.

11 Ibid., 90.

12 Deborah Gesensway and Mindy Roseman, *Beyond Words: Images from America's Concentration Camps* (Ithaca, N.Y.: Cornell University Press, 1987), 69.

13 United States Department of War, *Final Report: Japanese Evacuation from the West Coast 1942,* reprint (New York: Arno Press, 1978), 383. The army recorded the population of Topaz at 8,265 on October 31, 1942; however, the number incarcerated fluctuated daily.

14 The Staff, "Trek," *Trek* 1, no. 3 (June 1943): 37. The staff noted that they used mimeograph as well as multi-lith presses, which are small offset presses. The first issue had thirty pages, the second forty-two pages and a three-page supplement in Japanese, and the last forty-two pages.

15 Ibid.

16 Gesensway and Roseman, *Beyond Words,* 69.

17 *Trek*, 1, no. 2 (February 1943): 1.

18 For documentation, see United States, Commission on Wartime Relocation and Internment of Civilians, *Personal Justice Denied: Report of the Commission on Wartime Relocation and Internment of Civilians*, with a new foreword by Tetsuden Kashima (Washington, D.C.: Civil Liberties Public Education Fund; Seattle: University of Washington Press, 1997).

19 Yoshiko Uchida, *Desert Exile: The Uprooting of a Japanese-American Family* (Seattle: University of Washington Press, 1982), 53. See also Gesensway and Roseman, *Beyond Words*, 67. United States Department of the Interior, D. S. Myer, Director, War Relocation Authority, *Administrative Highlights of the WRA Program* (Washington, D.C.: U.S. Government Printing Office, n.d.), 2.

20 *Trek* contains considerable discussion about this. Taro Katayama analyzes the attitudes of the U.S. press in regional terms, indicating that in the late winter of 1942, midwestern and eastern publications were more favorable toward the internees than were those in the military areas that had been evacuated. See Taro Katayama, "Beyond the Gate," *Trek* 1, no. 2 (February 1943): 4–5; and Jim Yamada, "Falderol," *Trek* 1, no. 3 (February 1943): 42.

21 Yamada, "Falderol," 42.

22 Francis Stewart, War Relocation Authority Photographs of Japanese-American Evacuation and Resettlement, WRA No. b-330, March 12, 1943. "Editors on the *Topaz Times*, who have volunteered for combat duty in the army." This group included Taro Katayama, *Trek* editor.

23 Jack Yamaguchi, *This Was Minidoka* (Tacoma, Wash.: Yamaguchi, 1989), 27.

24 Charles Kikuchi, *The Kikuchi Diary: Chronicle from an American Concentration Camp, The Tanforan Journals of Charles Kikuchi*, ed. John Modell (Urbana: University of Illinois Press, 1993), 131, 200.

25 Okubo, *Citizen 13660*, 156.

26 Ibid., 157.

27 John DeFrancis, with the assistance of V. R. Francis, *Things Japanese in Hawaii* (Honolulu: University Press of Hawaii, 1973), 20–23.

28 Creef, *Imaging Japanese America*, 90–91.

29 Okubo, *Citizen 13660*, 26.

30 Ibid., 35.

31 Taro Katayama, "State of the City," *Trek* 1, no. 1 (December 1942): 2–3. See a similar drawing in Okubo, *Citizen 13660*, 149.

32 Katayama, "State of the City," 4–5.

33 City of Topaz map, *Trek* 1, no. 3 (June 1943): 18–19.

34 Illustration for Taro Katayama, "Beyond the Gate," *Trek* 1, no. 2 (February 1943): 8.

35 Katayama, "State of the City," 3.

36 Larry Tajiri, "Relocation," *Trek* 1, no. 3 (June 1943): 2–3.

37 Jim Yamada, "Guadeamus Igitur," *Trek* 1, no. 3 (June 1943): 20.

38 Toshio Mori, "Tomorrow Is Coming, Children," Japanese translation, *Trek* 1, no. 2, supplement (February 1943): 1.

11

MINÉ OKUBO'S ILLUSTRATIONS FOR *TREK* MAGAZINE

SITES OF RESISTANCE

LAURA CARD

Miné Okubo's illustrations in *Trek* magazine from December 1942 to June 1943 reveal the struggles of the Nisei incarcerated at Topaz over their feelings of betrayal by their government and their desires to be viewed as worthy citizens. Their struggle is portrayed through the subject matter of the illustrations as well as semiotic elements that communicate meaning through symbolism and form in Okubo's work and that may be viewed as a form of resistance against those who had power over her. Her act of breaking away from the censored camp newspaper to publish a magazine of her choosing, while still under the authority of the camp, frames her struggle between resistance and compliance while at Topaz. This chapter looks at Okubo's *Trek* illustrations through the lens of a critical rhetoric. It asks questions about the context of domination that produced a need for resistance and the rhetorical strategies Okubo used to express resistance. Because the illustrations are visual, elements of visual rhetorical theory will be combined with critical rhetorical theory as the context and strategies are examined.

Raymie E. McKerrow explains that "in practice, a critical rhetoric seeks to unmask or demystify the discourse of power. The aim is to understand the integration of power/knowledge in society—what possibilities for change the integration invites or inhibits and what intervention strategies might be considered appropriate to effect social change."[1] From what little Okubo wrote about the origin of *Trek* magazine, it seems that she and the other members of the staff understood the power dynamics of the camp and what they could and could not do to effect change within the limits imposed by the power structure controlling them. In a passage related to jobs in the camp, Okubo explains, in her book *Citizen 13660*, that she, her brother, and others understood that the camp "was a more or less permanent center" where it was desirable to find jobs for which they "had been trained or had some skill." Accordingly, following her arrival in Topaz, Okubo applied for and was accepted "for work on the Topaz *Times*." She states that the newspaper's purpose was to keep "the residents informed about the center and the outside" and that "all news passed the censorship of the administration staff." Then she relates, "After two months with the Topaz *Times*, a small group of us decided to break away and start a fifty-page art and literary magazine. We called it *Trek*. Three issues appeared."[2]

Okubo gives no reason as to why the group broke away, except perhaps for the comment about censorship and the phrase "decided to break away." Both pieces of information give the impression that the act of breaking with the newspaper was possibly more than just leaving one job for a different situation; rather, it was an act of resistance.

The staff's act of resistance did produce change. The most obvious change was in the location of their work. In the crowded confines of the camp, space was at a premium. For example, Okubo and her brother had to share a room with another young man, while whole families were crowded into one or two rooms.[3] Okubo's *Citizen 13660* illustration of the *Topaz Times* office shows a very crowded place.[4] However, the *Trek* staff was given space for another office and therefore granted legitimacy.[5] Not only were they provided with a place to produce the magazine; they were given access to materials, such as paper and a mimeograph, and to lithographs and lithographers. Their magazine was also accorded the status of an official publication of the Reports Division of the Central Utah Relocation Project.[6] Michel Foucault explains that space and place are functions of power.[7] By producing the magazine and claiming office space and a place in the Reports Division, the staff of *Trek* also claimed a certain amount of power—the power to express their views and perhaps to effect change among their fellow internees and camp administrators.

In gaining legitimacy and space, the staff would have also gained some prestige within the camp—mainly with other internees and also with camp administrators—but at a price. That price was the support for the War Relocation Authority's policies that they were required to convey throughout the magazine's text. The *Trek* staff had little choice. Expressing resistance within the confines of an internment camp was a perilous business. Protesters at the camps at Manzanar, Tule Lake, Heart Mountain, and elsewhere met with increased restrictions on personal freedom, transfer to camps for criminals and resisters, and even violence and death.[8] Additionally, officers of the Nisei-led Japanese American Citizens League (JACL) urged cooperation with the government, to the point of turning in their own people who were dissenters, as well as peaceful acceptance of internment. They felt that cooperation was necessary to dispel any stereotypes of disloyalty and "mitigate the present circumstances and perhaps have a lien on better treatment later."[9]

The major area in which Nisei were expected to collaborate was in supporting the WRA's agenda of moving the internees out of the camps and scattering them across the East and Midwest—away from the Little Tokyos of the West Coast, but also away from their homes. Eleanor Roosevelt wrote to the American people that loyal Japanese Americans would "gradually be absorbed" into society in an effort to return them to normal civilian life. She justified scattering them by saying, "We should never have allowed any groups to settle as groups where they created little German or Japanese or Scandinavian 'islands' and did not melt into our general community pattern."[10] The *Trek* staff duly echoed the official line, at least on the surface. Thus, as 1943 dawned and the WRA officials in charge of the internment camps focused more on convincing internees to leave the camps for the Midwest and the East, *Trek* paid more attention to the advantages and logistics of relocation. Articles such as "Beyond the Gate," "Campus Report," and "Relocation: Through the Gates of Topaz," all of which were illustrated by Okubo, appeared in the pages of *Trek*.[11]

From the number of articles on relocation, the *Trek* staff seem to have accepted the idea of resettlement. Certainly, the fact that Okubo herself illustrated these articles indicates a certain support on her part, since, as art editor, she could have assigned the illustration to Alfred Sawahata, listed as a contributing artist in the third issue. (Okubo quickly accepted resettlement when it was offered her soon afterward, and she "voted with her feet" by moving to New York, where she remained for the rest of her life.) A more important sign that the staff of *Trek*, and Okubo in particular, bought into the resettlement agenda is their commissioning of an article by Larry Tajiri, editor of the JACL newspaper *Pacific Citizen*. Tajiri's article "Relocation," illustrated by Okubo, appeared in the third issue.

Trek's support for relocation did not spring merely from government pressure. For the young Nisei who produced the magazine, relocation away from the camp meant breaking away from the domination of imprisonment. In addition, relocation away from the West Coast would also mean breaking with the traditional patriarchal control exercised within most Japanese American families at that time. It is worth pointing out that the WRA was not the only source of domination for the *Trek* staff. As Nisei, the staff would have experienced domination not only from the U.S. government but also from the traditional leaders of the older generation, the Issei.

Indeed, the image of resettlement as a means of resistance against these two forms of domination appears in explicit form in the third and last issue of *Trek*. An article written by the staff explains that the magazine's name was chosen as symbolic of "a pioneering movement of a people towards new lands, new homes, and a new future," especially in relation to "the projected publication of the out-standing young writers and artists group of Topaz, as they came eastward as evacuees from California to this desert settlement in Utah." The article goes on to state that the first issue of the magazine is about the "state of the city," the second issue is about possibilities of life "beyond the gate," and the final issue is about "the relocation movement, the exodus of the younger element still further eastward, no longer to stagnate as wards of the government, but to seek a new beginning as Americans."[12] This statement indicates the staff's resistance against their status as "wards of the government" and also perhaps demonstrates a breaking away from the Issei generation, who had ties to Japan, as staff members identify themselves with the "younger element" who laid claim to U.S. citizenship.

Yet, if the magazine's text was overtly supportive of WRA and camp administration and their agendas, the ironic tone and subtle (and sometimes not so subtle) digs at camp life and policies indicate that staff support was not entirely whole-hearted—that in their minds and hearts, while within the confines of the camp, they broke away from the domination of those over them. In order to gain the capability of peacefully expressing resistance against being viewed as possible enemy aliens or as subordinate to the older generation, Okubo and the staff of *Trek* would have had to employ careful rhetorical strategies. In other words, the staff would have had to evaluate their audience and the most effective means of persuasion—all the while using their knowledge of the power that was being exercised over them and the power they had access to so that they could express their views without getting into trouble. The contents of the magazine demonstrate that members of the staff were very much aware of their rhetorical context and adjusted their choice of topic and mode of expression so as to fit the situation. A similar mode of resistance was strategic silence. For example, the JACL was never mentioned in *Trek,* perhaps because many Japanese Americans in the camps blamed the JACL for their imprisonment. Even Larry Tajiri's author's blurb at the end of his article identified him as a "former San Francisco newspaperman and foreign correspondent" who was then the "editor of 'The Pacific Citizen.'"[13] Although the *Pacific Citizen* was the organ of the JACL, Tajiri's status as a leader of the JACL went unmentioned. Several other articles also appeared in the magazine in favor of relocation and military service, but they did not mention the *Pacific Citizen* or any other connection with the JACL.

Okubo's role in facilitating resistance in *Trek* also encompassed her work with the poets Taro Katayama and Toyo Suyemoto. The poetry was inserted on the page as a text box with the rest of the text flowing around it. As art editor, Okubo was responsible for arranging the layout of the pages, a task that included the placement of illustrations and text boxes. Katayama, as one of the magazine's editors, had an automatic venue for his poetry, which was often very supportive of WRA and military goals. Interestingly, Okubo sought out the poetry of Toyo Suyemoto, whose work was vehemently resistant to evacuation and internment. Suyemoto recalls Okubo stopping by and asking for a poem to be ready by that night. Suyemoto says, "I'd finish the poem, write it out neatly, tack it on the door to the barracks, and along about three o'clock I'd hear footsteps on the path, and I could hear Miné's voice talking to her brother, who always accompanied her, and . . . the poem would appear in the new issue of *Trek*."[14] In choosing to include Suyemoto's poetry in the magazine, it is possible Okubo was using it as another means of expressing resistance.

More importantly, Okubo's art enabled the *Trek* staff to express resistance to domination. From the beginning, her reputation as an artist lent a certain ethos to the magazine, an ethos that the staff absorbed and capitalized on. According to "Portrait of an Artist" by Jim Yamada, an article about Okubo in the first issue of *Trek,* she received an M.A. from the University of California at Berkeley in 1936. She was in Europe traveling on an art scholarship when Germany invaded Poland. Okubo also received numerous awards for her art and exhibited her work at the San Francisco Museum of Art and the University of California. Yamada quips, "A complete list of her prizes would cover a couple of typewritten pages—legal size at that." The article also tells about her work with Diego Rivera on a mural for the Golden Gate Fair after her return from Europe. Yamada quotes Okubo as saying, in self-deprecation, "Diego was up there on the scaffold, while I was near the bottom of the mural, answering dumb questions."[15]

The article could be viewed as an appeal to ethos as the staff established with readers that they had the credentials necessary to produce the magazine and to command respect. Such a move would be a form of resistance, a breaking away from both those who viewed them as unworthy and incapable of citizenship (the kind of people who should be put into an internment camp) and Issei who might view them as too young to know what they were doing. The staff's desire to be viewed as credible is validated by the statement that *Trek* is the "publication of the out-standing young writers and artists group of Topaz."[16] As the best writers and artists, they were the ones to be trusted to produce a product of high quality. Whatever the case, the staff of *Trek* were proud enough of Okubo's accomplishments to devote an entire article to her— something not done for any of the other people who worked on the magazine.[17]

Okubo, in turn, willingly lent her prestige to the project. As a fine artist, she may have felt demeaned by illustrating issues of the *Topaz Times,* which used mostly small cartoonlike images as illustrations or fillers.[18] She may also have felt constrained by the censorship imposed on the newspaper. Perhaps she viewed the illustration of a more elite literary and art magazine as preferable. Or she may have viewed it as an opportunity to express her opinions—to break away from a censored party line.

Okubo's illustrations permitted her to express resistance in a form more visually obvious than that which the magazine's writers could permit themselves, and her art informed and shaped their resistance. On one level, Okubo could avoid confrontation with the WRA over her illustrations and censorship of their subject matter because no words were used and her meaning might be harder to identify. Still, illustrations, by their very nature, are viewed in relation to the texts they explain. Because illustrations take a subordinate role, many fine artists do not view them as true art. Illustrating stories and articles in a literary and art magazine might have been something of a departure for Okubo, given her emphasis on fine art and her position as an up-and-coming fine artist. She had a gift for illustration that many fine artists do not develop. Her practice of sketching in pen or brush and ink lent itself well to the black-and-white line drawings used in the magazine. Her talent for expressing movement and mood also lent itself to magazine illustration, a skill that eventually moved her out of the camp and into New York City to illustrate a special issue on Japan for *Fortune* magazine.[19]

Nearly all of Okubo's *Trek* illustrations deal with camp life, except for those accompanying two of Jim Yamada's short stories, set before the war, probably at Berkeley. The range of styles she uses runs from realistic to highly stylized (reminiscent of the works of Diego Rivera and Pablo Picasso) to humorous cartoons—she admitted she especially liked reading comic books.[20]

The first illustrations seen upon picking up the magazines are on the front covers. At first glance, these illustrations look very much like Japanese wood-block prints.[21] But when all three are placed together, a theme is evident. All the covers seem to be structured according to Christian European art. The December 1942 cover shows a Japanese American family celebrating Christmas in one of the barracks. The February 1943 cover shows internees eating at a table in what is similar to a Last Supper painting of the 1400s by Dieric Bouts the Elder. The subject of the June 1943 cover looks very much like a Christian baptism.

Okubo was well versed in Christian European art, having spent several months in Europe for the purpose of studying great art just before the outbreak of World War II, as explained in the biographical article about her in *Trek*. It is possible that she appropriated the structure and subject matter of Christian art in an act of resistance to her situation. John Fiske states that those who are oppressed often must "poach" the resources of the elite in order to "make do" in conditions of "deprivation, oppression, or slavery."[22] Michael Omi and Howard Winant carry the idea of poaching one step further. They explain that "the effort to possess the oppressor's tools . . . [is] crucial to emancipation (the effort to possess oneself)."[23] Perhaps Okubo intended to appropriate the ethos of a white Christian artist by demonstrating that she knew how to structure a work symbolically in a way that only those educated in Western art could know. That she could claim membership in an elite group of educated and talented artists would not only establish her own credibility but also give credibility to *Trek* magazine and those Nisei associated with it. Her elite knowledge could also demonstrate her superiority over anyone, including white administrators, who did not have her high level of education.

Okubo clearly understood the importance, as well as the rhetorical uses, of symbolism and hierarchy of position and size, elements that are particularly apparent in Christian art. Her understanding is especially demonstrated in the cover of the December 1942 issue. Okubo chose to depict a Japanese family enacting the celebration of a Christian Christmas, thereby demonstrating complicity with common white practices and religion while also showing resistance, in that these people are capable of doing white things in spite of their race and the poverty and subjugation of their situation. She could also be making a statement about the imposition of white values on the internees. The composition and subject matter show an awareness of the characteristics of both her white audience and her Japanese American audience.

In the illustration, the father wears a Santa hat and plays with a homemade toy that is identical to a pioneer toy seen in Utah pioneer village reconstructions, such as Cove Fort. The toy could be a reference to the evacuees' pioneer journey into the wilderness of the Utah desert. Stockings are hung on an indoor clothesline that stretches, along with another one holding the family's laundry, behind the pot-bellied stove. The older boy holds a star, which he seems to be about to place on a small, bare tree on which hang two candy canes. A girl toddler also holds a candy cane. The mother, wearing an apron, is seated with something on her lap that could be a blanket for the baby or a cleaning rag. The baby is reaching for the bare Christmas tree. There are exactly five small presents under the tree on the table, the same number as the number of family members, indicating that even in their poverty they wish to celebrate the white religious tradition. The family is crowded into the picture just as, in real life, families are crowded into their rooms in the barracks.

The father's depiction, positioned higher in the picture and larger than the other figures, shows the importance of his patriarchal status in a traditional family, which would have been accepted in 1940s white society as well as in a patriarchal Japanese society. The next-largest figure is the mother, who is dressed for housework and faces the Christmas tree, reaching toward it or the baby, who is also reaching for the tree. The mother could be viewed as a Madonna figure with her hand raised in blessing, much like the figure in Andrea Mantegna's 1495 painting *Madonna of Victory*.[24] Everything is situated and sized in order to symbolize both the complicity and the resistance of the internees.

Hierarchy of size and position is traditional in Christian art, dating back to the third century. For instance, a fourth-century wall painting in the catacombs of the Via Latina shows Samson with the jawbone of an ass in the foreground of the picture, his body nearly twice as large as those of the Philistines. Another painting positions Abraham above and larger than everything else in the painting, except a heavenly presence. Such positioning indicates the level of importance of the characters in the painting.[25] This practice continued down through Renaissance times and sometimes is adopted by modern artists. Carl Bloch's painting of Christ healing the man by the pool of Bethesda is a good example, with Christ as the largest and foremost figure.[26]

The hand raised in blessing is a familiar gesture in European Christian art, and Okubo uses it more than once. It also appears on the cover of the third issue, which shows a child being bathed. Several paintings of Christ's baptism from the fifteenth and sixteenth centuries depict Christ standing in water while John the Baptist pours water on him or has a hand raised in blessing. To one side is often a figure, male or female, with a hand also raised in blessing. In this illustration, Okubo could be continuing the Christian theme of the other two cover illustrations, with possible interpretations such as those given for the first cover.[27]

One aspect of a rhetorical analysis is the assumption that in producing the text, the writers have intentions to communicate.[28] Through their association with texts, then, illustrators also have intentions to communicate. Illustrators and writers choose strategies for making meaning according to their rhetorical knowledge of certain characteristics of their audience, their context, and their own background in relation to the text. Charles Kostelnick and Michael Hassett explain, "Designers and readers shape visual language through the cultural lens of their own experiences and values."[29] Okubo might have assumed that her audience would understand her appropriation of Christian structure and symbolism because many of them were familiar with Christian traditions. Supporting this idea, the *Trek* article about the state of the city notes that "church attendance among all faiths has been large and consistent."[30] The *Topaz Times* of September 26, 1942, lists meeting times for the various faiths represented in the camp—Catholic, Protestant, Seventh Day Adventist, and Buddhist. The most meetings listed are for Protestants, and the largest number of clergymen listed are also Protestants.[31] Additionally, Okubo's audience included white camp administrators and staff, most of whom could also be presumed to be familiar with Christian traditions. With such a large population of Christians in the camp, Okubo could be assured that many in her audience would catch at least some of her symbolism.

Okubo uses symbolism in her illustrations throughout all three issues of *Trek*. One function of pictures combined with text is to "structure information" and "impose order on complex sets of quantitative and pictorial information."[32] Okubo's illustrations accomplish this for the magazine's readers through her interpretation of familiar scenes from camp life. For instance, in most of the illustrations, no one is smiling. Life is a serious business in the camp. Everyone is working hard or going about his or her business aware of the vicissitudes of being incarcerated. There are smiling people in only two illustrations; in both, it is the character who is innocent, who has no worldly knowledge, who is smiling.

The first drawing illustrates the article "Beyond the Gate."[33] A man is leaving camp bowed under the weight of a suitcase, and a little girl waves good-bye and smiles, not a large smile showing teeth, but just a little smile. The suggestion is that the little girl lacks the knowledge the adult male has of the problems he faces as he leaves the camp. To her, it is an adventure, while to him, it is a burden.

The second illustration in which a character smiles accompanies a short story by Jim Yamada, "Guadeamus Igitur."[34] The story is about a Nisei man who graduates from a university before the war. His Issei father comes to see the graduation and is inordinately proud of his son. Okubo illustrates the point in the story when the father gazes in admiration on the diploma and says how happy he is, while the son wonders what good it will do, since white employers never hire Japanese Americans except as gardeners or servants. The young man also knows that Nisei were often forced to help run family businesses, both because of circumstances and because of pressure from their Issei elders. In contemplating his own graduation, the young man "wondered if an A.B. in Econ was enough education to get a job clerking at some vegetable stand. Perhaps he'd better get a master's degree; how much more confidence that would give him while selling spinach."[35] Okubo portrays the smiling father as naive and the son as the worldly, cynical figure. Once again, in Okubo's illustration, the character who would least understand the serious reality of the situation is the one who is smiling.

Extremely stylized illustrations are the other obvious sites of struggle among Okubo's *Trek* illustrations. In these, the figures are constricted by the boundaries of the picture just as the evacuees are constricted by the boundaries of the camp. They are confined and unable to break away. Most of the extremely stylized illustrations are in the first two issues, perhaps because the less representational style could be considered sufficiently distanced from reality to pose no threat, although Okubo could still register a protest. Camp censors would then be less likely to shut down the magazine and take away the staff's means of expression.

Three such stylized illustrations accompany "State of the City," by Taro Katayama. The text is full of information and statistics about the camp and fills eleven pages. Although the tone of the article is favorable toward the camp as a successful endeavor, to the point of calling it a "city" rather than a "camp," the illustrations contrast sharply with upbeat phrases such as the one directly under the picture of a man bent over picking up coal: "Physically, then, Topaz is in fair shape at the present time."[36] The picture has no drawn-in borders, but the natural boundaries of the illustration do not allow the bent-over man to stand up straight. He is forever bent into an unnatural position, just as the internees had been placed in an unnatural position. The man's physical condition could not possibly be "in fair shape" while he is bent over.

As the art editor, Okubo probably had some control over the placement of pictures. The process of creating mimeographed pages involves a great deal of planning and design. Choices must be made while counting letters and spaces, measuring lines of text, and sizing illustrations and then pressing each mark, from typewritten letters to illustrations, into an ink-coated sheet of paper. During the planning stage, the art editor would position the illustration on the page for greatest effect, which makes it probable that an illustration's proximity to text is the result of a deliberate decision to associate the text and the picture in order to create some sort of message. Placing the illustration of the man picking up coal above the upbeat text informs the reader that the text is not telling the whole story. It is a site of resistance to the internment situation. It breaks away from the party line.

In contrast, the next illustration does represent the tone of the text, as the text itself expresses resistance. The picture shows four students in school, crowded one behind the other with only one book for all four. The student in front has his hand raised as if he is reaching for something out of the picture. In the column next to the illustration is one of the few paragraphs in the article that is truly critical of camp conditions. The text mentions the two thousand children and several thousand adults who need education, but because of "lack of adequate housing facilities and supplies," the "shortage of instructional supplies and equipment," and an insufficient number of "Caucasian teaching personnel," the schools are not up to full strength.[37] Once again, no one in the illustration is smiling. All the students are very serious. At this point, both the text and the illustration break away from compliance with a WRA agenda.

The most stylized "State of the City" illustrations appear at the end of the article. One shows a construction worker carrying what looks like sheetrock, and the second depicts a cook with a spoon in one hand and a plate in the other, which he shows to another man. The figures are stretched out of proportion and are in unnaturally tense positions. The expressions on the worker's and the cook's faces are strained and unhappy. The borders of the pictures cut off the legs of the worker and much of the cook and the other man. They are incomplete as are internees in the camp. While the struggle in these two pictures is evident from the straining of the figures, the accompanying text tells of the Topaz residents settling down—the older generation losing hope, people making fewer requests to change barracks, and teachers noticing the quietness of children. The illustrations do not seem to have anything to do with the text other than that they show stress. They take up an entire column on the page, so it is possible that they were intended merely to fill the page so that the next article could start on a fresh page. However, their silent message of struggle is still apparent.[38]

One of the recurrent themes in Okubo's illustrations is her depiction of guard towers or guardhouses, in an overt breaking away from the administration's practice of referring to the camp as a normal city or community. She seems to be saying, "Normal cities are not surrounded by guard towers." The first two issues have only two such illustrations per issue, perhaps because she wanted to avoid antagonizing the administrators too much. However, the third issue has five illustrations showing guard towers or guard stations.

The context surrounding each issue could offer an explanation for the increased number. At the time of the first and second issues, it must have seemed likely that internees would remain in the camp for a long time. The staff of the magazine knew that "the writers and artists must present facts in an interesting and illustrative way, recreate a mood or moment, and show a not-too-grim side of life in camp," as they were to explain in the issue.[39] However, by the time the third issue came out, most of the *Trek* staff had plans to leave or had already left Topaz.[40] There was no need to worry about the magazine being shut down or giving offense to the administration, because they were putting out the last issue. The grimmer side of life in camp could be shown or even made an object of fun.

In the first and second issues, the guard towers and guard stations are shown as either distant in space or with faceless guards and therefore distant in viewpoint. The tower closest in space is in the first issue, but the guard is staring off into the distance and is only barely recognizable as a white soldier. No one in the illustrations has a face with individual characteristics, giving the impression of isolation from the internees and the guards—breaking away from the policy of portraying Topaz as a normal city. The style is representational, serious, and somewhat stern, perhaps even threatening.

In the third issue, the illustrations of guard towers and guards depart sharply from their depictions in the first two issues. For the article "Relocation," Okubo illustrates a large group of people waiting for the train to take them away from the camp.[41] The faces of evacuees and guards have recognizable characteristics. One of the guards interacts in a friendly way with an evacuee. The figures border on being cartoonish and are therefore less threatening. The tone is no longer stern, but comfortable and even hopeful, although serious. Still, there are no wide grins or happy faces, except for the suggestion of a half-smile on one guard.

All but one of the other illustrations of guards or guard towers in this issue are also cartoonish. The one that retains the stern and dangerous tone found in the first two issues illustrates "One Happy Family," by Toshio Mori. This short story tells about a mother and young son anxiously awaiting news from the father, who is in a prison camp away from Topaz. The picture mirrors the story's sad and resistant tone.

Okubo's illustrations also accompany several nonfiction articles. Her style in these drawings looks most like the works of Rivera and of Picasso when he used rounded, solid forms. In these pictures, such as the one illustrating the article on the Pahvant Valley, the forms are simplified and shading gives the illusion of solidity.[42] Okubo uses this style in an impersonal way, reflecting the impersonal nature of a factual article. Of all her *Trek* work, these illustrations are also the closest Okubo comes to fine art. Of interest is the fact that this article is written by Frank Beckwith, Sr., publisher of the *Millard County Chronicle* and a resident of Delta, Utah. Beckwith also supplied informational articles for the other two issues of the magazine. According to his granddaughter, Jane Beckwith, he befriended some of the Japanese American internees who were connected with the *Topaz Times* and *Trek*. It is possible that Okubo appreciated Beckwith's friendship and therefore accorded his articles an extra effort as she illustrated them.

Okubo not only broke with the government and camp administrators in her art but also broke with some of her fellow prisoners. For instance, in camp, people who were perceived to be too cooperative with camp administrators were referred to as *inu*, or "dogs." The text of *Trek* contains occasional references to dogs and doglike behavior, such as tail wagging. The inference is that the people associated with these references are *inu*. A reference might even be taken as a warning to let people know they are being watched and action might be taken against them. At one point in an ironic essay titled "Yule Greetings, Friends!" by Globularius Schraubi (a pen name to disguise the author's identity), the text becomes threatening, especially since some *inu* had been secretly beaten so severely that they were taken to the hospital and transferred out of the camp:

> Dead men tell no tales. Dogs tell tales with their tails. Good dogs, however, wag them not at all when at a crucial moment, and as a result the merit of a dog is judged by the time, place, and manner of their tail-wagging. The best of them are enrolled, therefore, in the Tail-Waggers' Association together with such celebrities as Bette Davis. And, of course, the basis for judging the merit of little girls is the way in which they wag their pig-tails. When they grow up they are judged by the way in which they wag their tongues.[43]

Two pages later, in proximity to references to Tanforan and the way camp language evolved, Okubo inserts an illustration of two dogs in a strange configuration, showing only the hind end of one with a wagging tail and the front end of the other with a halo over its head. The second dog, the good dog, is sniffing the ground behind the first as if tracking it. The meaning seems to be that *inu* should be aware that they are known and are being watched.

Okubo, as mentioned previously, also broke with the Issei, the traditional leaders of the Japanese American community. She broke with them through the style of her art, through her promotion of relocation, and through associating herself with the younger generation, whose members were ready to move on, away from the traditional Japanese American community.

As McKerrow states in his explanation of critical rhetoric, the struggle for power between those dominating and those resisting can effect change. Perhaps, in part, because of *Trek*'s support of the relocation process, by the time the last issue of the magazine was published, more than eight hundred Topaz residents had relocated outside the camp to work in "a variety of skills, services, and professions."[44] Within months, Okubo joined them to establish her own career in New York City, a testament to the power of sustained resistance to domination.

NOTES

1 Raymie E. McKerrow, "Critical Rhetoric: Theory and Praxis," *Communication Monographs* 56 (June 1989): 91.

2 Miné Okubo, *Citizen 13660* (Seattle: University of Washington Press, 1983), 134. In the publications themselves, the names of the magazine and newspaper are formatted as *Trek* and *Topaz Times*. For instance, the table of contents page of *Trek*'s second issue (February 1943) states "*Trek* is a special publication of the Project Reports Division, Central Utah Relocation Center." Additionally, the front page masthead for the newspaper for the first several issues shows the words "Topaz" and "Times" in the same size and font, indicating that the two words were meant to go together.

3 Okubo, *Citizen 13660*, 132; and Toyo Suyemoto, "Another Spring," in *Last Witnesses: Reflections on the Wartime Internment of Japanese Americans*, ed. Erica Harth (New York: Palgrave, 2001), 30–31.

4 Okubo, *Citizen 13660*, 134.

5 *Trek* 1, no. 3 (June 1943): 25.

6 Ibid., no. 1 (December 1942): 1.

7 Michel Foucault, *Discipline and Punish: The Birth of the Prison* (New York: Random House, 1991), 140–46.

8 Eleanor Gerard Sekarak, "A Teacher at Topaz," in *Only What We Could Carry: The Japanese American Internment Experience*, ed. Lawson Fusao Inada (Berkeley, Calif.: Heydey Books; San Francisco: California Historical Society, 2000), 126–37.

9 Roger Daniels, quoted in Robert A. Wilson and Bill Hosokawa, *East to America: A History of the Japanese in the United States* (New York: Quill, 1982), 198.

10 Inada, *Only What We Could Carry*, 264–68. "A Challenge to American Sportsmanship" by Eleanor Roosevelt appeared in *Collier's* magazine on October 16, 1943.

11 "Beyond the Gate," *Trek* 1, no. 2 (February 1943): 2–11; "Campus Report," ibid.: 33–34; and "Relocation: Through the Gates of Topaz," *Trek* 1, no. 3 (June 1943): 8–11.

12 The Staff, "Trek," *Trek* 1, no. 3 (June 1943): 37.

13 *Trek* 1, no. 3 (June 1943): 2–7.

14 Susan Schweik, "The 'Pre-Poetics' of Internment: The Example of Toyo Suyemoto," *American Literary History* (Spring 1989): 89–109.

15 *Trek* 1, no. 1 (December 1942): 21–22.

16 Ibid., no. 3 (June 1943): 37.

17 Toshio Mori was the only other member of the staff with credentials impressive enough to brag about. He was the first Japanese American to have a book contract for a creative work

and was a friend of the Pulitzer Prize–winning author William Saroyan, yet even he was accorded only a blurb about his accomplishments at the end of his stories. Ibid., no. 1 (December 1942): 25.

18 *Topaz Times*, 1–3.

19 Okubo, *Citizen 13660*, ix.

20 *Trek* 1, no. 1 (December 1942): 22.

21 Lucille R. Webber, *Japanese Woodblock Prints: The Reciprocal Influence between East and West* (Provo, Utah: Brigham Young University Press, [1979]).

22 John Fiske, "Cultural Studies and the Culture of Everyday Life," in *Cultural Studies*, ed. Lawrence Grossberg, Cary Nelson, and Paula Treichler (New York: Routledge, 1992), 158.

23 Michael Omi and Howard Winant, *Racial Formation in the United States from the 1960s to the 1990s* (New York: Routledge, 1994), 67.

24 Richard M. Ketchum, ed., *The Horizon Book of the Renaissance* (New York: American Heritage Publishing, 1961), 80.

25 T. F. Matthews, *The Clash of Gods: A Reinterpretation of Early Christian Art* (Princeton, N.J.: Princeton University Press, 1993), 46–47.

26 D. L. Brown, *From Eden to Armageddon: A Biblical History of the World in Classic Art and Illustration* (Salt Lake City, Utah: Shadow Mountain, 1998), 158–59.

27 An additional level of meaning for the cover of the third issue could come from Okubo's resistance to a common epithet of the time—"Dirty Jap." The figures in the illustration are all engaged in cleansing something. The figure to the left front is a woman carrying dishes to be washed. A man is shaving while standing behind the child being washed, while the man behind him in the upper right-hand corner is washing clothes. The other female figure is washing the child.

28 Jeanne Fahnestock, and Marie Secor, "Rhetorical Analysis," in *Discourse Studies in Composition*, ed. Ellen Barton and Gail Stygall (Cresskill, N.J.: Hampton Press, 2002), 177.

29 Charles Kostelnick and Michael Hassett, *Shaping Information: The Rhetoric of Visual Conventions* (Carbondale: Southern Illinois University Press, 2003), 92.

30 *Trek* 1, no. 1 (December 1942): 10.

31 *Topaz Times*, September 26, 1942, 4.

32 Kostelnick and Hassett, *Shaping Information*, 100.

33 *Trek* 1, no. 2 (February 1943): 3.

34 Ibid., no. 3 (June 1943): 23.

35 Ibid.: 22.

36 *Trek* 1, no. 1 (December 1942): 7.

37 Ibid.: 8.

38 Ibid.: 11.

39 *Trek* 1, no. 3 (June 1943): 37.

40 Ibid.

41 Ibid.: 2–3.

42 *Trek* 1, no. 1: 17.

43 Ibid.: 13.

44 *Trek* 1, no. 3 (June 1943): 8.

12

PARADOXES OF CITIZENSHIP

RE-VIEWING THE JAPANESE AMERICAN
INTERNMENT IN MINÉ OKUBO'S *CITIZEN 13660*

STELLA OH

The subject who wants to avoid the melancholy insanity of the self-abstraction that is citizenship, and to resist the lure of self-overcoming the material political context in which she lives, must develop tactics for refusing the interarticulation, now four hundred years old, between the United States and America, the nation and utopia.

——LAUREN BERLANT, *THE ANATOMY OF NATIONAL FANTASY*

We return to those empty spaces that have been masked by omission or concealed in a false and misleading plenitude.

——MICHEL FOUCAULT, *LANGUAGE, COUNTER-MEMORY, PRACTICE*

We negotiate our "ways of seeing" and our ways of knowing through conflicting trajectories of representations that contain specific political values.[1] To gaze implies more than just looking at someone or something; it represents a relationship of power in which the gazer is superior to the object of the gaze. This chapter analyzes representations of public surveillance in regard to the ways Japanese Americans were seen and portrayed by print media and how they were placed under surveillance by the U.S. government during World War II. The spectatorship of the gaze is interlinked with power and the process by which knowledges are produced and circulated.

In considering the representations of Japanese Americans during World War II, the particular focus will be on Miné Okubo's autobiographical work *Citizen 13660*.[2] Through her personal recollection, Okubo intimately sketches the political climate of the nation during World War II as well as the reactions of and toward Japanese Americans. Okubo's text not only analyzes the internment and the propaganda that surrounded it but, in so doing, critiques the discrepancy between the abstract principles of citizenship and democracy and the practice of racism and exclusion in the United States. I argue that *Citizen 13660* is not merely another narrative of the Japanese American internment but a work of art that performs a theory of citizenship, one that is conceived through the irony and contestation found in the internment. *Citizen 13660* thereby offers us a different way of discussing the internment, one that underscores the tensions among nation, race, and representation.

Citizen 13660 is a compilation of narrative and pictorial illustrations that weaves together the author's experiences at the Tanforan Assembly Center and the internment camp at Topaz, Utah. The book's various textual and visual representations, which affirm, contest, and reproduce certain ideologies of citizenship, speak to the nexus of power within which Okubo's literary work is produced. *Citizen 13660* displays irony and a subversive critique of the internment, not simply in its narrative texts but especially through the gaps, inconsistencies, and contradictions between the texts and the accompanying drawn images. The composition of Okubo's autobiographical text is effective in that it sets both visual image and written text in tension over meaning and interpretation.

This contradiction in the compositional sequence expresses its own political agenda. The apparent inconsistencies in the text measure and reflect the contradictions between U.S. legal policies toward Japanese Americans and the discourse employed by the government to foster patriotism and jingoism during times of war. Okubo's text portrays the paradoxes of the U.S. government, which, though fighting under the banner of freedom and liberty, took those treasured values away from its own citizens and residents. In order to secure an image of a unified nation, the physical being of those of Japanese descent were placed in concentration camps scattered throughout Arizona, Arkansas, California, Colorado, Idaho, Oregon, Utah, Washington, and Wyoming.[3] For Okubo and other internees, their experience in the camps and the incongruity they encountered between the promise of citizenship and the reality of the camps speak to the inconsistencies in U.S. policies and the country's theories of citizenship. As will be further discussed below, the enforced invisibility of Japanese Americans in the public space of the nation stands in ironic counterpoise to their high visibility in the form of targets of surveillance in the internment camps.

In titling her work *Citizen 13660*, Okubo highlights the cruel paradox of being a citizen in a country that disregards the rights of her citizenship. The use of "Citizen" is ironic—in fact, the work exposes the contradictions regarding citizenship rights in the United States. Okubo experienced the bitter irony of being a Japanese/American[4] as she and her brother "tagged our baggage with our family number 13660, and pinned the personal tags on ourselves." The number replaces the Okubo family name and reduces the artist and her brother to mere numbers. Like prisoners, who, upon entering prison, exchange their personal belongings for prison uniforms and identification numbers, Okubo and her brother are given numbers, and their belongings are "stored by the government" in unsafe government warehouses.[5] Okubo's ironic use of the title *Citizen 13660* exposes the contradictions regarding citizenship rights in the United States in ways that pertain not only to Japanese Americans but also to other racial groups throughout the history of the United States.[6]

Okubo's ironic approach to citizenship also points to the tensions that lie in cultural representations and their effects on national psychologies. What America stands for and who is entitled to the rights of U.S. citizenship are juxtaposed and called into question in the scene in which she and her brother are forced to register themselves as dangerous persons who need to be kept under surveillance by the federal government. Abiding by the orders promulgated by the Wartime Civil Control Administration, Okubo goes to her Civil Control Station, located at "Pilgrim Hall of the First Congregational Church in Berkeley," to register her brother and herself.[7] In a rather bitterly ironic moment, Japanese American citizens are brought to Pilgrim Hall so that their legitimacy as Americans may be interrogated. Okubo points to the irony of going to a place named after those who fled political and religious persecution in Britain. Flanked by two armed soldiers, she enters Pilgrim Hall as a Japanese American who is singled out for racial prosecution by the U.S. government.

As Okubo waits to be interviewed by a government official at Pilgrim Hall, she reads the "funnies."[8] By reading the "funnies" at this juncture, Okubo hints at the almost laughable absurdity of the government that indiscriminately interned West Coast people of Japanese descent regardless of their citizenship status or cultural identity. Similarly, Okubo is evoking a political form: Cartoons do not merely function for simple amusement but also make subtly biting commentaries on contemporary economic, political, and social events. In her evocation of cartoons, Okubo foreshadows her own use of drawings. Calling into question the meanings of images and words, Okubo challenges how history is represented and by whom.

The impact of image productions on racial constructions was especially apparent during the 1940s. The xenophobic fear and panic that ensued from Japan's attack on Pearl Harbor created a political atmosphere that prompted a particular form of U.S. nationalism that viewed all Japanese Americans as a national threat.[9] During the 1940s, both the government and the media went to great lengths to construct an overall portrait of Japanese Americans as sly, suspicious, and dangerous individuals. Newspapers and magazines provided detailed physical descriptions of deviant Japanese bodies that were reviled by the American body politic. On December 22, 1941, *Time* magazine published a now-famous article on how to distinguish the Chinese "friend" from the Japanese "enemy." The following caption was accompanied by two illustrations, one of a Japanese and another of a Chinese man.

> How to Tell Your Friends from the Japs:
> Virtually all Japanese are short. Japanese are likely to be stockier and broader-hipped than short Chinese. Japanese are seldom fat; they often dry up and grow lean as they age. Although both have the typical epicanthic fold of the upper eyelid, Japanese eyes are usually set closer together. The Chinese expression is likely to be more placid, kindly, open; the Japanese more positive, dogmatic, arrogant. Japanese are hesitant, nervous in conversation, laugh loudly at the wrong time. Japanese walk stiffly erect, hard heeled. Chinese, more relaxed, have an easy gait, sometimes shuffle.[10]

Print media consigned the Japanese body to crude and obscure stereotypes. The "citizen Japanese" was singled out for exclusion and labeled as a danger to national security. As racial markers played an ever-increasing role during World War II in mapping the national body politic of America, Japanese Americans lost their legitimacy as political members of the same. The contestation over the representation of the American citizen subject is a relational one in which the American national body is defined against the bodies of Japanese Americans that threaten its hegemony. The abstract notion of the citizen subject is given materiality through the exclusion of physical bodies of Japanese Americans from the metaphorical body of the nation.

As the war abroad escalated, newspapers and magazines such as *Time* and *Life* not only informed Americans of news regarding the war but also helped to shape how Americans perceived the war and the Japanese, and, by erroneous extension, how they perceived Japanese Americans. The spread of insidious racist stereotypes through print media further aggravated the antagonistic feelings of most Americans toward Japanese Americans. These sentiments are portrayed in *Citizen 13660* as Okubo depicts herself reading a newspaper. Numerous media headlines are scribbled behind her: "Aliens-Citizens," "A Jap is a Jap," "Can't Trust Them," "Sabotage," "Bank Freeze Jap," "Stab in the Back," "We Don't Want Japs," "Dangerous Criminals."[11]

The surveillance and labeling of Japanese Americans as dangerous continued into and through the camps. Although Japanese Americans were not (initially) allowed to bring cameras to the camps, photographs of them were taken as they left the camps. As Okubo demonstrates, before she is released from the camp at Topaz, she is not only required to attend classes on "How to Make Friends" and "How to Behave in the Outside World" but to have her photograph taken.[12] The surveillance of the photographic lens captures the faces of the internees for governmental records. Here, the word "capture" means both to gain control of and to preserve in a lasting form. In her classic book *On Photography*, Susan Sontag makes reference to several aspects of "photographic seeing."[13] She argues that to photograph is to appropriate the thing photographed. Her notion of photography can be further read within the context of Michel Foucault's analysis, in *Discipline and Punish*, of the rise of surveillance in modern society.[14] Read in this way, the medium of photography operates as a controlling gaze that identifies and categorizes individuals who are to be punished.[15] Although Foucault does not make references to race, in such a case, the medium of photography imposed on Japanese Americans a hypervisibility through which American society isolates, judges, and punishes them.

In order to regain legitimacy for Japanese Americans and reinstall them in the American body politic, Okubo uses print-language and visual images, the same tools that had once stripped Japanese Americans of political and legal authority. In her foreword to the 1983 version of *Citizen 13660*, Okubo writes that cameras and photographs were not permitted in the camps: ". . . so I recorded everything in sketches, drawings, and paintings. *Citizen 13660* began as a special group of drawings made to tell the story of camp life for my many friends who faithfully sent letters and packages to let us know we were not forgotten. The illustrations were intended for exhibition purposes."[16]

As exhibition, Okubo's work publicly displays her personal memories of the internment and functions as a communal performance providing alternative images of the camps. Okubo's sketches draw attention to both the suffering and the bonds of community that were produced through the internment. In *The View from Within: Japanese American Art from the Internment Camps*, Karin Higa notes that Okubo uses "humor to indict her jailers, eliciting sympathy and compassion through her depictions of everyday life in the camps."[17] Okubo herself later wrote that "the humor and pathos of the scenes made me decide to keep a record of camp life in sketches and drawings." Remembering the "ridiculous, the insane, and the humorous" aspects of camp life, Okubo remarked that "I was an American citizen, and because of the injustices and contradictions nothing made much sense, making things comical in spite of the misery."[18] Like the musical form of the blues, which laments loss through its jaunty rhythm, the conflicting characteristics of humor and pathos function as instruments through which Okubo simultaneously unmasks the contradictions inherent in American citizenship and depicts the resilience of the Japanese American community.[19]

Working both within and against the restricting conditions of the camp, Okubo illustrates her views of the internment and publishes them in this volume as an "exhibition" to American society. She initially fragments the bodies of Japanese Americans in order to strip them of the incrustation of stereotypes and then reinvests these bodies with new meanings. Thus, in a manner that differs radically from photographs, Okubo uses her sketches to capture her experiences, as well as those of her fellow internees, and offers alternative ways of viewing the internment through her drawings. In all of her sketches, Okubo draws herself looking at other internees, camp police, and the campgrounds. By including herself in her drawings, she offers a perspective on the internment in which she looks at and is being looked upon by camp police as well as the audience reading the text. In doing so, she addresses the ways in which our visual productions shape our social perceptions along with our individual opinions.

For example, in one humorous vignette in *Citizen 13660*, Okubo depicts herself surreptitiously watching a Caucasian camp policeman who is spying on two Japanese American men in their barracks. The caption below the illustration reads: "Day and night Caucasian camp police walked their beats within the center. They were on the outlook for contraband and for suspicious actions."[20] The camp guard exercises a commanding gaze over two Japanese American men in the barrack while Okubo surveys the unsuspecting guard. The ironic sequence of surveillance in this scene signals a contestation over the construction of authority over particular subjects. In *Discipline and Punish*, Foucault argues that the panopticon was used as a mechanism of power by which to discipline subjects. For Foucault, the "panopticon is the architectural figure" of this composition of surveillance, knowledge, and power.[21] The panopticon induces in the inmate a state of constant fear that he or she is being watched, assuring the automatic functioning of power.[22]

Okubo, by playing with traditional narratives of surveillance, intervenes in and subverts the accepted body of knowledge imposed upon Japanese Americans. Although social control is exerted through the physical imprisonment of Japanese American bodies within the space of the internment camp, rhetorical control over representation is problematized by Okubo's sketches. The camp police constantly watch her and the other internees, but the images in *Citizen 13660* depict Okubo looking at other internees and looking back at the camp police. The rhetoric of images produced alongside Okubo's text subverts the sole narrative of the prison house of representation in which Japanese citizen subjects are the objects of regulation.

In the same way, *Citizen 13660* addresses and critiques the discourse that regulates and reproduces citizen subjects. Okubo writes that "a house captain" made rounds and checked on the internees twice a day.[23] In another drawing, she depicts the camp police checking on and jotting down notes about her. As the camp guard writes his notes regarding Okubo, she defiantly sticks out her tongue at him. The drawing also informs the viewer that Okubo is engaged in the process of writing when she notices the guard. Writing within and against the watchful eye of the camp police, she demonstrates that, although a prisoner of the camp, she refuses to be merely an object of the gaze and the compilation of governmental records and "knowledge" but writes her own version of the internment.

The process of writing and of "naming" became an important part of defining one's self within the restrictions of the camp. Okubo writes about other members of her camp who engage in the creative process of naming. Counterarticulating the discourse of the federal government, which euphemistically called the horse barns "barracks," Japanese Americans created their own literal signboards in an attempt to convert their "barracks" into homes. The assembly centers that were used as temporary camps were hastily constructed shacks built on old run-down racetracks and desolate desert lands. The living quarters at Tanforan, where Okubo and her brother were sent, consisted of horse stalls that "showed signs of a hurried whitewashing. Spider webs, horse hair, and hay had been whitewashed with the walls. Huge spikes and nails stuck out all over the walls. A two-inch layer of dust covered the floor, but on removing it we discovered that linoleum the color of redwood had been placed over the rough manure-covered boards."[24] Euphemistically referred to as "Barrack 16, Room 50," Okubo's living quarters were in reality a single, dirty stall, twenty feet by nine feet, split into two rooms.[25]

Despite the terrible living conditions in the camps, the internees tried to make the best of their situation. As Okubo relates: "On the barracks in the center field and on the stalls, ingenious family name plates and interesting signs were displayed with great pride. All signs in Japanese were ordered removed but many fancy names, such as Inner Sanctum, Stall Inn, and Sea Biscuit, lent a touch of humor to the situation."[26] Some names were invented, yet all referred to the outside world. For example, there were signs that read "Inner Sanctum," alluding to a popular radio series of the 1940s, and "Sea Biscuit," referring to the famous racehorse in whose stall at the Santa Anita Assembly Center many Japanese Americans later claimed to have been placed. At initial glance, the signs may simply represent individuals trying to assert their individuality and cope with their condition of imprisonment. Yet signposts such as those described above also represent broader cultural codes that signal toward national belonging.[27] Japanese Americans engaged in an appropriation of cultural space by giving names to their stalls. The signs, although eventually taken down by camp police, served as a medium of resistance to ascribed cultural codes of knowing and meaning.

Okubo, along with these internees, challenges established forms of cultural and national knowledge by creating her own signs that have other codes of meaning. When she first arrives at Topaz internment camp, she and the other passengers on board the bus are each handed a copy of the camp newspaper, the *Topaz Times*. Noticing the headline, "Topaz, the Jewel of the Desert," the internees chuckle at the ironic use of words.[28] Rather than being "the jewel," Topaz, like many of its counterparts, is in dismal condition. The misleading headline in the *Topaz Times* masks the material reality of the horrible conditions of the camp and the internment process. In contrast, once Okubo assumed the role of art editor of the *Topaz Times*, she and her staff imbued headlines and stories with illustrations that expressed different codes and knowledges from the vantage point of Japanese American internees. Both the signs on the barracks and the ostensibly innocent but subliminally subversive comic strips that survived the censorship of the *Topaz Times* functioned as codes through which the internees could strive to reconnect with the outside world and reaffirm through some means their participation in national events. Okubo's drawings in *Citizen 13660*, like the signs, serve as a medium of resistance to the assortment of signs that present dominant ideologies of knowing and meaning.

If the signposts signal the desire of Japanese Americans to connect with U.S. society, they also underline their inability to do so. Confined inside the walls of the camp, the internees were bombarded by signs that excluded them from the nation and labeled Japanese Americans as "enemies," as was done, for example, in the *Life* and *Time* magazine articles. One drawing shows internees who, at work in the scorching heat, see an advertisement for Acme Beer in the distance. The accompanying text reads: "A huge sign, 'Enjoy Acme Beer,' stood out like a beacon on a near-by hill. The sign was clearly visible from every section of the camp and was quite a joke to the thirsty evacuees, especially on the warm days." In a similar fashion, Japanese Americans could see far off the ideals of democracy and the inalienable rights that were supposed to be guaranteed to U.S. citizens, all of which were inaccessible to them. Okubo alludes to the mockery of justice, which taunts them just as the beer sign taunts the thirsty workers on a hot day. She writes, "[w]e were close to freedom but far from it."[29] Although Japanese Americans were guaranteed certain inalienable rights as citizens, they were nevertheless sent to internment camps without due process of law.

Okubo questions the principles of U.S. citizenship and problematizes abstract words such as "justice," "fair," and "freedom." In one vignette, she depicts the internees hiding their faces from the harshness of the wind and dust. The underlying caption reads: "The weather in Tanforan was fair. It was sunny on most days but always windy and dusty."[30] In this caption, Okubo questions the usage of the word "fair," urging us to reconsider its meaning. How "fair" was the internment in the light of military necessity? Words such as "fair" and "freedom" are commodified as fashionable currency and have long since lost substantial meaning. The dialogue between the image and the text produces a sequence of meanings and interpretations that are not present in the image or text alone.

Toward the end of *Citizen 13660*, Okubo depicts herself sticking her tongue out at the guards while she is granted "leave clearance" after having answered "yes" to loyalty question 28, which confirmed Japanese American loyalty to the United States.[31] Across from her is an old Issei who has been detained by camp police for having answered "no" to the loyalty question. Okubo answers "yes" to question 28 and thereby acceptably performs the discursive narrative of loyalty that the government expects. She is allowed to leave the camp, whereas the older Issei fails to execute the act and hence is detained. The defiant act of sticking her tongue out at the guard suggests that Okubo has consciously outsmarted the system through her performance. Through an initial submission to power, Okubo engages in a performative act that accords her productive power—a means of attaining her freedom from the camps. Read in this way, those who replied "yes" to the loyalty questions were not complying with the desires and conditions of the federal government but merely supplying government officials with what they wanted to hear.

After being singled out from other Americans and suffering through the cruelty of the internment, most Japanese Americans tried hard to assimilate into the mainstream way of life after their release from the camps. For several decades after the war ended, most Japanese Americans wanted to focus on rebuilding their lives and to forget their imprisonment experience. The McCarthy era of the 1950s also contributed to the silencing of attacks on the government. Originally published by Columbia University Press in 1946, right after the end of the Second World War, Okubo's text dropped from public consciousness until 1983.[32] As Cary Nelson argues in *Repression and Recovery*:

> . . . literary history is never an innocent process of recovery. We recover what
> we are culturally and psychologically prepared to recover and what we
> "recover" we necessarily rewrite, giving it meanings that are inescapably con-
> temporary, giving it a new discursive life in the present, a life it cannot have
> had before. A text can gain that new life in part through an effort to under-
> stand what cultural work it may have been able to do in an earlier time, but
> that understanding, again, is located in our own time.[33]

Okubo's text is now circulating again in ways that are unexpected and different from its presence in the context of the 1940s, when it was originally published. In the interim, the civil rights movement, the booming economy of the 1960s, and the Immigration Act of 1965 inspired the American nation to reevaluate the internment of Japanese Americans during the Second World War. Indeed, the revival of interest in this text occurred during a period that followed the Japanese American Citizens League's request to Congress that it appoint a commission to conduct extensive research into the internment—Okubo's text was submitted as an exhibit to the Commission on Wartime Relocation and Internment of Civilians. *Citizen 13660* was finally reprinted the same year in which the commission concluded that a "grave injustice" had been the result of "race prejudice and war hysteria" and a few years before Congress passed the Civil Liberties Act in 1988.[34]

In *Citizen 13660*, Okubo attempts to demystify the discursive formations of the fiction of racial categories and U.S. nationalism. The practice of power and discourse is tightly implicated in constructing and transmitting images regarding a specific racial group at particular moments in history. During World War II, the U.S. public sought to erase the presence of Japanese Americans from the imagined community of the nation, excluding them from the nation's public memory by confining them to internment camps where they would not be visible to the public eye. The 209 vignettes that compose *Citizen 13660* function as a reminder of the real political and economic issues of the internment as well as the systematic obliviousness to and forgetting of this event by the larger U.S. public. Okubo accords the Japanese internment ironic, mocking treatment that exposes the contradictions of the war, the injustices of the internment, and the propaganda that convinced the nation to intern its own citizens for the sake of national security. Through her sketches, laden with satirical contradictions, Okubo questions the ways of constructing historical narratives and the ideological implications in image creation.

In sum, Okubo's text is composed in relation to its absent contexts, and the gaps in her writing make room for other interpretations of the internment. The failure of text and image to correspond with each other in numerous places in Okubo's text is indicative of the text's incompatibility with the majority of society during the specific historical period of its composition. The text that is severed from the image testifies to the experience of Japanese Americans as they are severed from their homes and their country of citizenship. The gaps present between the text and the image in Okubo's text allude to the inability to contain or recall a complete historical recuperation, and they point to the difficulty of recording the traumatic memories of the internment and the impossibility of restoring past wrongs. We are left merely as witnesses to the contradiction of legal policies, loss of connection, and ultimately the loss of lives. Okubo's work testifies to the memories of the Japanese American community and exposes the gaps that will inevitably always exist in a community traumatized by such violence and betrayal. Like the shadows cast by the atomic bombs that devastated Nagasaki and Hiroshima, through the visual gaps of her text, Okubo remembers and memorializes the loss and signals to that which can never be articulated.

NOTES

Epigraphs are from Lauren Berlant, *The Anatomy of National Fantasy: Hawthorne, Utopia, and Everyday Life* (Chicago: University of Chicago Press, 1991), and Michel Foucault, *Lan-*

guage, Counter-memory, Practice, trans. Donald F. Bouchard and Sherry Simon (Ithaca, N.Y.: Cornell University Press, 1977).

1 In *Ways of Seeing* (London: Penguin, 1972), John Berger argues that "men act and women appear" (45). Focusing on European art from the Renaissance onward, Berger argues that men look at women while women watch themselves being looked at. Working under the assumption that the ideal spectator is male and that the object of the gaze is female, Berger argues that in European paintings from the seventeenth century onward, paintings of female nudes reflect the woman's submission to the owner of the painting as well as to the male viewer. He notes that "almost all post-Renaissance European sexual imagery is frontal—either literally or metaphorically—because the sexual protagonist is the specta-tor-owner looking at it" (56). Rather than focusing on the viewing practices of individu-als, in this chapter, I analyze how subject positions are constructed through the visual media of Okubo's text.

2 I examine the period roughly from the bombing of Pearl Harbor on December 7, 1941, to October 30, 1946, when the last detention center in Crystal City, Texas, was closed.

3 Japanese Americans on the West Coast were sent to one of ten internment camps: Amache, Colorado; Gila River, Arizona; Heart Mountain, Wyoming; Jerome, Arkansas; Manzanar, California; Minidoka, Idaho; Poston, Arizona; Rohwer, Arizona; Topaz, Utah; and Tule Lake, California. While the camps were hastily being built by government contractors, Japanese Americans were sent to assembly centers that served as temporary camps in Mayer, Arizona; Portland, Oregon; Puyallup, Washington; and Fresno, Marysville, Merced, Pinedale, Pomona, Sacramento, Salinas, Santa Anita, Stockton, Tanforan, Tulare, and Man-zanar, California. Manzanar was converted to a relocation camp on June 1, 1942. In addi-tion to the assembly centers and relocation camps under the supervision of the War Relo-cation Authority (WRA), there were also U.S. Department of Justice camps, which housed Japanese aliens considered "dangerous persons" (and in some cases their families). Japa-nese American community leaders, fishermen, or newspaper men were usually detained in these camps, located in Crystal City and Seagoville, Texas; Fort Missoula, Montana; Kooskia, Idaho; and Santa Fe, New Mexico. For further discussion, see Roger Daniels, San-dra Taylor, and Harry Kitano, eds., *Japanese Americans, from Relocation to Redress* (Salt Lake City: University of Utah Press, 1986).

4 I want to problematize the term "Japanese American" since it signals the tension between the ethnic Japanese and the national American as they come to bear on the term "Japanese American." Throughout this chapter, I allude to the tension between Japanese Americans as legal citizens and as racially marked pariahs.

5 Miné Okubo, *Citizen 13660* (Seattle: University of Washington Press, 1983), 22, 19. Under Executive Order 9066, Japanese Americans were forced to abandon their property, liqui-date their possessions, and move to the internment camps. The federal government offered no substantial protection for the property of Japanese Americans; most of the "government warehouses" were merely shacks, which were unsafe and unguarded against thieves. The majority of Japanese Americans had to leave their property behind, sell it for a meager amount, or entrust it to white neighbors—many of whom never returned it. The federal

government not only failed to offer U.S. citizens of Japanese ancestry protection for their goods; it did not offer any special aid for resettlement when the camps were finally closed in 1945–46. Estimates indicate that the Japanese American community's losses were "somewhere between $67 million and $116 million in 1945 dollars, which comes to a figure in excess of $500 million in 2001 dollars." See Greg Robinson, *By Order of the President: FDR and the Internment of Japanese Americans* (Cambridge: Harvard University Press, 2001), 144. This measure begs the question of what U.S. citizenship means for differently racialized subjects and for differently capitalized subjects as well. See also Cheryl Harris, "Whiteness as Property," in *The Judicial Isolation of the "Racially" Oppressed,* ed. E. Nathaniel Gates (New York: Garland, 1997). Harris argues that the concepts of race and property are intertwined with each other and explores the historical and ideological dimensions of viewing "whiteness and property"; she also contends that the exclusion of legal rights such as voting was specifically designed to disenfranchise minority individuals politically and economically. The cultural discourses that construct U.S. citizens influence and are influenced by preconceived material conditions.

6 Mexicans were promised citizenship when the United States acquired land after the Mexican-American War (1846–48). However, several factors such as the language barrier and an unfamiliar justice system prevented Mexicans from exercising their rights of citizenship. In addition, African Americans were granted citizenship after the Civil War but were prevented from actively participating in society as citizens due to the proliferation of Jim Crow laws.

7 Okubo, *Citizen 13660,* 18.

8 Ibid., 19.

9 Within minutes of the bombing of Pearl Harbor, several thousand Issei were taken to several detention centers in Hawaii and the West Coast. No one expected Nisei to also be directly affected. Yet, regardless of their American citizenship, Nisei were not spared from the internment.

10 "How to Tell Your Friends from the Japs," *Time,* December 22, 1941, 33. *Life* magazine published a similar article, "How to Tell Japs from the Chinese" (December 22, 1941). This article is cited in Ronald Takaki, *Strangers from a Different Shore: A History of Asian Americans* (New York: Bay Back, 1998), 370.

11 Okubo, *Citizen 13660,* 10.

12 Ibid., 207.

13 Susan Sontag, *On Photography* (New York: Farrar, 1977), 89.

14 Michel Foucault, *Discipline and Punish: The Birth of the Prison* (New York: Vintage, 1977).

15 In *The Burden of Representation: Essays on Photographies and Histories* (Amherst: University of Massachusetts, 1988), John Tagg offers a detailed analysis of how photography was used from the late nineteenth century onward to identify prisoners and mental patients.

16 Okubo, *Citizen 13660,* ix.

17 Karin M. Higa, "The View from Within," in *The View from Within: Japanese American Artists from the Internment Camps, 1942–1945,* exh. cat. (Los Angeles: Japanese American National Museum, 1992), 28–29.

18 Okubo, *Citizen 13660,* 53, ix.

19 The blues of Okubo's text adds to and revises the well-known historical facts surrounding the Japanese American internment. Like jazz, the blues is a musical form that evolved from African American musical tradition and covers a wide range of emotions, topics, and musical styles. The verses of the blues usually lament injustice and loss; however, the music of the blues is a jaunty rhythmic beat that celebrates life. Combined, the lamentations of the verses and the boisterous rhythm of the musical score offer a coping mechanism that overcomes sadness and despair.

20 Okubo, *Citizen 13660*, 60.

21 Foucault, *Discipline and Punish*, 200.

22 In *Discipline and Punish*, Foucault argues that public spectacles of punishment such as hangings and decapitations, which occurred before the Enlightenment, were replaced with surveillance within the prison-panopticon. Whereas during the medieval era, the body of the prisoner was tortured for public display, the body of the prisoner of the panopticon is simply alienated from society and other prisoners. The body of the prisoner is constantly watched. Realizing that he is always under surveillance, the prisoner internalizes the impulse of a surveyor. This prison-panopticon serves as Foucault's central metaphor for the rise of a society in which disciplinary knowledge constructs the behavior and beliefs of individuals. Foucault's model, it must be said, is somewhat problematically adapted to this case. Although Foucault effectively links the inspecting gaze with power and knowledge in this famous model of the panopticon, he does not offer an analysis of how this powerful gaze constructs racial categories of knowledge. In addition, Foucault's model of the panopticon isolates each prisoner in his individual cell, forming a collection of separated individuals who [are] seen, but [do] not see," who "[are] object[s] of information, never subject[s] in communication" (200). Although the panopticon model of the internment camp does create disciplined subjects through their fear of being watched, the internees have access to communication with other members of the camp. In fact, *Citizen 13660* presents several community events such as establishing churches, schools, and a small library; organizing talent shows, pageants, and dances; and electing a Center Advisory Council composed of Japanese Americans. All of these events demonstrate the ability of the Japanese American internees to continue or create a semblance of their previous lives within the confinement of the camps.

23 Okubo, *Citizen 13660*, 59.

24 Ibid., 35.

25 Ibid., 33.

26 Ibid., 83.

27 Roland Barthes argues that signs are codes that depend on different forms of cultural, national, aesthetic, and linguistic knowledges, which are invested in the image. See Barthes, *Image-Music-Text* (New York: Hill and Wang, 1977).

28 Okubo, *Citizen 13660*, 121.

29 Okubo, *Citizen 13660*, 2, 81.

30 Ibid., 56.

31 Question 27 asked: "Are you willing to serve in the armed forces of the United States on combat duty wherever ordered?" Question 28 followed: "Will you swear unqualified alle-

giance to the United States of America and forswear any form of allegiance or obedience to the Japanese Emperor or any other foreign power or organization?" Ibid., 175. Issei were placed in a difficult position. Even if they renounced their Japanese citizenship, they could not become naturalized citizens of the United States. The 1922 Supreme Court case *Ozawa vs. United States* ruled that Japanese were not Caucasian, and therefore not "white," and were ineligible for naturalization. If Issei pledged allegiance to the United States, they would be left without a country. Many of the Nisei, who were American-born citizens, felt that their loyalty to the United States was being questioned at the same time they were being asked to risk their lives and fight for their country. Riddled with inconsistencies, questions 27 and 28 provoked resentment from both Issei and Nisei.

32 Okubo states that *Citizen 13660* has never been out of print. It was published first by Columbia University Press in 1946, by AMCS Press in 1966, and by Arno Press in 1978 but remained rather obscure until the University of Washington Press reprinted it in 1983.

33 Cary Nelson, *Repression and Recovery: Modern American Poetry and the Politics of Cultural Memory, 1910–1945* (Madison: University of Wisconsin Press, 1989), 11.

34 United States, Commission on Wartime Relocation and Internment of Civilians, *Personal Justice Denied: Report of the Commission on Wartime Relocation and Internment of Civilians,* with a new foreword by Tetsuden Kashima (Washington, D.C.: Civil Liberties Public Education Fund; Seattle: University of Washington Press, 1997).

Popularly known as the Japanese American Redress Bill, the legislation officially acknowledged that the U.S. government had done a grave injustice to persons of Japanese ancestry; the bill mandated that each surviving victim of the internment receive $20,000 in reparations. The period of reparations lasted from 1988 to 1998. This delayed action on the part of U.S. government authorities to address the Japanese internment and assume responsibility alludes to the problem of legitimate representation of the war and underscores the paradox of U.S. racial politics and national policies. For more information on the Civil Liberties Act of 1988, please refer to Leslie T. Hatamiya, *Righting a Wrong: Japanese Americans and the Passage of the Civil Liberties Act of 1988* (Stanford, Calif.: Stanford University Press, 1994).

13

BIRTH OF A CITIZEN

MINÉ OKUBO AND THE POLITICS OF SYMBOLISM

GREG ROBINSON

itizen 13660, Miné Okubo's illustrated memoir of her personal experience during the wartime removal and incarceration of Japanese Americans (popularly known as the Japanese American internment), is a masterpiece of ambiguity. Like many works of art and literature by African Americans, *Citizen 13660* has often been assimilated by latter-day critics into the protest tradition.[1] These critics (including several in this volume) make much of Okubo's trickster nature and her use of double-sided combinations of words and images as weapons of resistance. Pointing to the disjunction between Okubo's narrative and her accompanying drawings, they contend that beneath the text's apparently clear (and supposedly inoffensive) surface narrative lurk various subversive and radical messages awaiting decryption by the attentive reader. For example, Pamela Stennes Wright finds that Okubo employs two narrative strategies throughout her book—an overt narrative that documents the story of a loyal American citizen who "must come to an understanding of her evacuation and internment," plus a covert narrative that suggests the injustices of official policy by depicting the massive disruption it wreaked on Japanese Americans.[2] "The genius of Okubo's book," Elena Tajima Creef adds, "is the unusual combination of visual and literary narrative that allows her to tell both stories . . . [pairing] its provocative, and subversive, use of the autobiographical 'I . . . with the observational power of the artist's 'eye.'"[3]

Even though I find the various critical explorations of subversive currents in Okubo's work engaging, they tend to privilege a rather recondite subtextual reading as *the* essential version. Worse, they focus so single-mindedly on locating resistance and agency as to obscure some of the complexity of the work.[4] This emphasis on Okubo's perceived resistance risks drawing attention away from the circumstances in which her work was created, as well as from her own original intentions. These are not simply matters of academic interest. The project that was to become *Citizen 13660* evolved within the specific political context of the wartime period, as Japanese Americans began to leave the camps and resettle throughout the United States. Okubo's work was promoted by the War Relocation Authority, the government agency responsible for running the camps, and its liberal allies outside of government, as part of a larger program of assimilation and absorption they had designed for the Nisei. She collaborated in this operation, not only in her choice of illustrations for the book, and in the brief texts she wrote to accompany them, but in her various public statements characterizing herself as a writer and fixing the meaning of her narrative. In sum, the conscious meaning that Okubo applied to the text and the critical readings it received at the time of its initial appearance deserve central consideration if the work is to be properly understood.

An examination of the gestation of *Citizen 13660* reveals the self-consciousness of Okubo's creation and how and why certain meanings became attached to it. Tracing the evolution of *Citizen 13660* requires a certain attentiveness. For her own reasons, Okubo tended to deny the intentionality that was a feature of her output more or less from the beginning. In the publicity for her book during the 1940s, she stated that the illustrations in *Citizen 13660* grew out of sketches she did throughout her confinement in order to document the story of camp life for her friends in Europe and the United States.[5] She continued in later life to affirm that she had intended the illustrations as a private gift for "my many friends who faithfully sent letters and packages to let us know we were not forgotten"[6] and only afterward thought of turning them into a public project. Only when the work was republished in 1983, in the heyday of the redress period, did Okubo reveal that her illustrations "were intended for exhibition purposes" from the first.[7] Even then, however, she remained silent regarding the particular stages and modifications through which the project evolved.

In fact, Okubo seems to have begun transforming her drawings into exhibition material by late 1942, not long after she left the Tanforan Assembly Center and arrived at the Topaz camp—or even earlier, if we are to believe a letter that University of California's vice president, Monroe Deutsch, sent Okubo at the time *Citizen 13660* was published: "You have done exactly what you said you would when you were in my office prior to the evacuation period—you kept your sense of humor and portrayed the amusing incidents in your life at Tanforan and Topaz."[8] In any case, Okubo's first effort to show her images of camp life publicly was her submission of two drawings to the spring 1943 show at the San Francisco Museum of Art (where she had frequently displayed her work in prewar years).[9] It is impossible to be certain as to when Okubo conceived of sending out art on the camps for display, but it can be assumed that this occurred well before the show actually opened. Whether or not the show's curators specially vetted her contribution in advance, it certainly would have been standard practice for them to ask artists to send in their drawings enough ahead of time to allow for the mounting of the show. Furthermore, Okubo would very likely have done all she could to get her work to the museum extra early, given the uncertainties of wartime mail service from Topaz.

The San Francisco Museum show opened in March 1943. Okubo's camp art drew special attention for both its style and its subject matter and received warm praise from a critic in the magazine *California Art and Architecture*.[10] *On Guard*, a study of two internment camp guards, won the Artist Fund Prize. A copy of the drawing was reproduced in the *San Francisco Chronicle*'s Sunday supplement *This World* on March 21, 1943. Such attention, especially from the West Coast press, lent Okubo special visibility among supporters of Japanese Americans. A school lesson plan that a Quaker group brought out shortly afterward in an effort to help raise public consciousness (to use a term unknown in the period) about the plight of Japanese Americans singled out Okubo for attention: "Miné Okubo is another artist who will some day be well-known as the others. She was given a traveling scholarship for her fine work and spent time in Europe studying art. She returned to the University of California to learn that she had been offered another year of study in Italy, but could not return to that country because of the beginning of the war."[11]

Meanwhile, the positive response to Okubo's drawing led the editors of the *San Francisco Chronicle* (a liberal newspaper with an editor, Chester Rowell, who had opposed evacuation) to commission further illustrations from the artist. Okubo obliged by sending a set of camp sketches. These, along with her brief commentary, were published in *This World* on August 29, 1943, as "An Evacuee's Hopes—and Memories" (see chapter 3 for the article text). In a prefatory note, the editors of the magazine explained that Okubo's "debut as a writer was accidental" and that they had incorporated into an article the explanatory notes she had sent with her sketches. At the same time, the magazine undertook "to document her objectivity" by interpolating a number of quotations from a speech Dillon S. Myer, director of the WRA, had delivered earlier at San Francisco's Commonwealth Club. As a result, Okubo's article bore the appearance of an officially sponsored publication.

Of course, even without the symbolic imprimatur of the WRA, Okubo's readers would have understood that she was speaking from confinement and was thus subject to official censorship. Although Okubo doubtless felt limited in what she could say, her article's text does not reveal particular reticence or sugarcoating:

The train trip from Tanforan to Topaz was a nightmare. It was the first train trip for many of us and we were excited, but many were sad to leave California and the Bay region. To most of the people, to this day, the world is only as large as from San Francisco to Tanforan to Topaz. Buses were waiting for us at Delta to take us to Topaz. Seventeen miles of alfalfa farms and grease-wood were what we saw. Some people cried on seeing the utter desolation of the camp. Fine alkaline dust hovered over it like San Francisco fog.[12]

The appearance of Okubo's sketches in *This World* occurred at an essential turning point in the history of incarceration. During summer 1943, the WRA completed its segregation of confined Japanese Americans into groups it judged "loyal" and "disloyal." With segregation completed—at a high cost to thousands of inmates who were arbitrarily displaced—and with the "no-no boys" confined in a high-security center at Tule Lake, California, the issue of winding down all the other camps became paramount. On September 14, 1943, just sixteen days after Okubo's article was published, the White House presented Congress with a report on Japanese Americans. In his transmittal letter, President Franklin D. Roosevelt stated that with the successful completion of segregation, the WRA could now redouble its efforts to resettle outside the camps those Japanese Americans "whose loyalty to this country has remained unshaken throughout the hardships of the evacuation." In particular, Roosevelt promised that Japanese Americans could return to the West Coast "as soon as the military situation will make such restoration feasible."[13]

This presidential pledge helped mobilize the WRA, which had been badly buffeted by hostile press campaigns and congressional investigations, to refocus its attention on a task it had already undertaken on a small scale: planning resettlement. Roosevelt's statement also capped the gradual transformation of the agency's mission during 1943, from constructing and managing camps in which to confine the excluded Japanese to opening regional resettlement offices and scouting out areas for resettlement so that internees could leave the camps. This new mission did not consist simply of finding sponsors who would provide Nisei with jobs or education or of helping migrants find housing.[14] Rather, it amounted to implementing an overall quasi-official policy of dispersion of ethnic Japanese throughout the United States and facilitating their absorption into the larger population.

The WRA, the War Department, the White House (notably First Lady Eleanor Roosevelt), and liberal and "fair play" groups—along with many Japanese Americans—broadly agreed that, by retarding assimilation and/or restricting economic opportunity, the prewar ghettoization of Japanese Americans in "Little Tokyos" had helped inspire the hostility that led to evacuation. Therefore, despite their continuing conflicts over the justice of removal and the morality of the government's operation of the camps, these disparate groups joined forces to facilitate the scattering of the Japanese American population across the rest of the country. This, they believed, would be the best solution to the "Japanese problem" as it had existed on the West Coast and would ensure that the tragedy of removal would never recur. WRA director Myer expressed a widely held view when he claimed that, on the whole, the Nisei were actually better off in the long run for their confinement experience and diaspora, since they could now establish themselves on an equal basis with other Americans.[15] As harsh and punitive as the destruction of ethnic Japanese communities may sound to present-day ears, these Americans—including many Japanese Americans, and not just the Japanese American Citizens League—looked upon the relocation process as a providential opportunity for Nisei to enter the larger society.[16]

Government officials realized early that the key to opening the doors of the camps and assuring the success of mass resettlement lay in remaking the Nisei's public image so as to reduce white suspicion and hostility toward Japanese Americans, for which the removal itself was largely responsible. Thus, although public relations figured only distantly, if at all, in the WRA's charter and initial mandate, the agency gradually shifted its program as the war proceeded. WRA staffers teamed up with colleagues from the Office of War Information to produce an enormous pile of propaganda for public consumption, focusing jointly on the achievements of the WRA and on the loyalty and American character of the inmates.[17] WRA efforts included informational pamphlets, documentary films, and speaking tours by WRA director Myer, former U.S. ambassador to Japan Joseph Grew, and Ben Kuroki, a Nisei war hero. The WRA and OWI also exerted pressure on publishers and film producers to promote responsible media images of Japanese Americans and avoid hostile depictions.[18]

Liberal groups outside the government, especially those opposed to incarceration, gladly collaborated with the government's media campaign. Some of them may well have privately deplored the WRA's heavy-handed management of the Nisei's public image and suppression of internal dissent—certainly many supporters of Japanese Americans with experience of the camps considered the official picture excessively rosy—but they obviously felt that it was in the interest of all to downplay their differences in light of the enormous public opposition to Japanese Americans.

It is not clear whether government censors ever vetted Miné Okubo's drawings or article text before they were published in *This World*. It is reasonable to assume as much, though, given the wartime restrictions on inmates and the interpolation of Myer's words in the text. Such review was in any case common practice. Notably, when Eleanor Roosevelt drafted an article in support of the Nisei for *Collier's* magazine, "A Challenge to American Sportsmanship," she first submitted her text to Myer for comment.

In any event, the positive reception of Okubo's article would have placed her squarely within the WRA's sights. In January 1944, barely four months after the article's appearance, Okubo was able to leave camp and relocate to New York.[19] According to her later testimony, she was solicited by the editors of *Fortune* magazine to illustrate their upcoming issue on Japan—although, as she explained, she had never been to Japan—and her release providentially followed: "I was planning on staying in camp. I didn't have any money and at least I was being fed. Then I got a telegram from *Fortune* magazine. I had always thought that if you are patient enough, the gods would answer your prayers. So I left for New York."[20]

There is no reason to doubt the basic truth of this story, which was recounted in publicity materials produced at the time. Yet it glosses over the degree of official cooperation required for such a move. Even ignoring the question of whether the government recommended Okubo to *Fortune*, it is unimaginable that government officials would not have been consulted. Moreover, the WRA's leave clearance process was cumbersome and time-consuming—even Interior Secretary Harold Ickes was forced to wait for some eights months during 1942–43 before he could obtain release and transportation for a pair of Japanese American laborers for his farm.[21] Although the WRA later streamlined its leave-clearance operations somewhat, the process remained an elaborate one. Okubo's remarkably rapid release therefore bespeaks official assistance, particularly since WRA officials would have been well aware of the nature of her future employment.

Okubo later claimed that when she arrived in New York and showed her sketches of the camp experience to *Fortune*'s editors, who knew nothing of the camps, they decided to do an additional piece on Japanese Americans using her sketches as illustrations and then urged Okubo to collect the sketches into a full-length book.[22] Again, Okubo's account may accurately reflect her own experience as far as it goes. Still, as undeniably powerful as her illustrations are, it is unlikely that they played as solitary a role in *Fortune*'s decision making as she contended. Even assuming that *Fortune*'s editors had not previously thought to devote any coverage to the plight of Japanese Americans—an implausible notion given the circumstances of the magazine's recruitment of Okubo—the final (unsigned) *Fortune* article contained significant data on resettlement and other aspects of the government's policy that were available chiefly from official sources. This fact, along with the substantially pro-government tone of the article—it was extremely mild in its criticism of the WRA even in its discussion of the injustice of segregation and the operations of the Tule Lake isolation camp—strongly suggests that there had been some official assistance backstage.[23]

In the months that followed the publication of the *Fortune* article, Okubo displayed a selection of her sketches at the San Francisco Museum of Art. Meanwhile, she worked on adapting the sketches into a full-length manuscript, which she evidently completed by March 1945.[24] Even as she supported herself by working as a freelance artist, she continued to publicize her work on the camps.[25] The *New York Times* printed three of the sketches alongside a review of her friend Carey McWilliams's book *Prejudice*, listing them as "Drawings of life in an internment camp made on the spot by Mine Okubo, artist, who after two years of internment is now working in New York City."[26]

At some point during these months, Okubo made the acquaintance of M. Margaret Anderson, codirector of the Common Council for American Unity, an organization dedicated to defending the rights of ethnic and racial minority groups, and editor in chief of its quarterly journal *Common Ground*. A warm friendship soon emerged between the two women. Anderson became Okubo's greatest patron and supporter, and Okubo in turn entrusted Anderson with the management of her career.[27]

Anderson was not a newcomer to the "Japanese problem." She had been interested in the condition of Japanese Americans even before Pearl Harbor, and she was a forthright opponent of evacuation. Once the removal became a fait accompli, she lobbied the WRA and other government agencies to take action against unjust treatment of the inmates and organized efforts to aid the Nisei—notably by scheduling a planning meeting in March 1943 that drew 120 people. Anderson also opened the pages of *Common Ground* to a range of Nisei writers, including Asami Kawachi, George Morimitsu, Mary Oyama, and Larry Tajiri. In early 1943, she hired journalist Eddie Shimano as editorial assistant so that he could leave camp.[28]

Anderson's efforts to help Japanese Americans were centered on her strong belief in the necessity of prioritizing resettlement. In "Get the Evacuees Out!" an editorial she published in *Common Ground*, Anderson stated flatly that resettlement of Japanese Americans outside the government camps and their "assimilation into the American scene" were pressing tasks for all Americans. "If we cannot solve so small and tidy a problem as the dispersal resettlement and assimilation of 110,000 people of Japanese descent within our borders, what hope is there for our own 13,000,000 Negroes and for the great masses of the people of the world who look hungrily to us for moral leadership?"[29] Anderson was not starry-eyed about the obstacles the newcomers faced. However, she felt that once resettled, Japanese Americans had in their own hands the capacity not only to foster their own absorption but to help the overall cause of equality. Her views are exemplified in a letter she wrote to Socialist Party leader Norman Thomas in late 1943: "I think there's a serious danger in the growing Nisei tendency to regard democracy as something entirely outside themselves—something that failed and will have to remedy its failures—the remedy to come to them as something of a gift package, not something they have to work for. For the final good of the group, I think they have got to see that they must get out of the centers and fight with us for democracy."[30]

It was therefore in conjunction with her primary interest in fostering Japanese American resettlement that Anderson took up Okubo's case. She threw herself into trying to persuade publishers to accept Okubo's manuscript. Meanwhile, she sponsored a large show of Okubo's camp artwork, which opened at the council's offices in March 1945. Anderson's goal was both to advance her protégée's career and to express a larger theme of racial tolerance. She carefully managed the construction of messages that the exhibit and Okubo embodied. Significantly, in her letter of invitation to the opening, Anderson underlined the human interest of the work and downplayed the injustice of the government's continuing policy.

> Caught in the evacuation of all Japanese Americans from the West Coast in the Spring of 1942, Miss Okubo made some 1,500 to 2,000 sketches of this episode in American history. . . . She has since developed some of these into finished paintings; others she has made into a series of drawings which tell the terrific story of evacuation with honesty, objectivity, and humor. . . . The United States has rarely produced a documentary record of any episode in its history to equal Miss Okubo's, and we wish to draw wide attention to this visit.[31]

Anderson received significant official cooperation for her project. WRA photographers visited the opening and shot several pictures of a smiling Okubo in front of her pictures—the quintessence of successful readjustment—for their documentary series on resettlement. Similarly, the WRA's April 1945 report listed Okubo's exhibit (which had moved by then to the New School for Social Research) as a highlight of its Area Public Relations program.[32]

Okubo readily went along with the line elaborated by Anderson and the WRA. In an interview with the *New York Herald Tribune* published soon after the exhibition opened, Okubo strained to emphasize the positive side of the experience and the creative adjustment of Japanese Americans.[33] "When we arrived there . . . the camp was only half-finished. It was a real pioneering life. We built all the community services ourselves—schools, churches, canteens, even a police department." Okubo stated that she had received letters while at camp from friends in Europe, telling her how lucky she was to be in the United States. "At the time it seemed strange . . . but at that, I guess I was lucky."[34]

In mid-1945, with the blessings of the WRA, the Common Council for American Unity sponsored a West Coast tour of the Okubo exhibition, "In an effort to create better understanding of the Japanese Americans and their problems."[35] The exhibition's first stop was San Francisco, where it was jointly sponsored by the International Institute and a group of liberal civic leaders.[36] While the show was widely and respectfully reviewed, one anonymous (presumably white) critic commented acerbically on both the show's establishment backing and its sanitized views of Japanese Americans:

This picture is at Mills [College], and it is the best imaginable commentary on the whole cockeyed situation that existed with reference to the Nisei during the war. You may be sure that no inmate of Dachau ever won a prize in a Leipzig annual during his confinement. Some of Miss Okubo's designs and stylizations are interesting, but the show is valuable mainly as a document [*sic*] record of an episode in the history of a group which was, apparently, quite as Americanized and quite as good-natured in adversity as any of the Kelly-Kaplan-Caruso combinations which traditionally symbolize the people of this country.[37]

After its run in San Francisco, the show moved to Los Angeles and then to Seattle.[38] The WRA closely followed Okubo's progress and reviewed the associated publicity. "In reporting an exhibit of paintings by Mine Okubo at the Seattle Art Museum," one internal memo reported, "*Time* magazine used a photograph of a painting taken by us some time previously at an exhibit of Miss Okubo's work under the auspices of the Common Council for American Unity which provided a print to *Time* for use in the story."[39] In fact, Okubo gained such a "respectable" image from her show that, in early 1946, *Glamour* magazine selected her to be among a set of Nisei women whom it wished to feature in brief biographical sketches.[40]

Meanwhile, Columbia University Press agreed to publish Okubo's manuscript. Although one later study of Okubo credited Nobuo Kitagaki, a fellow artist from *Trek*, with introducing Okubo to editor Harold Lasky of Columbia,[41] it seems likely that Anderson, with her various connections, played a decisive role. Certainly, it was Anderson who proudly wrote *Pacific Citizen* editor Larry Tajiri in January 1946 to give him the first news of the upcoming book publication and invite him to sell the work through the newspaper.[42]

Citizen 13660 was published in September 1946. Okubo would later refer to the work as a "personal documentary"—since the internees had not (at first) been allowed cameras in camp, she stated, she had taken on the task of illustrating the inmates' day-to-day existence through her sketches.[43] However, in contrast to the approach taken by classic documentary photographers such as Walker Evans and Dorothea Lange, or even Ansel Adams in his study of Japanese Americans, *Born Free and Equal*, Okubo's strategy was precisely *not* to seem detached or distanced from any part of the experience she chronicled. Rather, she presented herself as an eyewitness of camp life and placed her self-portrait in virtually all of the pictures. In its final form of first-person narrative and self-portrayal in sketches, *Citizen 13660* thereby, whether intentionally or not, evokes Taro Yashima's (i.e., Jun Iwamatsu's) well-regarded 1943 book *The New Sun*, an illustrated narrative of the author's experience in a Japanese prison.[44]

In any case, both the text and illustrations for *Citizen 13660* bore the mark of the book's wartime publication. Although Okubo's work was not subject to official censorship, it was written and accepted for publication at a time when Japanese Americans were leaving the camps and trying to reestablish themselves in mainstream U.S. society. It was of central importance to Okubo to humanize herself and other Nisei in order to underline their acceptability as new neighbors to a largely Caucasian audience. Thus, while Okubo's work describes the tragedy of mass incarceration, her narrative strategy is to portray the camp experience primarily as an absurd, humorous predicament that Japanese Americans faced and overcame. She did this through both her comments in the text and her use of a comic-book-like drawing style (almost fifty years before Art Spiegelman's *Maus*) to portray camp life.

For example, on one page, Okubo remarks, "We had to make friends with the wild creatures in the camp, especially the spiders, mice and rats, because they outnumbered us." Similarly, alongside a sketch of an adult flying a tiny kite, she notes, "Kite-making and flying was not limited to the youngsters."[45] In one picture, Okubo shows an Issei man threatened by a gang of pro-Japan inmates, but she undercuts the menace of the actual situation by including in the drawing an image of herself sticking out her tongue at the attackers.[46] This is confinement—and hence confinement narrative—as picaresque adventure.

The book's prevalent tone is droll and sad—certainly not angry or bitter—and it is at times almost nostalgic. The volume ends with Okubo's departure from Topaz:

> I looked at the crowd at the gate. Only the very old or very young were left. Here I was, alone, with no family responsibilities, and yet fear had chained me to the camp. I thought, "My God! How do they expect those poor people to leave the one place they can call home!" I swallowed a lump in my throat as I waved good-by to them.
>
> I entered the bus. As soon as all the passengers had been accounted for, we were on our way. I relived momentarily the sorrows and joys of my whole evacuation experience, until the barracks faded away into the distance. There was only the desert now. My thoughts shifted from the past to the future.[47]

This approaches the confinement narrative as elegy.

The book's publicity was carefully orchestrated. Nowhere in the promotional material released by Columbia University Press was the government or the WRA attacked for their policies, and the sufferings of Japanese Americans under official rule were downplayed. On the contrary, the book received the WRA's seal of approval. Director Myer contributed a blurb directed at West Coast bigots: "[Okubo] tells her story not with rancor but with quiet eloquence. The book is a reproof to those who would malign any racial minority, and it should help to forestall any future mass movements of the type she portrays." M. M. Tozier, former WRA Reports Division chief, added his own admiring assessment, in which he unconsciously revealed his astonishing lack of direct contact with the inmates and their experience:

> By an unusually happy combination of pictures and text, Miné Okubo has succeeded in giving the reader a strong sense of participation in the evacuation and relocation center experience. She makes you feel that this actually happened, that it might have happened to you, and that it should never happen again. After reading this book, I felt that I knew for the first time what camp life looked like, smelled like, and felt like to the evacuated people.[48]

The book's reviewers concurred. Critiques of *Citizen 13660* in national newspapers and magazines spoke warmly of the wit and pathos Okubo had brought to her study of Japanese American survival and adjustment to difficult circumstances and lauded the lack of bitterness she displayed. The reviewers did not suggest that the government or the army had been primarily responsible for the incarceration of Japanese Americans or for the tragic consequences of the loyalty questionnaire and segregation policy. Rather, like Okubo, they blamed the hysteria on West Coast bigots. Margaret Anderson reviewed her protégée's book for the *New York Times* (today this would no doubt be considered unethical behavior).[49] In her review, "Concentration Camp Boarders, Strictly American Plan," she wrote, "Anti-Oriental prejudice, always profitable to certain groups, was fanned by the emotions of war into a hysteria that finally led the Federal government into acceptance of racial discrimination as an instrument of national policy." Staying firmly on message, she added, "The drawings reveal a two-way process at work, the gradual demoralization of a group where family ties had ceased to matter under the system of mass living and mass feeding, and the resourcefulness and resilience of these fellow-Americans who tried desperately to turn negative living into something positive."[50] *Christian Herald* reviewer Daniel A. Poling commented, "Humor and pathos, both of which are at times profound, season the volume from cover to cover. I personally visited these centers. . . . What I found there is dramatically confirmed in this timely but also timeless volume."[51] Ironically, among Okubo's readers, Harold Ickes, the former Secretary of the Interior who had overseen the WRA in its last years, took the most critical stand toward the government. Ickes wrote in his syndicated column that *Citizen 13660* gave a clear account of the horrendous wartime treatment of Japanese in the United States. "As a member of President Roosevelt's administration I saw the United States Army give way to mass hysteria over the Japanese." Ickes described how army officials, who had not taken precautionary measures on the mainland, lost their cool and, in response to self-interested public clamor, began rounding up Japanese Americans indiscriminately and sending them to concentration camps in the desert. "We gave the fancy name of 'relocation centers' to the dust bowls, but they were concentration camps nonetheless, although not as bad as Dachau or Buchenwald."[52] Yet even Ickes strongly praised the WRA for helping Japanese Americans and congratulated President Roosevelt on his appointment of Myer as director.

The Nisei press, which had devoted extensive coverage to Okubo's show and other achievements, was less unanimously positive about her book. On the one hand, a reviewer for the *Pacific Citizen* noted with satisfaction, "The book has captured all the bumbling and fumbling of the early evacuation days, all the pathos and humor that arose from the paradox of citizens interned."[53] However, two radical New York newspapers, *The Nisei Weekender* and the Japanese American Committee for Democracy's *Newsletter*, panned the book, berating Okubo for soft-pedaling the hardships of evacuation and its impact on the inmates. Anderson remarked sadly to Larry Tajiri that Okubo's Nisei critics did not realize "the whole impact of the book which made its point with consummate skill," a description that speaks volumes.[54]

In a review in the *American Journal of Sociology*—one of the few scholarly commentaries on Okubo's book at the time it was published—Nisei sociologist Setsuko Matsunaga Nishi, who had herself been confined at Santa Anita, perceptively summed up both Okubo's goal and the constraints on her:

> Because the book is entertaining, *Citizen 13660* will undoubtedly serve an important propaganda function to a public that would perhaps be more comfortable to forget the treatment of Japanese-Americans during the war. For all but the most careful reader, the very facile nature of the book detracts from the deep subjective meaning of the drawings. If the reader were to verbalize the significance of some of the illustrations, he might be surprised at the bitter irony. It seems unlikely that the author intended to be funny. . . . What is not evident to most readers is the disillusioning torment that evacuation meant. . . .[55]

In the years after *Citizen 13660* was first published, Okubo pursued her independent art career, which she subsidized for a time with freelance book and magazine illustration work (including illustrations for *Common Ground*, until that magazine's demise in 1949–50). She preferred not to focus on her camp experience in her later work, although she was generous in sharing her story with interviewers, most famously as part of the 1965 CBS television documentary *The Nisei: The Pride and the Shame*. Nevertheless, she was impatient about being identified primarily as a Nisei rather than as an artist. "I have enough headaches of my own," she said in one interview. "I don't have to worry about race. I'm an individual."[56]

Although Okubo always insisted that she was not bitter about her wartime experience, she became far more outspoken in later years about the trials she had undergone, even as public sentiment regarding the camp experience changed dramatically. Okubo was active in the Japanese American redress movement of the late 1970s and 1980s and joined in protests. Roger Daniels has pointed out that Okubo also shifted her language during these years. Whereas in the original edition of *Citizen 13660*, Okubo had spoken of "evacuees" and "relocation centers," by the 1980s she was using the terms "internment camp" and "internee."[57] Similarly, in her 1983 introduction to the book, Okubo asserts that "There were untold hardships, sadness, and misery" in the camps, although in her original version of thirty-seven years earlier, she described her experience more neutrally as a mixture of "joys and sorrows."[58]

How then should we understand *Citizen 13660* and the political messages its author meant to deliver at the time of its creation? It is fair to wonder how willingly Okubo played the part of model citizen and how much of that role was forced on her by circumstance. The evidence is mixed. On the one hand, she remained proud of her work on *Citizen 13660* in later years, and she was especially gratified by the letters she continued to receive about it from readers around the world. Further, when she testified before the Commission on Wartime Relocation and Evacuation of Civilians, she offered the book as testimony.[59] On the other hand, Okubo later described herself as having been "very green" at the time she emerged from camp,[60] and she referred obliquely to the restrictive field of discourse in which she felt able to operate in 1946. "It was still too early. Everything that was Japanese was still rat poison so the book became a souvenir for [former inmates]."[61] Clearly, the burden of diluting mass anti–Japanese American hostility at that point was at least as stifling in its way as any officially derived censorship, and its impact on the author was telling. Okubo may not have been referring simply to her camp experience when she remarked in an interview shortly after the book's release, "You had to work hard to keep yourself going, and to keep from thinking."[62]

In sum, Miné Okubo's original text and illustrations for *Citizen 13660* were consciously arranged and publicized to respond to a particular historical moment, the exodus from camp. Although the immediate crisis of resettlement soon faded, the work remained and remains no less powerful in the changed political context of later decades. Perhaps the true greatness of Okubo's work of art can be judged by its power to transcend a particular agenda, even one in which the author was complicit, and to deliver many varied, and sometimes contradictory, meanings.

NOTES

1   The debate over the production of protest fiction and its stifling effect on creativity is memorably dissected in James Baldwin's essay "Everyone's Protest Novel," in his *Notes of a Native Son* (New York: Harper & Row, 1956), 13–23, and in Ralph Ellison's polemical dialogue with

Irving Howe, "The World and the Jug," in Ellison's *Shadow and Act* (New York: Random House, 1964), 107–44.

2 Pamela Stennes Wright, "'Hitting a Straight Lick with a Crooked Stick': Strategies of Negotiation in Women's Autobiographies from the U.S. 1940s: Zora Neale Hurston, Mine Okubo, and Amelia Grothe" (Ph.D. diss., University of California, San Diego, 1993), cited in Elena Tajima Creef, *Imaging Japanese America: The Visual Construction of Citizenship, Nation, and the Body* (New York: New York University Press, 2004), 78.

3 Creef, *Imaging Japanese America*, 78.

4 The theme of locating resistance has been a common element in accounts of Japanese American incarceration. Lane Hirabayashi, in the introduction to his selection of sociologist Richard Nishimoto's reports from Poston, offers a classic statement of this trend: "My selections and interpretations are highly motivated by my conclusion that popular resistance by Japanese Americans in WRA camps during World War II has been highly underreported and misinterpreted." Richard S. Nishimoto, *Inside an American Concentration Camp: Japanese American Resistance at Poston, Arizona* (Tucson: University of Arizona Press, 1995), cited in *Journal of American History* 82, no. 4. (March 1996): 1629.

5 See, for example, the introductory biographical paragraph in "Issei, Nisei, Kibei," *Fortune*, April 1944, 21.

6 Miné Okubo, "Preface to the 1983 Edition," in *Citizen 13660* (Seattle: University of Washington Press, 1983), ix.

7 Ibid.

8 "Excerpts from Comments on 'Citizen 13660' by Miné Okubo," press release, Columbia University Press, September 20, 1946, 6, collection of Aiko Herzig-Yoshinaga. Deutsch may have been exaggerating Okubo's fixed goals and comic purpose, although Okubo did not disagree enough to forbid the use of the letter in her publicity.

9 In 1939–40, Okubo exhibited her paintings at the Palace of Fine Arts built on Treasure Island for the San Francisco World's Fair. In November 1940, she contributed four paintings to the San Francisco Society of Women Artists' fifteenth annual show. *San Francisco News* critic Emile Hodel praised Okubo as "[A]n accomplished artist whose Japanese tradition fuses beautifully with American forthrightness." "Art Work of Mine Okubo, Berkeley Nisei Artist, Given High Praise at Show," *San Francisco Nichi Bei*, November 11, 1940, 1. In the 1941 painting show, Okubo won the $200 Anne Bremer Memorial Prize for her painting *Miyo and Cat*. Okubo would continue to contribute to the San Francisco Museum of Art shows as her principal means of showing her work. In 1944, she won the Art Association Purchase Prize and in 1948 the Museum Annual Prize. In spring 1946, she won praise for her contributions to a show of watercolors. See "Nisei Artist Has Watercolors on Exhibit," *Utah Nippo*, April 26, 1946, 1; "Artists Take Part in S.F. Exhibition," *Rafu Shimpo*, September 28, 1941, 1.

10 "[T]wo entries of Miné Okubo, one of which was given the Artist Fund Prize [deal with the war]. [*On Guard*] is a fine monumental drawing of two sentries guarding a Japanese Internment camp, done solidly as a mural, in black and white tempera on paper. The two soldiers with their guns on a hilltop make a bold and strong design against the small bare

barracks of the distant camp. *Evacuees*, done in the same medium and style, is a similar muralesque treatment of a Japanese family struggling with the problems of baggage and removal. Both of these drawings have a simple rich pattern of blacks and grays that is very fine." Dorothy Fuccinelli, "Review of the Art Association's Annual Exhibition of Drawings and Prints," *California Art and Architecture* 60, no. 3 (April 1943): 12.

11 Ruth Hunt Gefvert, "American Refugees: Outline of a Unit of Study about Japanese Americans," pamphlet (Philadelphia: Committee on Educational Materials for Children of the American Friends Service Committee, 1943), 47–48.

12 Miné Okubo, "An Evacuee's Hopes—and Memories," *San Francisco Chronicle, This World*, August 29, 1943, 12–13 (reprinted in chapter 3 of this volume). See also "Miné Okubo's Art, Article, Published in Coast Magazine," *Pacific Citizen*, September 11, 1943, 4.

13 U.S. Senate, 78th Congress, First Session, Document Number 96, "Message from the President of the United States Transmitting Report on Senate Resolution No. 166 Relating to Segregation of Loyal and Disloyal Japanese in Relocation Centers and Plans for Future Operations of Such Centers," September 14, 1943, 2.

14 The WRA's strong efforts in these fields nevertheless led historian Kevin Leonard to compare the agency's role to that of the Freeman's Bureau in supporting African Americans during Reconstruction in his "Years of Hope, Days of Fear: The Impact of World War II on Race Relations in Los Angeles" (Ph.D. diss., University of California, Davis, 1992), chapter 5.

15 On the "providential" nature of Japanese American resettlement as defined in government circles, see Greg Robinson, *By Order of the President: FDR and the Internment of Japanese Americans* (Cambridge, Mass.: Harvard University Press, 2001), 236–39.

16 For a recent restatement of this thesis, see Bill Hosokawa, "Afterword 2002," in *Nisei: The Quiet Americans*, rev. ed. (Boulder: University Press of Colorado, 2002), 529.

17 WRA teams also compiled press clippings and added sociological data on Japanese Americans collected in the camps by government social scientists and members of the University of California's Japanese Evacuation and Resettlement Study. The methodological and ethical faults of these studies have nevertheless been analyzed and justly critiqued. See, for example, Yuji Ichioka, ed., *Views from Within: The Japanese American Evacuation and Resettlement Study* (Los Angeles: Resource Development and Publications, Asian American Studies Center, University of California at Los Angeles, 1989).

18 A notable example of these efforts is the WRA's protest over a story in the serialized newspaper comic strip *Superman*, which was set in a Japanese American internment camp. See Gordon H. Chang, "'Superman Is About to Visit the Relocation Centers' and the Limits of Wartime Liberalism," *Amerasia Journal* 19, no. 1 (1993): 37–59. For official influence on film images, see also Clayton R. Koppes and Gregory D. Black, *Hollywood Goes to War: How Politics, Profits, and Propaganda Shaped World War II Movies* (Berkeley: University of California Press, 1990).

19 Paul La Rosa, "An Artist Remembers," *New York Daily News*, October 3, 1983, M3. Okubo claimed in her "Statement before the Commission on Wartime Relocation and Internment of Civilians" (reprinted in chapter 4 of this volume) that she was released in March 1944, but this is almost certainly a misstatement, as a contemporary issue of the *Topaz Times* lists

her as having departed for New York in the last two weeks of January 1944. "Keep Posted," *Topaz Times*, February 1, 1944, 3. Certainly, planning for the April 1944 issue and Okubo's preparation of the numerous new illustrations for the articles on Japan would have made a short deadline impracticable.

20 Quoted in Deborah Gesensway and Mindy Roseman, *Beyond Words: Images from America's Concentration Camps* (Ithaca, N.Y.: Cornell University Press, 1987), 74. The story of how *Fortune* became interested in Okubo's work shifted somewhat over time. In a later interview, Okubo recalled being told that, by a lucky chance, a *Fortune* staff member had seen some of her paintings in a Los Angeles art gallery and was able to track her down and arrange for her release to New York. Dennis Dugan, "Artist Gets a Second Look," *Newsday*, September 21, 1983, 35. Her *New York Times* obituary stated, with greater plausibility, that the prize awarded Okubo's drawing *On Guard* in the 1943 San Francisco Museum of Art show catalyzed *Fortune*'s interest. "Miné Okubo, 88, Dies; Art Chronicled Internment Camps," *New York Times*, February 25, 2001, 29.

21 Robinson, *By Order of the President*, 187.

22 Okubo, "Statement before the Commission."

23 In the same month that *Fortune*'s article appeared, the weekly photomagazine *Life*, published by Time, Inc., ran a story on harassment of Japanese American resettlers in New Jersey. See Robert Shaffer, "Mr. Yamamoto and Japanese Americans in New Jersey," *Journal of American History* 84, no. 1 (Spring 1998): 454–56. While it may be coincidence, the timing of the two articles could reflect an overall push by Time, Inc., to run stories on Japanese American resettlement.

24 "New Yorkers Honor Miné Okubo," *Colorado Times*, March 24, 1945, 1.

25 Ibid. Her illustrations appeared in such diverse publications as the *Saturday Review of Literature*, the *New York Times, Survey Graphic*, and *Lamp*, the house organ of the Standard Oil Company.

26 *New York Times Book Review*, October 15, 1944, 7. Some months later, the *Times* published another Okubo drawing alongside a review of a book by Alexander Leighton.

27 Okubo later claimed, with some exaggeration, that Anderson was the only person who had ever really worked to advance her career, without selfish motives. Okubo also recalled with gratitude that she had often been invited to Anderson's summer home in upstate New York, where she was able to relax and beat the New York City heat. Miné Okubo, comment to author, September 1998.

28 For more on M. Margaret Anderson and *Common Ground*, see Deborah Ann Overmyer, "Common Ground and America's Minorities, 1940–1949" (Ph.D. diss., University of Cincinnati, 1984).

29 M. Margaret Anderson, "Get the Evacuees Out!" *Common Ground* 3, no. 2 (Summer 1943): 65–66.

30 Letter, M. Margaret Anderson to Norman Thomas, December 27, 1943. Correspondence file, microfilm reel 15, Norman Thomas Papers, New York Public Library.

31 Letter, M. Margaret Anderson to Eleanor Roosevelt, February 28, 1945. Series 100 correspondence, Eleanor Roosevelt Papers, Franklin D. Roosevelt Library.

32 Monthly report, Reports Division, New York Office, War Relocation Authority, April 1945. War Relocation Authority Papers, RG 210, National Archives.

33 "Nisei's Drawings of Life in a War Relocation Center," *New York Herald Tribune*, March 14, 1945, 32. Two of Okubo's sketches accompanied the interview. One sketch portrayed the arrival at Topaz, and the other showed a Japanese American woman teaching school at the camp. Interestingly, Okubo's description of the school image changed drastically in the eighteen-month period between its appearance in the *New York Herald Tribune* and its final publication in *Citizen 13660*. In the earlier version, Okubo's caption reads simply "Discipline was lax at Topaz, Utah, when schools were first opened." Conversely, in her book, Okubo accompanied the same image with a more positive but pointed commentary: "School organization was an improvement over Tanforan. The curriculum followed the requirements of the state of Utah and the school was staffed by Caucasian teachers and by teachers selected from among the evacuees; the latter received only the standard camp wages." Okubo, *Citizen 13660*, 166.

34 "Artist Tells of Her Internment in Horse Stall," *New York Herald Tribune*, March 14, 1945, 32.

35 "Display Art Work Done by Nisei," *Utah Nippo*, September 18, 1946.

36 "Nisei Art Exhibit Opens in San Francisco," *Utah Nippo*, July 12, 1946.

37 Review, cited in "Life of the Nisei," *Utah Nippo*, April 26, 1946, 1.

38 "Display Art Work Done by Nisei," 1.

39 "Stories in Area Newspapers," monthly report, Reports Division, New York Office, War Relocation Authority, June 1945, 11. War Relocation Authority Papers, RG 210, National Archives.

40 "Biographies of Nisei Women in 'Glamour' Magazine," *Colorado Times*, January 23, 1946, 1.

41 Shirley Sun, *Miné Okubo: An American Experience*, exh. cat. (San Francisco: East Wind Printers, 1972), 29.

42 Letter, M. Margaret Anderson to Larry Tajiri, January 14, 1946. "T" Correspondence File, Common Council for American Unity Files, American Council for Nationalities Service Papers, Immigration History Research Center, University of Minnesota (hereafter "Anderson papers").

43 Okubo, *Citizen 13660*, viii.

44 Naoko Shibusawa, "'The Artist Belongs to the People': The Odyssey of Taro Yashima," *Journal of Asian American Studies* 8, no. 3 (October 2005): 257–75. Okubo later recalled having met Yashima at the time she resettled in New York, although she was unable to say whether his work had influenced the style of her book. Miné Okubo, conversation with author, New York, 1999.

45 Okubo, *Citizen 13660*, 68, 172.

46 Ibid., 177.

47 Ibid., 209.

48 "Excerpts from Comments on 'Citizen 13660,'" 4, 5.

49 Two other book reviews, one by *New York Herald Tribune* columnist Gerald W. Johnson and one by an anonymous critic in the *Saturday Review of Literature*, also used the term "concentration camp" to describe the government's camps.

50 M. Margaret Anderson, "Concentration Camp Boarders, Strictly American Plan," *New York Times Book Review*, September 22, 1946, 7.

51 Cited in "Miné Okubo to Exhibit at Basement Shop," *New York Nichi Bei,* September 29, 1983, 2.

52 Harold L. Ickes, "Mass Hysteria Hits Harmless Jap Residents," *Austin American*, September 23, 1946, 1.

53 MOT (Marion O. Tajiri), "Citizen 13660," cited in "Bookshelf," *Pacific Citizen*, November 4, 1983, 5. Also reprinted in *The New Canadian*, December 22, 1946, 3.

54 Letter, M. Margaret Anderson to Larry Tajiri, December 12, 1946. Anderson papers.

55 Setsuko Matsunaga Nishi, "Book review of *Citizen 13660*," *American Journal of Sociology* 52, no. 5 (March 1947): 463–64.

56 La Rosa, "An Artist Remembers."

57 Roger Daniels, "Words Do Matter," in *Nikkei in the Pacific Northwest*, ed. Louis Fiset and Gail M. Nomura (Seattle: University of Washington Press, 2005), 202–3.

58 Okubo, "Introduction to the 1983 Edition," in *Citizen 13660*, vii.

59 See Okubo, "Statement before the Commission."

60 "Miné Okubo to Exhibit at Basement Shop," *Hokubei Shimpo*, September 29, 1983, 2:1.

61 La Rosa, "An Artist Remembers."

62 "Miné Okubo, 88, Dies."

REMINISCENCES

AND TRIBUTES

14

HOLDING CENTER: TANFORAN RACE TRACK, SPRING 1942 —FOR MINE OKUBO

JAMES MASAO MITSUI

Dinner was cold: one boiled potato,
a can of Vienna sausage,
and rice with cinnamon & sugar.
Outside the fence
a dog barks in the cricket-filled night.
You stay in your horse stall,
sitting on a mattress stuffed with straw,
and stare at white grass
growing up through the floor.
Hay, horse hair and manure
are whitewashed to the boards.
In the corner
a white spider is suspended
in the shadow of a white spider web.

From James Masao Mitsui, *From a Three-Cornered World: New and Selected Poems* (Seattle: University of Washington Press, 1997)

15

A REMEMBERING

SOHEI HOHRI

Lovely, lovely Miné.
Your work remains with us.
And remaining is the memory of
your enormous strength of spirit,
and unyielding stamina; for stamina is
the mainstay of a lifetime devotion to art.

We see in your work ties to the great masters
you named: Mexican Diego Rivera;
French Raoul Dufy, Henri Matisse, Fernand Léger:
Their light, their color, their order, their humanity.
And we see the unannounced influences:
1000 year old Chinese brush drawings,
and Japanese Utamaro, Hokusai, Hiroshige.

Miné, your work endures.
And we remember your final, wonderful drawing,
a thank-you sent to each of us—
Miné, her cat, and her balloon (floating away).
Lovely, lovely Miné.

This poem was read at the Miné Okubo Memorial Service in New York City,
April 7, 2001.

16

A TRIBUTE TO MINÉ OKUBO

GREG ROBINSON

Perhaps I was better off not knowing who Miné Okubo was when I first met her in 1998. She was such a commanding personality that I was intimidated enough by her as it was. If I had realized her place in history, I might have been totally overwhelmed. My friend Shirley Geok-lin Lim was visiting New York, and we were to meet in Manhattan and go off to lunch. "Come pick me up in Greenwich Village," she told me. "I am going to spend the morning visiting a friend of mine, this elderly Japanese artist named Okubo." Promptly at 11:00 A.M., I arrived at a brownstone walkup on Ninth Street and rang the bell.

I caught my first glimpse of Miné Okubo as she answered the front door and ushered me upstairs. She was a small, slightly bent woman with a lined face dominated by two large eyes and a sideways smile that gave her the appearance of eternally sizing up the world. Her hair was pulled back from her face in a severe braid. Her hands were thrust into the pockets of her worn jacket. I would soon see them emerge as they lashed out to smack her hip as she laughed. I started slowly up the stairs in deference to her age, but she blithely hopped up the old staircase behind me, muttering greetings. The apartment was a studio, with little light save the daylight pouring in through a pair of French windows. The floor, bed, and the few folding chairs were a battleground of newspapers, mail, and papers in various piles. Miné went into the kitchen to bring us cake and tea. Of all the small kitchens I have seen in a lifetime of New York apartment visits, Miné's was the unchallenged prize-winner for the tiniest. Some general conversation ensued, during which I discovered that Miné was Nisei and not Japanese, and that she was the author of *Citizen 13660*, a book I had heard of but not then read. After regaling us with some of her stories about life in New York, Miné asked if we wished to see some of her paintings. Although I am no art expert, I politely agreed.

Miné moved to a section of the room where a number of canvases were lined up with their faces to the wall. Carefully, she set about dismantling the odd picture-puzzle arrangement she had made of her works, with smaller canvases housed within the backs of larger ones, and turning different paintings around for viewing. The sight of the canvases made me immediately giddy with delight. Their bold colors engulfed me, and their deceptively childlike design intrigued me. I tried unsuccessfully to think of what well-known artist's work they seemed to resemble, and after repeatedly failing, gave in and shared in the general admiration. As she displayed the canvases, Miné provided a running commentary, explaining how she had returned to first principles and was going far beyond the talentless frauds who dominated the art world. Feeling a bit gauche, I wondered how much the paintings sold for and whether I could afford one. However, when Shirley took out her checkbook and asked to buy a work that particularly struck her fancy, Miné shook her head and said, a bit haughtily, "I won't have these things separated. If you want to buy, you have to buy everything." I joined in the pleading and told Miné how much I would like to buy something too, but she was adamant. Like a traveling salesman packing her valises, she reassembled her painting gallery and pushed it back away against the wall. But then, as if to make up to us for her refusal to sell, Miné provided us with a copy of her latest Christmas card, featuring a print of a tiger that she had designed.

At our urgent request, Miné ended up joining Shirley and me for lunch in Chinatown and then for a walk through Soho. I was so captivated by this lively woman and her stories that at the end of our time together, I asked her whether I might interview her in order to learn more for my own historical work on Japanese Americans. "Oh God," she replied, "people are always bothering me, never letting me alone. This is why I can't get any work done!" This was not an attitude guaranteed to ease the path of a budding researcher, and so I delayed calling Miné back for a few months, hesitating even after Shirley assured me that Miné loved to complain but was actually pleased to have people contact her and to help them. It was only after I finally picked up *Citizen 13660*, and found the work moving, that I resolved to contact her again. Miné had told me that she worked at night in order to be free from distraction and slept into the afternoon. Thus, I waited until late one evening, and then, with great trepidation, I found her telephone number in the book and summoned the courage to call. After she answered, I explained my wish to come talk to her, making sure to explain who I was and how we had met. She did seem to remember me, and after once again complaining about how stupid people were always bothering her, she agreed to see me a few weeks later.

Just before I was to meet Miné, I caught a bad cold. Deciding it was wiser not to risk infecting a woman of advanced age with my germs, I canceled the interview. Although I promised to reschedule once I got better, I felt a guilty relief at postponing my confrontation with this formidable personality. The evident indifference with which she greeted my cancellation only confirmed my belief that my presence was not wanted. About two weeks later, however, I returned home late from my job to find a message on my answering machine: "This is Miné Okubo—*where the hell are you!?*" I need not say that I called her back immediately and set a date. In fact, from then on, I was a little less afraid of bothering Miné, and I went to visit her a number of times.

The visits conformed to a general pattern. Miné would sit me down and give me tea. After a while she would unpack her paintings and show me works she had done in a variety of styles. I would tell her of my latest discoveries about Franklin Roosevelt and the Japanese American internment, and then ask her questions about her experience or about Japanese Americans she had met. Although I never formally interviewed her or taped our sessions, I learned a lot from these dialogues. Miné, in her last years, had some trouble with her memory, but she had a wonderful fund of stories that she would produce in response to specific questions.

After spending an hour or two in Miné's house, I would proceed to take her to lunch in the area. Although Miné told me of her nightly walks and prowls around the neighborhood, I sensed that she often was too busy to eat or did not care about food. Feeding her thus became for me an act of devotion. Furthermore, since I had grown up in Greenwich Village myself, I was familiar with the local restaurants. Miné's respect for me rose exponentially when I took her to Japonica, her favorite Japanese restaurant, and the headwaiter came over to greet me as a familiar and ask after my parents.

As I got to know Miné, I began to find articles or documents about her career, and when I visited, I would bring along material I had dug up to show her. Miné was delighted when I told her that I had located two letters she had written to Isamu Noguchi during 1942 at the Isamu Noguchi Foundation. When I read her copies of the letters' texts, she erupted into gales of laughter. "He must have thought I was really nuts!" she exclaimed with satisfaction. As I began to realize Miné's historical importance, I became even more impressed by her, and I tried repeatedly during our conversations to explain to her what a hero she was and how influential *Citizen 13660* had been for so many people. As proud as Miné clearly was of her artwork and talent, she always scoffed when I insisted on her status as a historical figure. At first I thought Miné was being modest, and I persevered in assuring her of her worth. At length I realized that while she certainly enjoyed and even craved recognition, she was not overly interested in being a historical role model. A free spirit—a "misfit," in her own words—she was more interested in her own life and in the progress of her latest work than in judging her legacy.

Even though Miné touched my life so strongly, I never quite thought of myself as her friend. I did not meet her until late in her life, when she already had a group of friends. I did not see her regularly, and I was never certain how much she remembered me from one visit to the next, especially after her health declined. I was always a little intimidated by her powerful presence. Still, I do feel that I managed to get at least a little bit inside Miné's tough exterior. One of the last times we met was at the funeral of Motoko Ikeda-Spiegel, a friend of Miné's whom I knew slightly. After the service, Miné grew agitated because she could not remember what she had done with her coat and did not know how she would get back home. I managed to find the cloakroom stub for her coat, and I volunteered to find a taxi and take her back home before returning uptown. Miné protested weakly that I did not need to go out of my way to escort her, but I insisted that it was a pleasure for me to have some time with her. When the taxi arrived at Miné's house, she gave me a big hug and a kiss, something she had never done before.

I feel that my work on this collection is my last chance to speak to Miné. I would love to use this volume to prove to her once again how strongly she has influenced both Japanese Americans and others, and how she lives in people's hearts. At the same time, I hope that all the people who were not fortunate enough to meet Miné can still benefit from the work and example of this great woman.

17

A MEMORY OF GENIUS

SHIRLEY GEOK-LIN LIM

Miné Okubo would have grimly enjoyed this irony: that I am composing a memorial to her at the same historical moment as the United States is mourning the deaths of some three thousand Americans and other nationals in the terrorist attacks on the World Trade Center Towers and the Pentagon. For, as numerous commentators have repeated, September 11, 2001, shares parallels with December 7, 1941, a day "that will live in infamy," when the Japanese air force attacked Pearl Harbor and pulled the United States into the Pacific War.

Miné lived through the consequences of Pearl Harbor and was interned between 1942 and 1944, first at the Tanforan Assembly Center, then at the camp in Topaz, Utah. Like almost 120,000 Issei and Nisei, innocent of any treason to the United States, she was deprived of her civil rights on account of her ethnicity, despite being an America-born U.S citizen. In 2001, the country has learned from this bitter injustice. Thus, over and over again as well, commentators have drawn parallels to the fate of the Japanese Americans falling under racial discrimination and prejudice and the plight of Arab Americans now reviled by some because of their ethnicity.

I think of what it might be like if Miné were still alive and I were to visit her now in her fourth-floor walk-up apartment on Ninth Street in the Village. I would call her first, as I always did, to ask for an invitation, for Miné never invited on her own. Each time I called, however, I knew she would welcome my self-invitation. Indeed, once I moved to California in 1990, I called less often, and my guilt at my decreasing contacts motivated me to introduce her to other scholars on the East Coast who would be able to replace my visits to her.

Miné was gruff. She was suspicious. She always wanted to know *why* you were calling. But all you had to say was that you wanted to visit, to talk to her, and she immediately yielded, although with apparent reluctance. "Oh, all you people just take up my time," she'd growl. "I am busy, you know, doing my art for the world. One day the world will know all that I am doing, and you are taking up my time." But you knew she was pleased that you were coming to call on her, for you were also part of that world that Miné anticipated would acknowledge her genius.

It always alarmed me that Miné made a fuss each time I visited. I would ring the doorbell and she would walk down to let me in, because the mean old landlord who had been trying to get rid of her for decades had shut off the electricity that would have permitted her to buzz in a visitor. A stocky woman with gray rather than snowy hair even in her eighties, Miné came down the steep wooden stairs slowly.

Her face was square; her eyes large and deep set. It was the face of an iron woman, ironic in cast, strong-boned, with a straight gaze and nothing self-conscious or soft about it. You could easily forget her age. She was in her seventies when I first met her, but I never thought her frail or weak. She was independent, determined, self-willed, indeed, full of herself, and very wonderful. Wonderful in that you had to wonder on meeting her what kind of woman she was. What kind of spirit and intellect resided in that balanced, centered body that walked down the four flights of stairs, more slowly with the years, it is true, and then walked you up to her one-room apartment, more like an attic than a studio. What kind of California-born, nativized New York Nisei is this who seemed perfectly at home in the Village in the apartment where she had lived as a rent-control tenant for more than fifty years? What kind of woman could walk at eighty years of age through the Village from grocery store to restaurant to apartment, unafraid of muggers, burglars, loneliness, isolation, ill health, or poverty?

When I first met Miné, she told me with relish about her fight against the landlords who had come and gone and come again. One had tried to get rid of all the tenants in her building in order to put up a large co-op in its place. A landlord had bribed tenants with generous sums of money to move elsewhere. Then, when Miné had refused more and more exorbitant offers, the landlord had turned off the water and electricity. Miné finally got the city to force the return of water and light, but only in her walk-up studio. The stairs and the rest of the building, untenanted, remained dark, gloomy, and forbidding. Miné lived alone in this abandoned building for years. Finally someone bought the building and renovated the rest of it, leaving her walk-up strictly alone, with its unpainted walls and window casements, its falling-down pipes, and dirty creaky stairs.

Miné had a large window looking out to the back, and when I first visited, it was possible to go through that window to perch on a kind of balcony created by the roof of the room below. She would sit out there and paint on many days. That room was torn down, the little open makeshift studio outside her window disappeared, and her apartment and life grew that much smaller and constrained. Outside the window through the years, I watched the brownstone and limestone townhouses across the back gardens grow brighter. They were gutted, and hypermodern track lights illuminated interiors full of expensive kitchen equipment and lovely-looking families with children dining and reading. Miné never appeared to notice them or the newness of her neighbors. She never talked about the gentrification of the Village.

Instead she shuffled her canvases in private exhibitions for me, showing off stacks of canvases with years of changing painterly styles. I worried about the oils smearing or scraping against each other as she moved each painting from its stack. The canvases were placed one on top of the other on the floor space behind her bed and table and between the tiny gallery that served as her kitchen, which held a small stove and a sink, and her bathroom, with its pull-chain toilet. I never asked how she took her bath, as she must have done frequently, for Miné was always clean and never smelled anything but fresh. The canvases were stacked so they nestled one on the other, and even then there were too many canvases for the floor, and she had large canvases, quite large, about five by four feet, placed up above on a ceiling contraption. She never allowed me to help with the exhibition. I was not allowed to touch her canvases or help her bring them down or restack them. Over the visits, I saw many of the same paintings, but I never tired of these private shows. She always began with the early representatives, my favorites. Still lifes, of cats, vases of flowers, and young girls with hats, in colors like watercolor gouaches and in pinks and purples and yellows. There were abstracts, large and small, in bright slashing colors.

She was proudest of these. Showing the abstracts, she talked about how her philosophy of art would one day overwhelm the world, and everyone would know and agree with her vision. Only she never used the word "vision." "They will know," she repeated, but what they were supposed to know I never figured out.

I never tried to cross-examine her or to question her for fuller elaboration. Miné was suspicious of questions. "Why do you want to know?" she'd ask, fixing you with what was close to a glare, and I knew better than to press her. "You people all want something out of me," she'd declare, looking at you as your eyes shifted and you turned to cross-examining your motives.

Of course she was right. We all wanted something out of her. I wanted something out of her. An article I could publish on her work. A boast to someone that I knew the famous Miné Okubo. I wanted to buy her paintings, to show her off to the world.

"I don't sell my paintings like that," she growled.

Some agents had offered to sell her paintings, but they were all out to steal from her, she said. Someone had once requested that she loan her paintings for an exhibition. She had to pay for the cost of packing and shipping. The museum had not offered to reimburse her, and when the paintings were returned, she found a number missing. People had ripped her off; she had lost some of the most famous of her early works that had appeared in her book, *Citizen 13660*.

Citizen 13660 had made her famous. From the first appearance of her illustrations as part of a catalog, with photographs of the "relocation camps" by Dorothea Lange, Francis Stewart, and Tom Parker in 1942, her black-and-white illustrations had been published and reissued more than half a dozen times. *Citizen 13660* first appeared in 1946, published by Columbia University Press, then by a variety of smaller presses, and finally by the University of Washington Press in 1983. But Miné did not seem aware of who was using her work, copyrights due her, or other such contractual matters. She knew only her distrust of museums, universities, gallery owners, professors, scholars, anyone who offered to exhibit her paintings and to make her famous.

No, she would not sell me even one work, although I took out my checkbook and told her I would pay whatever price she asked. "I will sell only if someone buys all of them. They must stay together," she said over and over again through the years.

You wondered if she knew something you did not. Was there really out there an individual, a foundation, an institution with the money and the desire to buy all her paintings and keep them together forever? I had dizzy visions of the Getty warehousing her canvases, rotating them in special Miné Okubo rooms. I knew it would never happen. But I never said any such thing to Miné.

Now that Miné is no longer living in that walk-up, I wonder what has happened to her paintings. Did her landlord put them out in the trash? Did he save all of them, knowing her genius? Did she have family on the West Coast who went to her apartment and packed away her works to preserve them for a more knowledgeable generation? Whatever, Miné never allowed me to walk away with a single painting.[1]

But she gave me little ink drawings. For each New Year, she inked the Chinese astrological creature for the year—a goat, a tiger—on white cards. She gave me a few large cards, mailed me small ones. I have kept them all.

She fed me. Each visit, she had plates of cold cuts, presliced cheese, grapes, cut vegetables—carrots, celery—and crackers. She boiled water in her kettle and made me cups of tea, Lipton teabags hanging from china cups. The food was plentiful.

"Enough, Miné. You shouldn't buy so much," I'd plead.

"Oh, you eat so little," she'd scoff and munch away on the cheese, the crackers, the ham, and bologna. No exotic sushi or udon noodles from Miné.

"These are bad for you," I'd say, worrying about her cholesterol, her living alone at eighty, eighty-two.

"Oh, I never worry about these things," she'd say, chomping on another slice of Kraft's cheese. She had strong white teeth. You never worried about osteoporosis with Miné—her bones and teeth would outlast yours.

Later, I insisted on taking her out to meals, early dinners so I could catch the train home to Katonah or meet up with younger friends for late-night talks. Miné was always reluctant to see me leave, just as she was reluctant to have me visit. She'd take out some books for me to read, books that featured her life or her work. She had a small area curtained off to the right in her single-room apartment, and I could see it was piled with boxes of papers and had a shelf of books. I wondered about her papers—what treasures of archives for the scholar, the library, tied with string lay among them? But I wondered very briefly, because to raise this question with Miné was to set her eyes glinting with suspicion, to hear her say, "You people always want something out of me." Her books could not detain me long; so, reluctantly, Miné would accept my offer of dinner. It was not because she was hungry or needed to have someone buy her food. It was to keep the time longer between us, for I was part of that world she knew was visiting her because we were arriving at an understanding of her genius.

Miné never, within my hearing, doubted her genius. "Oh, I know," she said. "I know something great, and it is all in my paintings, and the world will also know it someday when they see my paintings."

Miné never needed fame, never courted it, although she was pleased when people like me came by to confirm it. For me, this belief in her genius was what made her eccentric. Instead of normal, everyday, sad paranoia, Miné knew she was different, no, unique. Only she knew the great thing, and the world, so ignorant, would catch up with her one day.

Well, the day has come and gone. I knew she would die. Even a strong-boned, strong-willed Nisei who survived the internment camp and went to work at *Fortune* magazine immediately after internment, could not live forever.

Was Miné a genius? I don't know. Was she a character? Yes. But more than a character. Miné was a young student at the University of California in the 1930s, traveling on a great adventure to Europe in 1939, when she was called back to the States. She documented her internment at the Tanforan Assembly Center and later in the Topaz internment camp in graphic, funny, sad, pathetic, memorable sketches. These black-and-white drawings still haunt U.S. history. As a compilation, *Citizen 13660* has no equal in evoking a series of sharp penetrating views of the internment history. No poem, no memoir, no novel approaches its comic, its tragic view of Japanese Americans living through that most painful period in the community's history. Miné's text—seemingly factual, bald, concrete, detailed—chronicles with deadpan accuracy the humanity of the experience in ways that more lavish, emotion-loaded prose cannot mime. For example, the simple statement "The birth rate in the center was high" fills an entire page below a sketch of pregnant women surrounded by infants and toddlers. And the page is set beside one illustrating the sick in a hospital, noting, "The dead were sent to Salt Lake City for cremation, and the ashes were held for burial until the day of return to the Bay region."[2]

Miné lived almost sixty years past that experience and that art. But she never dwelt on these drawings or on the historical moment they documented. In fact, she never talked to me about that period of her life. Each time we talked, it was about the grand, totalizing concepts of painting and art. She was passionate about her unsold, unexhibited paintings, not her achievement in *Citizen 13660*. It was the art in her soul she was convinced about, not politics, not her landlords, not the U.S. state, not even justice. Her life and work have made a difference to how we look at a community and a history. That is genius enough, if genius is wanted in the reception of her life.

NOTES

1   Okubo requested that after her death, her artwork be divided between the Oakland Museum of California; the Japanese American National Museum; her alma mater, Riverside Community College; and her family members in California.

2   Miné Okubo, *Citizen 13660* (Seattle: University of Washington Press, 1983), 163, 162.

A PARTIAL CHRONOLOGY OF
MINÉ OKUBO'S LIFE AND WORK

1912	Born June 27
1935	B.A. in Art from University of California, Berkeley.
1936	M.A. in Art from University of California, Berkeley.
1938	Winner of Bertha Taussig Traveling Scholarship.
1938–39	Travels in Europe.
1939	Returns home to California and works on Federal Arts Program mural project.
1941	Japan bombs Pearl Harbor on December 7.
1942	Sent to Tanforan Assembly Center, San Bruno, California, as a result of Executive Order 9066.
1942	Sent to Central Utah Relocation Camp in Topaz.
1944	Recruited to New York City by *Fortune* magazine to work as an illustrator.
1945–61	Works as a freelance commercial artist and book illustrator.
1946	*Citizen 13660* published by Columbia University Press.
1948	Paints four murals for American Export Lines.
1948	Receives the San Francisco Museum Annual Prize.
1950–52	Lectures in Art at University of California, Berkeley.
1957	Exhibits in "Art in Asia and the West," San Francisco Museum of Art.
1965	Appears in "The Nisei: The Pride and the Shame," Twentieth Century TV, CBS News.
1968	One-woman exhibition at Image Gallery, Stockbridge, Massachusetts.

1972	Retrospective, "Miné Okubo: An American Experience," Oakland Museum, California.
1972	Group exhibition on Japanese American relocation camps. Sponsored by the California Historical Society.
1974	Riverside Community College retrospective.
1975	Exhibits in "Transcendental Blossoms," Syntex Gallery, Palo Alto, California.
1981	Gives testimony in New York City before Congressional Commission on Wartime Relocation.
1983	*Citizen 13660* reprinted by the University of Washington Press.
1984	*Citizen 13660* wins the American Book Award.
1984	*Citizen 13660* is translated and published in Tokyo by Ochanomizu Shobo.
	"Miné Okubo: Forty Year Retrospective," Catherine Gallery/Basement Workshop, New York.
1987	Sent by New York's *Nichibei* newspaper to Washington, D.C., to record proceedings of National Council for Japanese American Redress class action lawsuit.
	Honored by the California State Department of Education, which selects her as one of twelve women pioneers for its poster "California since 1800."
1989	Exhibits in "From Bleakness," a show of art and artifacts from Tanforan Assembly Center, Gallery at Hastings-on-Hudson, New York.
1990	Receives $20,000 reparation check.
1991	"Miné Okubo: National Museum for Women in the Arts," Washington, D.C. Sponsored by the Women's Caucus for Art of the College Art Association.
1992	Exhibits in "The View from Within: Japanese American Art from the Internment Camps, 1942–1945," Wight Art Gallery, University of California, Los Angeles. The exhibition also travels to San Jose, Salt Lake City, Honolulu, New York, and Tokyo.
1993	"Into the Light: Miné Okubo: A Fifty Year Retrospective," Sky Gallery, Boston. Sponsored by the Japan Society of Boston and the Bank of Boston.
1993	Selected to appear in Japan's National High School textbook.
1995	Exhibits in "The View from Within: Japanese American Art from the Internment Camps, 1942–1945," Queens Museum of Art in Flushing Meadows Park, New York
1998	"Miné Okubo: A Fifty Year Retrospective for Bay Area Collectors," Oakland Museum of California.

2001	Miné passes away on February 10, 2001, in New York City.
2006	Debut of play based on Okubo's life, *Miné: A Name for Herself*, by Mary H. Curtin and Theresa Larkin.
2006	Riverside Community College debuts Miné Okubo Drive on campus.

NOTE

This chronology is based on one compiled by Shirley Sun in the catalog *Miné Okubo: An American Experience* (San Francisco: East Wind Printers, 1972) for the exhibition at the Oakland Museum, July 18–August 20, 1972.

SELECTED BIBLIOGRAPHY

Americans of Japanese Ancestry and the United States Constitution: 1787–1987. San Francisco: National Japanese American Historical Society, 1987.

Barton, Ellen, and Gail Stygall, eds. *Discourse Studies in Composition.* Cresskill, N.J.: Hampton Press, 2002.

Brown, D. L. *From Eden to Armageddon: A Biblical History of the World in Classic Art and Illustration.* Salt Lake City, Utah: Shadow Mountain, 1998.

Cheung, King-Kok, ed. *An Interethnic Companion to Asian American Literature.* New York: Cambridge University Press, 1997.

Chin, Frank, ed. *Born in the USA: The Story of Japanese America, 1889–1947.* Lanham, Md.: Rowman & Littlefield, 2002.

Creef, Elena Tajima. *Imaging Japanese America: The Visual Construction of Citizenship, Nation, and the Body.* New York: New York University Press, 2004.

Daniels, Roger. *American Concentration Camps.* New York: Garland Press, 1989.

Daniels, Roger, Sandra Taylor, and Harry Kitano, eds. *Japanese Americans, from Relocation to Redress.* Salt Lake City: University of Utah Press, 1986.

DeFrancis, John, with the assistance of V. R. Francis. *Things Japanese in Hawaii.* Honolulu: University Press of Hawaii, 1973.

Dower, John. *War without Mercy: Race and Power in the Pacific War.* New York: Pantheon Books, 1986.

Foucault, Michel. *Discipline and Punish: The Birth of the Prison.* New York: Random House, 1991.

Gates, E. Nathaniel, ed. *The Judicial Isolation of the "Racially" Oppressed.* New York: Garland, 1997.

Gesensway, Deborah, and Mindy Roseman. *Beyond Words: Images from America's Concentration Camps.* Ithaca, N.Y.: Cornell University Press, 1987.

Gornick, Vivian. *The Situation and the Story: The Art of Personal Narrative.* New York: Farrar, Straus & Giroux, 2001.

Grodzins, Morton. *Americans Betrayed: Politics and the Japanese Evacuation.* Chicago: University of Chicago Press, 1949.

Harth, Erica, ed. *Last Witnesses: Reflections on the Wartime Internment of Japanese Americans.* New York: Palgrave, 2001.

Hatamiya, Leslie T. *Righting a Wrong: Japanese Americans and the Passage of the Civil Liberties Act of 1988.* Stanford, Calif.: Stanford University Press, 1994.

Hibbett, Howard. *The Chrysanthemum and the Fish: Japanese Humor since the Age of the Shoguns.* New York: Kodansha International, 2002.

Hirabayashi, Lane Ryo. *The Politics of Fieldwork: Research in an American Concentration Camp.* Tucson: University of Arizona Press, 1999.

Hosokawa, Bill. *Nisei: The Quiet Americans.* Revised edition. Boulder: University Press of Colorado, 2002.

Ichioka, Yuji, ed. *Views from Within: The Japanese Evacuation and Resettlement Study.* Los Angeles: Resource Development and Publications, Asian American Studies Center, University of California at Los Angeles, 1989.

Inada, Lawson Fusao, ed. *Only What We Could Carry: The Japanese American Internment Experience.* Berkeley, Calif.: Heyday Books; San Francisco: California Historical Society, 2000.

Ketchum, Richard M., ed. *The Horizon Book of the Renaissance.* New York: American Heritage Publishing, 1961.

Kiyama, Henry Yoshitaka. *The Four Immigrants Manga: A Japanese Experience in San Francisco, 1904–1924.* Berkeley, Calif.: Stone Bridge Press, 1999.

Koppes, Clayton R., and Gregory D. Black. *Hollywood Goes to War: How Politics, Profits, and Propaganda Shaped World War II Movies.* Berkeley: University of California Press, 1990.

Kostelnick, Charles, and Michael Hassett. *Shaping Information: The Rhetoric of Visual Conventions.* Carbondale: Southern Illinois University Press, 2003.

Lee, Anthony W. *Painting on the Left: Diego Rivera, Radical Politics, and San Francisco's Public Murals.* Berkeley: University of California Press, 1999.

Lee, Robert G. *Orientals: Asian Americans in Popular Culture.* Philadelphia: Temple University Press, 1999.

Lent, John A., ed. *Illustrating Asia: Comics, Humor Magazines, and Picture Books.* Honolulu: University of Hawaii Press, 2001.

Marvis, Barbara J. *Contemporary American Success Stories: Famous People of Asian Ancestry.* Volume 4. Childs, Md.: Mitchell Lane Publishers, 1994.

Matthews, T. F. *The Clash of Gods: A Reinterpretation of Early Christian Art.* Princeton, N.J.: Princeton University Press, 1993.

McWilliams, Carey. *The Education of Carey McWilliams.* New York: Simon & Schuster, 1979.

Minear, Richard H. *Dr. Seuss Goes to War: The World War II Cartoons of Theodore Seuss Geisel.* New York: New Press, 2000.

Mitsui, James Masao. *From a Three-Cornered World: New and Selected Poems.* Seattle: University of Washington Press, 1997.

Morse, Anne Nishimura, J. Thomas Rimer, and Kendall H. Brown, eds. *Art of the Japanese Postcard: The Leonard A. Lauder Collection at the Museum of Fine Arts, Boston.* Boston: Museum of Fine Arts, 2004.

Myer, Dillon S. *Uprooted Americans: The Japanese Americans and the War Relocation Authority during World War II.* Tucson: University of Arizona Press, 1971.

Muller, Eric L. *Free to Die for Their Country: The Story of the Japanese American Draft Resisters in World War II.* Chicago: University of Chicago Press, 2001.

Nelson, Cary. *Repression and Recovery: Modern American Poetry and the Politics of Cultural Memory, 1910–1945.* Madison: University of Wisconsin Press, 1989.

Nomura, Gail, Russell Endo, Stephen H. Sumida, and Russell C. Leong, eds. *Frontiers of Asian American Studies.* Pullman: Washington State University Press, 1989.

O'Brien, Robert W. *The College Nisei.* Palo Alto, Calif.: Pacific Books, 1949.

Okubo, Miné. *Citizen 13660.* Seattle: University of Washington Press, 1983.

Omi, Michael, and Howard Winant. *Racial Formation in the United States from the 1960s to the 1990s.* New York: Routledge, 1994.

Palumbo-Liu, David. *Asian/American: Historical Crossings of a Racial Frontier.* Palo Alto, Calif.: Stanford University Press, 1999.

Persistent Women Artists: Pablita Velarde, Mine Okubo, Lois Mailou Jones. Videotape. Presented by Betty LaDuke, directed by Brian Varaday. Wilton Art Appreciation Programs. Botsford, Conn.: Reading & O'Reilly, 1996.

Ricoeur, Paul. *Oneself as Another.* Translated by Kathleen Blamey. Chicago: University of Chicago Press, 1992.

Robinson, Greg. *By Order of the President: FDR and the Internment of Japanese Americans.* Cambridge, Mass.: Harvard University Press, 2001.

Schodt, Frederik L. *Manga! Manga!: The World of Japanese Comics.* New York: Kodansha International USA, 1983.

Shirane, Haruo, ed. *Early Modern Japanese Literature: An Anthology, 1600–1900.* New York: Columbia University Press, 2002.

Sontag, Susan. *On Photography.* New York: Farrar, 1977.

Sun, Shirley. *Miné Okubo: An American Experience.* Exhibition catalog. San Francisco: East Wind Printers, 1972.

Takaki, Ronald T. *Strangers from a Distant Shore: A History of Asian Americans.* Boston: Little, Brown & Company, 1989.

Tateishi, John. *And Justice for All: An Oral History of the Japanese American Detention Camps.* New York: Random House, 1984.

Taylor, Sandra. *Jewel of the Desert: Japanese-American Internment at Topaz.* Berkeley: University of California Press, 1993.

tenBroek, Jacobus, Edward N. Barnhardt, and Floyd W. Matson. *Prejudice, War, and the Constitution.* Berkeley: University of California Press, 1968.

Uchida, Yoshiko. *Desert Exile: The Uprooting of a Japanese-American Family.* Seattle: University of Washington Press, 1982.

United States. Commission on Wartime Relocation and Internment of Civilians. *Personal Justice Denied: Report of the Commission on Wartime Relocation and Internment of Civilians.* With a new foreword by Tetsuden Kashima. Washington, D.C.: Civil Liberties Public Education Fund; Seattle: University of Washington Press, 1997.

United States Department of War. *Final Report: Japanese Evacuation from the West Coast 1942.* Reprint. New York: Arno Press, 1978.

United States War Relocation Authority. *Nisei in Uniform.* Washington, D.C.: U.S. Government Printing Office, 1945.

————. *Wartime Exile: The Exclusion of Japanese-Americans from the West Coast.* Washington, D.C.: U.S. Government Printing Office, 1945.

Varley, Paul. *Japanese Culture.* 4th edition. Honolulu: University of Hawaii Press, 2000.

The View from Within: Japanese American Artists from the Internment Camps, 1942–1945. Exhibition catalog. Los Angeles: Japanese American National Museum, 1992.

Webber, Lucille R. *Japanese Woodblock Prints: The Reciprocal Influence between East and West.* Provo, Utah: Brigham Young University Press, 1979.

Wright, Bradford W. *Comic Book Nation: The Transformation of Youth Culture in America.* Baltimore, Md.: The Johns Hopkins University Press, 2001.

Wu, Frank H. *Yellow: Race in America beyond Black and White.* New York: Basic Books, 2002.

Yamamoto, Traise. *Masking Selves, Making Subjects: Japanese American Women, Identity, and the Body.* Berkeley: University of California Press, 1999.

Yoo, David K. *Growing Up Nisei: Race, Generation, and Culture among Japanese Americans of California, 1924–49.* Urbana: University of Illinois Press, 2000.

CONTRIBUTORS

LAURA CARD teaches rhetoric, writing, and critical analysis at Brigham Young University in Provo, Utah. She is a former newspaper and magazine editor and has had hundreds of articles and several short stories and poems published. Her doctoral dissertation is titled "Trek Magazine 1942–1943: A Critical Rhetorical Analysis."

FAY CHIANG is the author of two volumes of poetry, *In the City of Contradictions* (Sunbury Press, 1979) and *Miwa's Song* (Sunbury Press, 1982), and a children's book, *A Railroad on Gold Mountain* (Macmillan/McGraw-Hill, 1997). Her poetry and prose have been published in numerous small press magazines and anthologies. Currently, Chiang is a staff member at Project Reach and is working on her third volume of poetry, *Chinatown*, a book-length poem. She lives in the East Village with her daughter Xian.

VIVIAN FUMIKO CHIN teaches in the Ethnic Studies Department at Mills College in Oakland, California. Her mother was interned at Heart Mountain, Wyoming, and introduced her to *Citizen 13660*.

ELENA TAJIMA CREEF is an associate professor in women's studies at Wellesley College, Massachusetts. She is the author of *Imaging Japanese America: The Visual Construction of Nation, Citizenship, and the Body* (New York University Press, 2004). Her work is included in Darrell Y. Hamamoto's and Sandra Liu's *Countervisions: Asian American Film Criticism* (Temple University Press, 2000) and Gloria Anzaldúa's *Making Face, Making Soul/Haciendo Caras: Creative and Critical Perspectives by Feminists of Color* (Aunt Lute Fundation Books, 1990).

HEATHER FRYER is assistant professor of history and co-coordinator of the American Studies program at Creighton University in Omaha, Nebraska. Her forthcoming book *Enclosed Worlds in Open Space: Freedom, Security, and Citizenship in America's Inverse Utopias* (University of Nebraska Press), examines the political and social impact of four federally run bounded communities—including Topaz—on the American West. In addition to contributing essays on ethnicity, encounter, and visual culture to journals and anthologies, she served as principal curator and catalog editor for the 2002 exhibition "Cowboys, Indians, and the Big Picture," at the McMullen Museum of Art at Boston College.

MASUMI HAYASHI was born at the end of World War II in an American concentration camp at Gila River, Arizona. She earned critical plaudits for her series of photographic collages. By assembling small photographs in a 180- to 360-degree panoramic rotation, Hayashi created one large-scale collage, an image of remarkable detail that also captured the vastness of the landscape. Exploring the hidden aspects of the North American landscape—from Environmental Protection Agency Superfund sites, the U.S. War Relocation Authority camp sites, and Canadian camp sites— Hayashi's work encourages viewers to reexamine the physical landscape and its histories. Hayashi was a professor in the art department at Cleveland State University, Ohio. She was killed by an assailant in Cleveland in 2006.

SOHEI HOHRI was born in 1925 in Salinas, California. From 1942 to 1944, he was interned at Manzanar and has lived in New York City since 1956. He is interested in things maritime and the arts.

LYNNE HORIUCHI is a visiting assistant professor at the University of North Carolina in Charlotte. She holds an M.A. and Ph.D. in Art History from the University of California at Santa Barbara, an M.A. in Italian from Middlebury College, and a B.F.A. from the University of Colorado. She has directed research, exhibits, and book projects sponsored by the National Endowment for the Humanities and the California Council on the Humanities on Japanese American family albums. She is a recipient of the Bancroft Library Study Award and Civil Liberties Public Education Fund Fellowship. Her interdisciplinary research interests include ethnic studies, architecture, urbanism, race critical theory, and diasporic studies with a special focus on the built environments of the U.S. government's internment of Japanese and Japanese Americans during World War II.

CLEMENS KALISCHER has been working as a photographer for more than fifty years, ever since he arrived in New York City in 1942 after fleeing Germany with his family via Switzerland and Paris. His work has been published in Edward Steichen's *Family of Man* (Museum of Modern Art, 1955) and in magazines such as *Time, Life,* and *For-*

tune. He worked on assignment for the *New York Times* for thirty-five years. Kalischer now lives in Stockbridge, Massachusetts.

SHIRLEY GEOK-LIN LIM is professor of English at the University of California, Santa Barbara. She has published criticism on postcolonial, feminist, diasporic, and Asian American cultural productions. Her book of poems, *Crossing the Peninsula & Other Poems* (Heinemann Educational Books, 1980), received the Commonwealth Poetry Prize. She has published four poetry collections, two novels, *Joss and Gold* (Feminist Press at the City University of New York, 2001) and *Sister Swing* (Marshall Cavendish Editions, 2006), and three books of short stories. *The Forbidden Stitch: An Asian American Women's Anthology* (Calyx Books, 1989), which she co-edited, received the American Book Award, as did her memoir *Among the White Moon Faces* (Feminist Press at the City University of New York, 1996). Among her honors, Lim has received the UCSB Faculty Research Lecture Award and the Chair Professorship of English at the University of Hong Kong (1999–2001).

JAMES MASAO MITSUI recently moved to Surprise, Arizona where he has taken up watercolor painting and returned to teaching creative writing at Arizona State University's Osher Lifelong Learning Institute in Sun City Grand. He received his M.A. in English at the University of Washington in Seattle. His latest book is *From a Three-Cornered World* (University of Washington Press, 1997).

STELLA OH is assistant professor of Women's Studies at Loyola Marymount University in Los Angeles. Her areas of specialization include Asian American literature, postcolonial theory, and feminist theory. She is currently working on the manuscript for her book, which explores the relationship between visibility, citizenship, and national belonging.

KIMBERLEY L. PHILLIPS is Frances L. and Edwin L. Cummings Associate Professor in History and American Studies at the College of William and Mary in Williamsburg, Virginia, where she teaches courses on African American and American cultural and social history. She is the author of *Alabama North: African American Migrants, Community, and Working-Class Activism in Cleveland* (University of Illinois Press, 1999) and is currently working on *War! What Is It Good For?: African American Culture and the U.S. Military.*

IRENE POON was born and educated in San Francisco. She received her B.A. and M.A. in art and photography from San Francisco State University. Her photographic work has appeared in museums and galleries. She is the author of *Leading the Way: Asian American Artists of the Older Generation* (Gordon College Press, 2001). Poon currently serves as an adviser to the National Endowment for the Humanities project *Asian American Art: Starting from Here,* a biographical directory to be published in 2007. She is also on the board of the Chinese Historical Society of America Museum and Learning Center in San Francisco, where she has curated and co-curated several exhibitions. She is the visual resource specialist in the Art Department at San Francisco State University.

GREG ROBINSON is a professor of history and associated researcher at the Centre for United States Studies, Université du Québec à Montréal. He is the author of *By Order of the President: FDR and the Internment of Japanese Americans* (Harvard University Press, 2001). His upcoming book, tentatively titled *The Japanese Camps,* is a transnational study of Japanese confinement and experience during World War II. He is also an editor of the *Encyclopedia of African American Culture and History* and its supplement (Gale/Mcmillan, 1995–2009), and of the memoirs of Ayako Ishigaki and Kathleen Tamagawa. He is a regular columnist for the San Francisco *Nichi Bei Times* newspaper.

ILLUSTRATION CREDITS

COLOR PLATES

Courtesy of the Leeper and Hall Collection

PORTFOLIO

p. 15: cover of *Trek 1*, no. 1, December 1942

p. 16: cover of *Trek 1*, no. 2, February 1943

p. 17: cover of *Trek 1*, no. 3, June 1943

pp. 18, 19, 20: illustrations for Grace W. McGavran, *Where the Carp Banners Fly* (New York: Friendship Press, 1949); courtesy of Presbyterian Historical Society

p. 21: illustrations for Marianna Nugent Prichard, *Ten Against the Storm* (New York: Friendship Press, 1957); courtesy of Presbyterian Historical Society

p. 22: illustrations for Peggy Billings, *The Waiting People* (New York: Friendship Press, 1962); courtesy of Presbyterian Historical Society

p. 23: illustrations for Toru Matsumoto, *The Seven Stars* (New York: Friendship Press, 1949); courtesy of Presbyterian Historical Society

p. 26: photograph by Toge Fujihira

pp. 27, 28, 29: photographs by Clemens Kalischer; collection of the artist

p. 30: photocollage of Mine Okubo by Masumi Hayashi; courtesy of the estate of Masumi Hayashi

p. 31: photograph by Irene Poon; collection of the artist

Chapter 3 illustrations reproduced, with permission, from the *San Francisco Chronicle*, August 29, 1943

Figs. 10.1, 10.2, 10.3, 10.4 reproduced, with permission, from *Citizen 13660* (Seattle: University of Washington Press, 1983)

Figs. 10.5, 10.6, 10.7, 10.8, 10.9, and 10.10 reproduced, with permission, from *Trek*, nos. 1–3, 1943

INDEX

Adams, Ansel, 71, 105, 167, 196
American Civil Liberties Union, 83
Anderson, Margaret M., 165–66, 169, 174n.27

"barbed-wire democracies," 87–88, 92
Barthes, Roland, 157n.27
Beckwith, Frank, Sr., 123, 141–42
Berger, John, 155n.1
Berlant, Lauren, 145
Biddle, Francis, 83
Bloch, Carl, 138
blues, as musical form, 157n.19
bricolage, 74

censorship, 115–16, 139
Central Utah Relocation Project, 132
Chang, Gordon, 103–4, 173. See also
    Superman
Chiang, Fay, 5
Citizen 13660: comic book style,

99–101, 147; depiction of religion,
88; evolution of memoir, 160–68;
ironic citizenship, 147; and physical
gestures, 67, 69, 71–79, 150, 152–53;
pioneer metaphors, 85–87, 96n.6,
106, 137; politics of the gaze, 145–51,
155, 157; reviews of, 92–95, 168–70,
175
Civilian Exclusion Order No. *19,* 108n.2
Civil Liberties Act of *1988,* 154
Columbia University Press, 47, 153,
    167–68
comic strips/cartoons, 99–101, 109n.9,
147
Commission on Wartime Relocation
    and Internment of Civilians, 46–49,
    95, 153, 171
Common Council for American Unity,
    165–66
Creef, Elena T., 104, 119, 159
Curtin, Mary H., 37, 193